OLD TESTAMENT
EVANGELISTIC SERMONS

Old Testament Evangelistic Sermons

D. Martyn Lloyd-Jones

THE BANNER OF TRUTH TRUST

THE BANNER OF TRUTH TRUST
3 Murrayfield Road, Edinburgh EH12 6EL
PO Box 621, Carlisle, Pennsylvania 17013, USA

*

*

Typeset in 11/12pt Erhardt MT
Printed and bound in Great Britain
at The Bath Press, Avon

CONTENTS

OLD TESTAMENT EVANGELISTIC SERMONS

INTRODUCTION

The Evangelistic Use of the Old Testament in the Preaching of Dr Lloyd-Jones

Much has been said and written about the ministry of David Martyn Lloyd-Jones since his death in 1981. His work has become a matter of history and there is an impression abroad that its main features are now well-known and understood. His memory has become identified with such things as the practice of expository preaching, the need for doctrinal Christianity, the danger of ecumenism, and the necessity of a recovery of the power of the Holy Spirit. But as a summary of his work this common impression is wrong, and wrong because it leaves out of account what came *first* in his own understanding of his calling. Dr Lloyd-Jones regarded himself primarily as an evangelist. Those who knew him best also saw him in the same way. Mrs Lloyd-Jones was once present with a group of men who, in her husband's absence, were paying compliments to his abilities. As she listened to them she evidently thought that they were missing the main thing and surprised them by quietly remarking, 'No one will ever understand my husband until they realise that he is first of all a man of prayer and then, an evangelist.'[1]

It is not entirely the fault of the Christian world that it has, since his death, tended to take up a wrong impression. The people who have wanted Dr Lloyd-Jones' sermons in book-form have obviously been Christians and therefore those responsible for publication assumed that the books to be issued from his ministry should be those taken from sermons intended for believers. If, therefore, people's impressions are based on the content of his published works, they can hardly be blamed for thinking that, for him, preaching was mainly a matter of exposition directed to those who

---

[1] See my *David Martyn Lloyd-Jones: The Fight of Faith 1939–1981* (Edinburgh: Banner of Truth, 1990), p. 322.

already believe in Christ. But the impression is quite wrong. The fact is that at least half of his preaching was evangelistic and only a fraction of that preaching has so far been published.

Publishers are therefore partly to blame for the current mis-conception. But there is another reason. Dr Lloyd-Jones' known opposition to features of modern evangelism led those who wanted to defend those features, and who were uncomfortable under his strictures, to allege that he was 'a teacher, not an evangelist'. In other words, he was not qualified to speak about evangelism. This was an assessment of him which gained some popularity and it still survives today. A spokesman of that viewpoint once took the opportunity to question his commitment to evangelism with the question, 'When did *you* last have a campaign at Westminster Chapel?' The answer, 'I have one every Sunday', was not intended to be humorous. It was true. Speaking to students for the ministry ML-J could say, 'I contest very strongly and urge that there should always be one evangelistic service in connection with each church every week.'[1] In his case it was the Sunday night service which had this purpose, and he continued that practice from the beginning of his ministry in 1927 until he concluded his pastoral oversight in 1968.

Many people became Christians at Westminster Chapel. Like Whitefield's Tabernacle of an earlier day, the place could be called a 'soul-trap'. But the contrary opinion no doubt gained some credence from Lloyd-Jones' unwillingness to make any announce-ment on the numbers converted under his ministry. Indeed, he deliberately avoided any attempt to ascertain that number for him-self. It was one of his most deeply held convictions that no public action should be required *as a part* of coming to faith in Christ. Converts were never asked to identify themselves publicly.[2] Years

---

[1] *Preaching and Preachers* (London: Hodder and Stoughton, 1971), p. 151. See, also, p. 63.

[2] He knew that the practice of calling for public 'decisions' was too easily confused with conversion, and that it was entirely unsafe as a means of recog-nising true converts. See his *Preaching and Preachers*, pp. 265–82. In this area, as in others, his thinking was the same as that of Whitefield who warned of 'mushroom Christians' and of the danger of 'dubbing people converts so soon. I love now to wait a little and see if people bring forth fruit; for there are so many blossoms which March winds you know blow away, that I cannot

might pass before he heard of particular cases and there were many, I am sure, of which he never heard. I was reminded of this a few years ago when I met an old friend of Westminster Chapel days in a country village in Suffolk. Although I was myself close to the work at Westminster in the period of which we began to speak (which was more than thirty years before), it did not surprise me that I had heard nothing of two conversions of which my friend now told me for the first time.

The first concerned his aunt, a worldly woman, twice divorced, who had no time for spiritual things. One Sunday, when my informant was having lunch with her, she asked about his movements for the rest of the day. Hearing that he was going to a chapel, she surprised him by saying that she would come as well. The sermon that night proved to be far from 'appealing' to a non-Christian and about her only comment afterwards was the exclamation, 'I love darkness!' But, unknown to her nephew, she returned alone in succeeding weeks, slipping in at the back of the building, and before long she was brought to hate forever what once she loved so much.

The second case was that of a younger woman who had, in those days, recently arrived from the Continent to study architecture in London. My friend was one of her instructors and, noticing how she was struggling with her English, he took the opportunity to advise her that her language problem would be eased if she could hear more of the best-spoken English, as it might be heard, for example, at Westminster Chapel! She took the advice, though at first with results which were sometimes humorous. It was noted that her vocabulary was being enlarged by the word 'abomination' and other terms equally improbable in modern London! Before long this foreign student came to rejoice in something far more important than better English. Had these and other such testimonies been gathered together years ago they would have made a large book, but it would never have gained the approval of the minister of Westminster Chapel. He assured all who sat under the preaching of the gospel that he would be more than willing to talk privately with any troubled soul. Other than that, he left all in the hands of God.

---

believe they are converts till I see fruit brought forth. It will do converts no harm to keep them a little back; it will never do a sincere soul any harm.' *Sermons on Important Subjects by G. Whitefield* (London, 1825), p. 603.

As background to this book there are some things which it may be helpful to state by way of introduction.

The Source of these Sermons

Of the twenty-one sermons in this volume, fifteen are printed from the preacher's own handwritten copy and they all belong to the period of his first pastorate at Sandfields, Aberavon, in South Wales (1927–38). It was normal for him at that time to write one sermon per week in full, though of course it was not read in the pulpit and was undoubtedly expanded at certain points in delivery. In particular, his hearers would have been called back to his text more often than his manuscript would indicate. The remaining six sermons were preached at Westminster Chapel and taken down in shorthand; four of them have previously been published in single form.[1] The reader will notice some difference between the sermons he wrote in full and the looser style of the remainder.

It may be of interest for some to add a few words here on the more technical side of his sermon preparation. Once he had selected his text, ML-J's chief concern was to arrive at a division of his subject in the form of an outline or 'skeleton' which satisfied him. He regarded this as the most demanding, creative part of the preacher's work and might often have two or more attempts at forming an outline on the back of an envelope or some other scrap of paper before he was satisfied. The sixteen Sandfields sermons in this book were probably all first prepared in this way. In later years he prepared fuller outlines – usually four sides of paper – and did not write in full.

Dr Lloyd-Jones put much emphasis on the need for a sermon to have a sound structure. In his view, it is the outline which does much either to make a sermon succeed or fail. A poor outline is hardly likely to provide a clear, convincing presentation of a text. The reason the questions which he so often directed to his hearers were so compelling was that they followed a case logically argued.

[1] They are those on Psalm 107; Isaiah 22:8–14; 35:7; all in the *Westminster Record*, and on 1 Samuel 5:1–4, published from a hearer's notes, in the report of the International Congress for Reformed Faith and Action, held in France in 1953. Some of the Sandfields sermons in this volume were also preached a second time at Westminster Chapel.

He excelled Spurgeon in this regard though the last-century preacher understood the need and could write: 'I am not an admirer of the peculiar views of Mr Finney, but I have no doubt that he was useful to many; and his power lay in his use of clear arguments.'[1]

In ML-J's later Sunday morning preaching to Christians, as is well-known, he increasingly preached consecutively through a passage of Scripture over a period of time. But he was much slower to do this in preaching to the unconverted.[2] On a Sunday night, or when he was preaching around the country as he so often did, he had to treat each occasion as possibly the only one he might have with his hearers. He had therefore to be sure that they heard the complete message of the gospel. The idea that he was always 'expository' in the sense of consecutive is therefore erroneous. For evangelistic preaching he mainly used individual, single texts – texts likely to bring to mind the necessity of salvation even when all else was forgotten. This book thus presents a type of textual preaching which is at the present time too often neglected in the interest of being 'expository'.

Why Evangelistic Preaching?

ML-J believed that evangelistic preaching ought to exist *as a special category of preaching*. For him, as already said, gospel preaching was the main part of preaching and the priority which he gave to it can be seen by the fact that it was his Sunday night evangelistic sermon which he generally wrote in full while he was at Aberavon. Today there is a need to re-establish the recognition that the type of sermon most likely to be used to aid the non-Christian is not the same as one intended for those who already believe. Of course, all true preaching has common elements to it. Preaching is the orderly presentation of the Word of God; it must therefore always contain instruction; and it should bring men into the presence of God. But

[1] *Lectures to My Students*, Second Series (London, 1877), p. 185.
[2] One of his earliest evangelistic series of sermons based on a passage was on Matthew 11 in 1948–49, and now published as *The Heart of the Gospel* (Eastbourne: Crossway Books, 1991). For one of his evangelistic series available on tape we draw attention to fourteen sermons on Ezekiel 36 preached in 1956 (Lloyd-Jones Recordings Trust, 25 High Street, Ashford, Kent; and Sound Word Associates, PO Box 2035, Michigan City, Indiana 46360, USA).

it is a serious mistake to think that, provided the content of a sermon is biblical, the preacher need not be concerned whether his text is likely to be used of God to help the converted or the unconverted. There is too much preaching today which suggests that the preacher has no definite conviction about the persons to whom his text and sermon are primarily intended. Spurgeon warns against this in an address to his students on 'Sermons Likely to Win Souls'. He says: 'God the Holy Spirit can convert a soul by any text of Scripture apart from your exposition; but there are certain Scripture passages, as you know, that are the best to bring before the minds of sinners, and if this is true about your texts, much more is it so in your discourses to your hearers.'[1]

Lloyd-Jones believed, as all evangelists have believed, that there ought to be a distinct difference in the approach of the preacher when he is speaking to the unconverted. For one thing, when a sermon is directed to Christians the existence of some measure of interest can be assumed. But to awaken and hold the attention of the non-Christian is a different matter. Here nothing can be assumed. There may be no real interest at all. Some may be present without any intention of actually listening – mere casual onlookers; and some may mean to listen only to be silent critics. It is no use preparing to address non-Christians as though they were all waiting to hear the Word of God. Their real interests presently lie in an altogether different direction, and evangelistic preaching has to break into the world where they are. This was one reason why ML-J regarded the preparation of a true evangelistic sermon as making more demands upon the preacher than any other type of preaching.

But, more important, the evangelistic sermon is a sermon much narrower in its intention than one addressed to Christians. Preaching directed to Christians has to deal with their many and varied needs – it may be of more faith and love, more strength and patience, or whatever. Christians need a wide range of help and instruction. But the non-Christian needs only one thing: he needs to be convicted, to be humbled, to be brought to an end of himself. All preaching ought to be *more* than teaching, but in the case of

[1] *The Soul-Winner* (London, 1895), p. 92. See also his chapter 'On Conversion as our Aim' in *Lectures to My Students*, Second Series.

evangelistic preaching it is imperative. It *must* reach the heart and the conscience or it will fail. It has got to be personal and pointed, and awakening. It will need to have something alarming about it. Men have to be made to face the fact of their spiritual condition. Even in cold print this element will be found often in these pages and, sadly, it contrasts with much that goes for preaching today.

Theodore Cuyler, a well-known nineteenth-century preacher in Brooklyn, on one of his visits to London, was struck by the question Spurgeon put to him: 'How far do your ablest American ministers aim mainly at the conversion of souls?'[1] We are not told the answer but we know what it was both in the case of Spurgeon and of Lloyd-Jones.

Dr Lloyd-Jones' Use of the Old Testament in Evangelistic Preaching

A volume of ML-J's evangelistic sermons preached at Aberavon has already been published.[2] It is made up exclusively of sermons on texts in the four Gospels. Those in this volume are taken exclusively from the Old Testament and I believe that gives them special value at the present time. It may be surprising to note the large use which he made of the Old Testament in the course of his ministry, and the fact that it was very often an evangelistic use. In his first pastorate in Aberavon approximately a third of his texts were taken from the Old Testament. At Westminster Chapel the percentage was only slightly lower with around 430 Old Testament texts. These texts were drawn from all over the Old Testament. When Wilbur M. Smith heard him one Sunday night in 1955 he tells us that the preacher's text was one that he had never noticed before. It was Jeremiah 17:14, 15 ('Heal me, O Lord, and I shall be healed; save me, and I shall be saved . . .') and, as usual on a Sunday

---

[1] Theodore Cuyler, *The Young Preacher* (London, 1893), p. 76. Alexander MacRae, commenting on this same subject as it affected Scotland, quotes Lord Overton who, when laying the foundation stone of the Free Church of Scotland at Fearn, said: 'It is one thing for the Church to be evangelical, and another to be evangelistic. The Church might be evangelical, and hold sound doctrines, but, if the Church was not living in Christ, and leading many souls to Him, it might hold these evangelical truths in vain' (*Revivals in the Highlands and Islands in the 19th Century*, London, n.d., p. 16).

[2] *Evangelistic Sermons at Aberavon* (Edinburgh: Banner of Truth, 1983).

night, the sermon was evangelistic. Smith wrote:

You cannot hear him preach for three minutes without realising that he
believes God is speaking in His Word, that the Word is infallible, and that
what we do with the Word of God will determine our eternal destiny . . . I
have not heard such preaching for years. One thing I determined in my
own soul. I would never be satisfied again, as long as I live, with preaching
but the very best that I have in deadly earnestness and, pray God, in the
power of the Holy Spirit.[1]

It has also to be remembered that as well as the work of his
settled ministry, ML-J was constantly preaching in many other
places and in this field also his use of the Old Testament was
striking. When he took a mission at Oxford University in 1943 his
main addresses were from Jeremiah 6:14–16. Invited to speak at the
International Congress for Reformed Faith and Action in France in
1953, his text was 1 Samuel 5:1–4, with its subject, Dagon, fallen
on his face in the temple of the Philistines. One of the most solemn
evangelistic sermons he ever preached was at a civic service in
Cardiff in 1957. The text was Isaiah 22:8–14, with the words, 'In
that day did the Lord God of hosts call to weeping, and to mourning, and to baldness, and to girding with sackcloth.' These two
sermons are included in the present volume. Again, on his very last
tours in Scotland and mid-Wales the year before his death his
preaching was supremely evangelistic and was based on the words
of Psalm 2. These references are enough to illustrate the extent of
his use of the Old Testament but the question is, why did he attach
this degree of importance to it? Let me offer two reasons:

1. *Because he saw the neglect and near disappearance of the Old
Testament as a powerful influence in contemporary Christianity.*
Here was one of the great contrasts between historic Christianity
and the ministry of the twentieth century. In the writings of the
Reformers or of the Puritans one of the first things which tends to
surprise us is the extent to which they employed the whole Bible.
The same is true of such last-century preachers as Spurgeon.
An index exists of all the texts from which Spurgeon preached

---

[1] *The Fight of Faith*, p. 330.

and it shows that about half of all his texts were from the Old Testament.[1]

A very different position obtained when Dr Lloyd-Jones began his ministry. And today Old Testament preaching, let alone of an evangelistic nature, is hard to find. Those of us who are preachers are probably very conscious of our deficiency in this regard. But why should it be? One reason has to be that we have been living in the after-shock of the assault which was made on the Old Testament by an unbelieving scholarship towards the end of the last century. At the beginning of this century the Scottish Presbyterian minister and higher-critic, Professor George Adam Smith, gave eight lectures at Yale which were subsequently published as *Modern Criticism and the Preaching of the Old Testament*. Smith's case was that higher criticism had provided a new understanding of what was dependable in the Old Testament. Ministers would therefore now be able to deal with the Old with more confidence and the result could only be beneficial to their preaching. There could not have been a greater delusion. N. L. Walker, reviewing Smith's Yale lectures, said:

The book is fitted to do a great deal of mischief . . . Written apparently for the purpose of relieving the perplexities of such preachers as have been disturbed by the higher critics, it has unquestionably failed in that aim. Many preachers will continue to have as many difficulties as before. Professor Smith fails to meet the situation. He has done worse than that. He has awakened doubts where none previously existed and seriously hindered the evangelistic work of the Church.[2]

Walker was more right than he knew. Higher Criticism almost silenced the evangelistic use of the Old Testament. Even evangelicals became so conscious of the general disregard for Old Testament Scripture in the modern world that they were to be, in measure at least, inhibited from using it as truth for unbelievers. They were tempted to think that they could hardly speak of Adam

---

[1] *Commenting and Commentaries* (London: Banner of Truth, 1969), pp. 201–12 lists O.T. texts, and pp. 212–24 those from the N.T.
[2] 'The Case of Prof. George Adam Smith' in *The Presbyterian and Reformed Review* (Philadelphia, October 1902), p. 596.

and Eve, or of such events as the Flood and the parting of the Red Sea, without being a little defensive, if not apologetic.

Perhaps, however, it was chiefly for other reasons that the decline in the use of the Old Testament affected evangelicals. We have been so subjected to the cry for the contemporary and the relevant, so pressured by the insistence that modern life, with all its problems, is uniquely different from anything that has gone before, that we fear the very mention of the Old Testament sounds remote and archaic.[1] And in case that were not enough to deter us, evangelicalism has been assailed from within by those who claim that, in any case, the Old Testament has little to do with Christians: 'The Old Testament was for the Jewish dispensation'; 'There is no grace in the Old Testament', etc. So we can manage well enough without it. Reflecting on this situation, ML-J once gave an address on 'How evangelicals unconsciously deny the Word of God'. One of his headings was, 'Too much separation of the O.T. and the N.T.' He spoke of the feeling that the Old Testament has nothing to do with us now, of the failure to see that there is but one covenant, and of how this attitude led to the ignoring of the Old Testament except as devotional literature.[2]

2. *Dr Lloyd-Jones viewed the disuse of the Old Testament as serious because, being an essential part of divine revelation, such neglect is bound to have far-reaching practical consequences.*
The Bible is contained in two parts, the first given during the millennia between the creation and 400 B.C., the second, during the redemptive history of the first century A.D. But these two parts form one whole. In a typical comment on this point, ML-J said: 'This book is one. We call them Old Testament and New Testament, but it is only one book, you know. Some people say this

---

[1] A. W. Tozer wrote: 'One of the most popular current errors, and the one out of which springs most of the noisy, blustering religious activity in evangelical circles, is the notion that as times change the church must change with them. That mentality which mistakes Hollywood for the Holy City is too gravely astray to be explained otherwise than as a judicial madness visited upon professing Christians for affronts committed against the Spirit of God.' *Renewed Day by Day: A Daily Devotional* (Camp Hill, Pa.: Christian Publications, 1980), February 7.
[2] *The Fight of Faith*, p. 388.

is a library of books; that is a terrible fallacy. This is not a library, this is one book, sixty-six sections in it, but only one book as there is only one theme, one message.'¹ The difference, he would say, lies only in the form in which the message is presented.

So strong was his conviction about this that he says in another place, 'I have never been happy about the practice of printing the two Testaments apart; it leads some people to read only the New Testament.'²

But to understand the practical consequence of the disuse of the Old Testament we have to ask, What is the special purpose of the Old Testament? Why was the revelation before Christ spread through such a long preparatory period? Why did God permit such a delay between the fall of man and the coming of his Son into this world for the work of redemption? Is not the answer that the Old demonstrates at length and in detail that man is in a condition from which only a divine Saviour can deliver him? The Old is a voice crying in a wilderness of sin, 'Prepare ye the way of the Lord' (*Isa.* 40:3). Its purpose is, 'that every mouth might be stopped, and all the world might become guilty before God' (*Rom.* 3:19).

If that is so then we may surely deduce an obvious lesson: to suppose that we can expect to find people ready to take up Christianity though ignorant of the message of the Old Testament is to make ourselves wiser than God. Men need to know that it is the Creator of the universe, the Lord of the nations, the God of Abraham and Isaac and Jacob – this God and no other, who so loved the world that he gave his only-begotten Son. B. B. Warfield once wrote an article on 'How to Get Rid of Christianity'.³ The way it is done, he argued, is this: evaporate the facts out of the Bible; set aside and ignore the historicity of the narratives; and the result will be that men will see no need for Christianity. They will be left unconcerned and indifferent.

Early in the nineteenth century there were some earnest but poorly instructed missionaries who went to Tahiti in the South

---

¹ On 2 Kings 5:8–16; 21 February 1950.
² *Romans, Exposition of Chapters 3.20–4.25: Atonement and Justification* (London: Banner of Truth, 1970), p. 157.
³ *Selected Shorter Writings of B. B. Warfield*, ed. John E. Meeter (Nutley, N.J., 1970), vol. 1, pp. 51–60.

Pacific with the thought that the natives were waiting in childlike simplicity for the gospel. They had a terrible shock. But the same error is to be found in the evangelical world today where the idea exists that all we need to do is to tell people about Christ and salvation and they will want to accept him. Were that true there would have been no need of any Old Testament revelation at all. To by-pass the Old Testament is to ignore the fact that men must be awakened to the sinfulness of sin. Where its testimony is unknown we should not be surprised that men remain indifferent, apathetic and unconcerned.

It was inevitable that a mighty change should take place in the Christian world when the Old Testament was no longer faithfully preached. The inevitable consequence was a loss of the sense of sin and of reverence for God. Sometimes witness to this loss was to be heard in unexpected quarters. R. W. Dale was the successor to John Angell James in Birmingham, and to one of the great evangelical pulpits of the last century. But sadly Dale, along with many others, was one of the many who abandoned the historic Christian view of the Old Testament. He lived to see the result and before the end of his life he confessed one day to a friend, 'Ah, Rogers, no one fears God now'.[1]

When Dale's confession is taken in conjunction with a statement by W.G.T. Shedd it cannot but be related to the absence of revival in twentieth-century Christianity. In a sermon on 'The Use of Fear in Religion', Shedd wrote: 'All the great religious awakenings begin in the dawning of the august and terrible aspects of the Deity upon the popular mind, and they reach their height and happy consummation, in that love and faith for which the antecedent fear has been the preparation.'[2] On the same subject Lloyd-Jones noted,

---

[1] Quoted by G. H. Morrison, *Flood-Tide* (London, n.d.), p. 108. Seeking to counter the tide of popular opinion, Morrison spoke of the O.T. as 'preserved to counteract a natural tendency of man. For God in the Gospel comes so near us, and the love of God shown in the love of Jesus is so brotherlike, that only to realise it is to run the danger of forgetting reverence and growing very familiar with God . . . O living Spirit, open our eyes and give us back again something of the fear of God! For we shall never learn to love or serve Thee well till we have learned to reverence Thee more!'

[2] W. G. T. Shedd, *Sermons to the Natural Man* (1876; Banner of Truth, 1977), p. 331.

'The importance of keeping your eye on the Old Testament emerges here in the whole question of evangelism and revivals.'[1]

How Dr Lloyd-Jones came to his use of the Old Testament in preaching

If neglect of the Old Testament had become common early in this century, how did it come about that Dr Lloyd-Jones made such major use of the Old Testament in his preaching from the very outset of his ministry? Where did he learn this? Had he observed, perhaps, models of this type of preaching in his childhood which he now began to follow? The answer, very definitely, is, No. In the denomination in which he grew up, and in which he early became a communicant, all were encouraged to regard themselves as Christians. 'It was not', he writes, 'a true assessment of my condition. What I needed was preaching that would convict me of sin and make me see my need, and bring me to true repentance and tell me something about regeneration. But I never heard it. The preaching we had was always based on the assumption that we were all Christians.'[2] Such preaching as he did hear in his youth from the Old Testament was sentimental and moralistic. His own preaching was to be entirely different.

Can it be, then, that he acquired his insight into the evangelistic use of the Old Testament from Christian literature, old or modern? In 1925, the very year when ML-J was struggling over the call of God to the work of the ministry, two articles appeared from the pen of O. T. Allis in the *Princeton Theological Review* entitled 'Old Testament Emphases' and 'Modern Thought'. Speaking of these emphases, Allis wrote:

The most striking thing about them is the extent to which they are ignored or denied, even by those who call themselves Christians. This fact makes it only the more evident how necessary it is that the minister of the Word should set himself in all earnestness to restore these lost emphases to their rightful place in the faith and life of 'modern' man who needs them no whit less than did the men of yesterday and of years and centuries that are gone.[3]

[1] *Romans, Exposition of Chapter 1* (Edinburgh: Banner of Truth, 1984), p. 95.
[2] *Preaching and Preachers*, p. 146.
[3] *Princeton Theological Review* (Princeton, N.J.), July and October, 1925.

Can it be that ML-J saw these two fine articles by Allis and was influenced by them? Again, the answer has to be, No. It is certain he read and knew nothing of the Princeton theologians in 1925. Nor did he read anything else on the subject which was formative in his thinking. While books were to be a major aid in his future ministry I believe that they played no part as far as this issue was concerned. The conclusion has to be that ML-J learned the application of the Old Testament to the unconverted from an entirely different source and what that source was is patently clear: he saw the history of the Old Testament being repeated in the London of the early 1920s! In those years he was on the threshold of what would have been a very eminent career in medicine. He was already rubbing shoulders with the successful and the great, with some of the most brilliant medical minds of his day. And through his chief, Sir Thomas Horder, he had access to medical notes and personal observations on kings and prime ministers. What did this experience and information reveal? Why, here was human nature precisely as depicted in the Word of God – arrogant, proud, unhappy, covetous, lustful, and dissatisfied. More than that, the testimony of Old Testament Scripture had come powerfully alive in his own conscience. His was the heart deceitful above all things and desperately wicked. He was the fool who thought he could live without God. He was the restless unbeliever who wandered in the wilderness in the solitary way and found no city to dwell in. Then, when he at last cried unto God in his trouble, God intervened and brought him from darkness into the kingdom of his dear Son.

We know little of the details of Lloyd-Jones' conversion but we know that his new life and his call to the ministry were close to each other. He saw the need of others almost as soon as he saw his own, and when he went straight from medicine to a mission pulpit it was supremely clear to him that nothing had changed in human nature since the Old Testament was written. Its characters under different names were all alive in Port Talbot. Let the Book, therefore, be held up like a mirror and, in God's mercy, men would come to see themselves and discover their need of a Saviour. The certainty and authority with which he preached this was born straight out of his own experience.

It was typical of ML-J's view of preaching that in the pulpit he generally said nothing about himself. In his Old Testament

evangelistic sermons at Port Talbot we recall no personal references, no parallels drawn between characters in his texts and his
own life. Yet it is certain he first saw himself in the text before he
applied it to anyone else.[1] And this habit was lifelong as can be
seen below in a sermon which he preached as late as 1960. His
subject was Naaman, captain of the host of the king of Syria, as
described in 2 Kings 5:1–14, 'Naaman was a great man . . . a mighty
man in valour, but he was a leper.' Perhaps it can be anticipated how
ML-J would handle this. He began by proving that there is always a
'but' in human experience, some trouble, some disappointment,
some running sore. No life is whole, unspoiled and complete in
happiness and peace. Sin is the universal problem, affecting even
the greatest and the most successful, and it is a problem beyond all
human remedy. Here are two kings, of Syria and of Israel, and both
utterly incapable of finding a solution to Naaman's disease. The
problem is too deep for them, the disease is too foul for them and
the medicaments are inadequate. But in the midst of human helplessness there came the report of an Israelite kitchen girl who
declared that there was a prophet of the living God in Samaria,
Elisha, and she knew that through him God could recover even the
leper. So at length the great Naaman goes to Elisha only to be en-
raged by the way the prophet treats him. Naaman feels humiliated
and insulted. He will not have a cure on the humbling terms which
the prophet proposes.

It is at this point in the second sermon that ML-J becomes most
experimental and blazing. Naaman was offended because he
received no special treatment, and, said the preacher, 'There are
many in this congregation who are in that precise position at this
moment.' They disliked the way the gospel treats all alike and gives
special attention or respect to none. Naaman was only a leper like
any other leper, why should he have special treatment? Because the
prophet's message hurts his pride he will not have the cure that is
offered:

---

[1] His wife, whom he married the year he went to Port Talbot, had misgivings
about his being able to sustain a ministry. 'How do you know you can preach?'
she asked him before he took up the work. His significant answer was, 'I know
I can preach to myself'.

Look at this man Naaman. Here he is, a leper, he cannot cure himself, the physicians, wise men and astrologers cannot cure him, his king cannot cure him, the king of Israel cannot cure him and yet, look at the fool, what else can you call him; though he is helpless and hopeless as a leper and everybody can do nothing for him, he is fool enough to criticise what Elisha does and to argue and to put up his objections and protestations. What can you say of the man but that he is a fool and a lunatic?

The preacher is then fairly carried away as he applies the point further both to Naaman and to his unbelieving listeners. All men, he says, are miserable failures yet they have the folly to criticise the salvation which has been sent into the world by God. But then, after more such words, ML-J allowed a brief and certainly unpremeditated personal reference which speaks volumes: 'You know I am sounding harsh about this man Naaman, I am really very sorry for him because I understand him so well. I have *been in Naaman's position*, like everyone else you see.'[1]

In those words we have the key to his evangelistic preaching from the Old Testament: it came out of his own experience. As with John Bunyan, he preached what he 'smartingly did feel'.

Lloyd-Jones' Understanding of the Chief Emphases of the Old Testament

1. *Scripture reveals sin in its true nature.*
Dr Lloyd-Jones believed that the difference between moralising preaching on the Old Testament and true evangelistic preaching is that moralising deals only with sin in terms of its symptoms and secondary features. The essence of sin, the true seriousness of sin, can only begin to be understood when it is seen in terms of a wrong relationship and attitude to God himself. Sin is revolt and rebellion against God. It is man asserting his will against God's will. It means defying God, fighting against God, refusing to live for the glory of God. Scripture speaks of man being in a state of 'wrath' against the true God. Preaching on 'Surely the wrath of man shall praise thee' (*Psa.* 76:10), ML-J said:

Man has turned his back upon God and has enmity in his heart towards God and is trying to live his life in this world without God and apart from God, and he regards God as one who interferes and upsets everything . . .

[1] See below p. 137.

That is what our author means by referring to the 'wrath of man'. And of course you find this great story unfolded in the pages of the Bible and it is the whole key to the understanding of secular history, man fighting God, man refusing to humble himself before God, and arrogantly and proudly doing the exact opposite, so that what you have in the Bible is an account of the conflict between this glorious God and man in sin.

Unless men are brought to know that because of the fall their entire relationship to God is wrong, they cannot begin to understand how their problem is to be dealt with. As a point of contact with unconverted hearers, ML-J often introduced sermons by speaking of the various problems of life and of the world. He used them to show that there was something profoundly wrong, but the tragedy of man is that he continues to be blind to the real nature of his problem. He can recognize something of his troubles but he cannot see that his fundamental problem has to do with God himself.

In 1947, at a time when the whole western world was agog with the issue of the atom bomb and the possibility of atomic warfare, ML-J preached two sermons on the conversion of Jacob at Penuel, both printed for the first time in these pages. Here is Jacob, returning to Canaan after his long absence and afraid of the anger of Esau which he deserved. He sees his problem as the threat of Esau, and Esau's four hundred men, and so makes his various arrangements to deal, as he hoped, with the danger. But Jacob had to be shown something far more fundamental. He had to be brought to forget all about Esau:

Jacob discovered there at Penuel that his real problem, if I may put it with reverence, was not Esau, but God. You see this man's primary error was, 'How can I appease Esau?' but what God said was, 'My dear Jacob, what you need is not to be reconciled to Esau, but to be reconciled to me', and that, I say, is the essence of the modern difficulty and the modern problem . . . Man was made by God, in the image of God – man was meant for companionship with God. . . The gospel comes to us and makes us see that by living a life apart from God, and apart from Christ, we are living a life which is a travesty of human nature and we are doing something that is utterly insulting to God . . . There is the danger of the atomic bomb – I am not here to say that there is not a danger but, my dear friends, infinitely greater and more important than the danger of being killed perhaps in a few years with an atomic bomb is this danger that my everlasting and eternal soul may go to hell and spend itself there in misery and torment because I am wrong with God – that is my danger! Esau isn't the problem, the atomic bomb isn't the problem – No, no, you yourself are the problem ultimately, not Esau but God, not Esau but myself, not being what I am meant to be; not land and possessions and goods but the loss of my immortal soul.[1]

This was Dr Lloyd-Jones' starting point and he held it to be the only sound starting point for true evangelism. By one historic fall the whole human race stands alienated from God. This emphasis ran right through his entire ministry. He was constantly bringing his hearers to such questions as these:

Have you ever faced the question of your attitude to God? Are you a rebel against God? Are you a hater of God? Do you feel you know better than God? If so, well, I tell you what you are suffering now is nothing to what you will have to suffer. That is the root cause of all ills and troubles, it is the cause of all suffering, all pain, all confusion. The only hope is to acknowledge it, to face it, to go to God in utter contrition and repentance.[2]

There are two deductions which he constantly made from this starting point:

(i) Sin must never be preached as though it were *primarily* a matter of actions. *Sinfulness* is a graver problem than sins. 'The carnal mind is enmity against God' (*Rom.* 8:7). A 'religious' church member who remains self-centred will be as surely lost as the most profligate.

(ii) Until a person comes to know the truth about himself he can never approach the gospel in the right spirit. Without self-knowledge he may investigate, discuss and reason but it will do him no good at all. Because the real need is for a personal meeting with God and until we come to him in submission we cannot come at all. A typical example of the way ML-J insisted on this can be read below in his sermon on Moses at the burning bush.[3]

[1] See below pp. 28–30.
[2] MS of unpublished sermon on Isaiah 1:1–2, 3 February 1963.
[3] See below p. 33.

2. *Scripture reveals the absolute futility of life without God.*

It was Lloyd-Jones' conviction that the gospel itself is not necessarily the main subject in true evangelistic teaching, rather the main subject must often be truth which brings home to men and women their need of the gospel. That was exactly how he saw much of the purpose of Old Testament history. Here is a record of people as individuals and as nations. With one voice they tell us that all human existence is the story of weakness, failure and death. Man is a feeble, ruined creature whose inner longings can never be satisfied apart from God. Man aims to restore himself and others to paradise but he will never succeed. His hopes of final peace can never be fulfilled. This is what the Holy Spirit proves in Scripture and ML-J saw it as the preacher's calling to prove it too. He never had a problem in moving from an Old Testament character to his own day. It is characteristic of his thinking that when, for instance, he is preaching on Adonijah from 1 Kings 1:41, he asserts, 'What explains the story of Adonijah is precisely the same thing as explains the lives of hundreds of people living at this present time.'

Sometimes he took the history of nations in the Old Testament as declaring the same lesson. Man cannot deal with his problems. The power of Egypt, of the Canaanites, of Babylon of all the great empires is transitory and soon gone for ever. These great civilisations came up one after another, but they all failed.[1] And the history of Israel itself, far from showing that the chosen people possessed some natural religious genius, as liberals claimed, reveals how men, even when highly privileged, constantly depart from God.

On this subject his preaching in his early days in South Wales shows only one difference from his later preaching in London. In his later ministry he made more direct use of the supporting testimony of modern non-Christians to show the emptiness of all human expectations.

So far was ML-J from being intimidated by the popular idea that the Old Testament was too far behind modern times to speak to us, that he would often meet that argument head-on. He did so memorably in a sermon in 1961, at a time when the world was agog with the news of the Russian cosmonaut, Major Yuri Gagarin, and

[1] *Romans, Exposition of Chapter 1*, p. 84.

his first manned flight in space. The text for that sermon was Job chapter 38: 'But where shall wisdom be found? and where is the place of understanding?. . . And unto man he said, Behold, the fear of the Lord, that is wisdom; and to depart from evil is understanding'. In the course of developing the interest of his hearers, he conceded that mankind across the centuries had accumulated much information and, alluding to the Russian exploit, confessed that Job had never heard of Major Gagarin. Never heard of him. But then he proceeded to demonstrate that wisdom was a very different thing from mere knowledge or information. What had the modern man really got, what was all his knowledge producing? What is the use of being able to travel from London to New York in five hours if man does not know how to live when he gets there? The modern view of man is that he is just an animal who is in the world to eat or drink or to indulge in sex. It is the part of wisdom to ask, What is life? Where is it leading? How can I put my head down on the pillow and rest in peace, and not be afraid that I am going to die suddenly? How can I look into an unknown eternity? Then the preacher proceeded to prove man's ignorance of God until, at the end of a long sermon, he shut his hearers up to the sure conclusion:

'The fear of the Lord, that is wisdom'. What does this mean? My dear friend, it is as simple as this, you have to submit yourself utterly, entirely, and absolutely to God and his way. There is no wisdom apart from God. Money cannot buy it. You can have it for nothing. It is the free gift of God!

3. *Above all else, the Old Testament is a book about God.*
Nowhere was his thinking more contrary to the modern view of the Old Testament than at this point. According to the modern view the Old Testament is the story of man's religious development, a record of the Jews' progress of discovery. To say that, ML-J believed, was sure proof of blindness. The Bible is revelation. Its answer to the question, 'Canst thou by searching find out God?' (*Job* 11:7) is an emphatic, No! 'Behold, God is great, and we know him not' (*Job* 36:26). God has come to us and made himself and his will known in Scripture which is his Word: 'When men come to the Bible, and find all this history about kings and people, they say, What is the meaning of it all? This is the meaning of it all, it is just to manifest the sovereignty and glory and the might and majesty and the dominion of God. The assertion of the Bible is that God is

over all and, whether we like it or not, God will remain over all. The man who does not submit and recognize and accept it joyfully, and glorify God, is the man who sooner or later will be forced to do so.'[1]

The purpose of preaching is to confront men with this vision of God, not the gods which the nations have conjectured – 'the gods of the people of the earth, which were the work of the hands of men' (*2 Chron.* 32:19) – but the living God, almighty, infinite and eternal. Our maker, who knows us individually and yet who upholds all things by his power; our sovereign ruler, who has our breath in his hand; our holy judge, whose image we have lost, and to whom we must all soon give an account. Jonathan Sacks, the British Chief Rabbi, wrote recently that 'God has been exiled by much of our culture. But He exists where we let Him in.'[2] Such words represent a view of God alien to the Bible. Rather, God speaks to us as One altogether above our actions and decisions, and whose will can never fail. Christ charges his disciples to fear God on the grounds that he 'is able to destroy both soul and body in hell' (*Matt.* 10:28). Modern religious man affects to despise a message which comes to us with words of warning and threat but that is precisely how God addresses us. He spoke in that way before the Flood. He spoke in that way before fire fell on Sodom and Gomorrah. He spoke in that way at Sinai and so he continues to speak: 'For the wrath of God *is* revealed from heaven against all ungodliness and unrighteousness of men' (*Rom.* 1:18). We have wilfully withheld from God the glory which is his due and we all stand deserving of hell.

Lloyd-Jones believed that there can be no true evangelistic preaching where the wrath of God is not being made known. Any such preaching has to be unscriptural. 'In the Old Testament alone more than twenty words are used to describe the wrath of God, and these words in various forms are used 580 times in the Old Testament . . . If you take out of the Bible this idea of the wrath of God against sin there is very little Bible left.'[3]

---

[1] Psalm 70:10; 25 March 1951.
[2] 'Credo: God exists where we let Him in', *The Times*, 8 May, 1993.
[3] *Romans, Exposition of Chapters 3.20–4.25,* pp. 74, 79.

To hide this truth from men is to hide biblical proof that our present relationship to God is wrong and that it must be changed if we are not to perish. False views of God's character inevitably cause men to misread what Scripture reveals. Thus men turn the Old Testament into a code of ethics, a book calling for our moral effort and endeavour. But to do this is to be blind – as the unbelieving Jews were blind – to its greatest and most glorious theme, namely, the acts of God. The Old Testament is divine testimony to redemptive history. So ML-J, preaching from it, can say:

If we fail to realise that the gospel and all it professes is primarily an activity on the part of God and not on the part of man, we have entirely failed to understand it. Of course, man has something and indeed much to do in the scheme of salvation, but all that is secondary. Man only begins to act after God has first acted and has rendered man capable of action. What is the Bible after all but an account of God's activity and action in the matter of human salvation.[1]

The preaching of the gospel is not meant to be an appeal to men and women to do something that will make them Christian – it is an announcement, a proclamation to them about something that God has done and that will make them Christian.[2]

For ML-J the rejection of the note of judgment in the Old Testament led inevitably to the suppression of the true glory of redemptive love. From Genesis 3 onwards there is the disclosure of salvation from judgment by the wonderful provision of God – there is a promised Substitute; expiatory sacrifice and 'the blood of sprinkling' are the means whereby sinners are to be restored to God at amazing cost. The way of Isaac's deliverance is the only way for us all: 'My son, God will provide himself a lamb for a burnt offering' (*Gen.* 22:8). On this subject a certain Professor Lofthouse wrote earlier in this century: 'At the present day it must be confessed that to large numbers sacrificial teaching has no appeal at all . . . The evangelical "plan of salvation" strikes them as cumbrous and artificial.'[3] Of course! ML-J would have replied. Men unconvinced of sin will remain disinterested in the gospel.

[1] Port Talbot sermon on Jeremiah 30:18, 19. See below p. 243.
[2] Genesis 32:24; 27 April 1947. See below p. 24.
[3] Quoted by O.T. Allis in *Princeton Theological Review*, October 1925, p. 600.

'They that be whole need not a physician, but they that are sick' (*Matt.* 9:12). The whole position changes when an individual recognizes his true condition in the sight of God, when he learns that he cannot save himself, and feels, with Naaman, the leprosy that is destroying him. Let these things be understood and the knowledge of how God can both be just and 'delight in mercy' is knowledge which is life eternal.[1]

For ML-J all the essential elements of the gospel are present in Old Testament revelation. He regarded any idea that the new birth only belongs to the New Testament era as 'thoroughly unscriptural'.[2] Foremost among these elements, and foremost in his preaching, was that because salvation is the work of God it is something large and vast, something 'which completely and entirely changes us', and something, therefore, which leads men to wonder and amazement. A 'gospel' which merely exhorts men to live a better life, to be good and kind, has no such effect: 'it ceases to be something which breaks in upon us and overwhelms us with its majesty and graciousness. But such is always the effect of the gospel which announces God's action. He amazed Abraham and Jacob and David and the prophets and all the New Testament saints.'

I quote these words from the introduction to one of his most memorable sermons of the 1930s. The text was the words of Jeremiah 30:18,19: 'Thus saith the Lord; Behold, I will bring again the captivity of Jacob's tents, and have mercy on his dwelling places; and the city shall be builded upon her own heap . . .' His divisions of his subject were as follows: '1. The task with which the gospel is faced.' Man in ruins, just as Jerusalem was a ruined heap in the time of Jeremiah. All that man was meant to be has been ruined and demolished. '2. A task with which only the gospel can deal.' The children of Israel with their city destroyed were captives in Babylon, powerless to help themselves. So too all men are failures, unable to deal with their past, and defeated in the present. They are no more able to renew their own souls than were the Israelites able to rebuild Jerusalem. '3. The task to which the gospel alone is equal.' The words of the text were actually fulfilled, God brought

---

[1] For the way he handles this from the Naaman passage see below pp. 135–42.
[2] *Romans, Exposition of Chapter 1*, p. 95.

the people back, and on the very site and ruins of the old city the new city was built:

God offers to do the impossible. And he does the impossible. He comes to us and speaks to us in our deepest trouble and woe. He comes to us when we are defeated and helpless and miserable, realising what we have done and our desperate plight. He comes to us and announces what he purposes to do. It is his moment, his action, his initiative. He announces that he is going to work a miracle upon us – 'the city shall be builded upon her own heap'. He promises us life and joy. Just when we are most unhappy and forlorn the wondrous word comes. How does it come? In and through Jesus Christ, the Son of God.[1]

Lloyd-Jones was one of a triumvirate of famous preachers in London in his day. Describing these three, the shrewd remark was once made that Soper preached love, Weatherhead preached Jesus, while the minister of Westminster Chapel preached God. That was what Lloyd-Jones believed every preacher is called to do as he follows the mind of God in Scripture. But it is the balance of his evangelistic preaching that is so marked. God is proclaimed as 'the high and lofty One that inhabiteth eternity, whose name is Holy', yet he dwells 'with him also that is of a contrite and humble spirit, to revive the spirit of the humble and to revive the heart of the contrite ones'. The thunder of justice and (still more) the tenderness of love, are both present. To the critic there is an inconsistency in ML-J's gospel preaching. He preaches man's inability and absolute dependence upon God but then he speaks of the arms of divine mercy thrown open to all, of the love of God in Christ as ready to embrace all, of an atonement freely offered as a gift for all. But such an 'inconsistency' belongs in Scripture itself. Certainly there is a universal love revealed in Scripture and its wonder is not to be belittled. But the love that *saves* is the love made known to those who, having heard of their lost condition and entire undeservedness, are ready to be saved by grace alone. One emphasis in preaching belongs to men unhumbled in their natural pride and another to those who have come to an end of themselves. When it comes to addressing the latter the preacher has to be as unfettered as Scripture is unfettered in the proclamation of salvation to all.

[1] See the whole sermon below, p. 242ff.

The theorist may analyse such preaching but it was supremely wonderful to those who passed from death to life under its message. This writer will never forget a man sharing the same pew with him at Westminster Chapel one evening and weeping tears of joy at the sense of God's love shed abroad in his heart. As though to apologise for his emotion, he explained to me that he came from an area where such preaching was not to be heard. True gospel preaching will always leave some saying, 'How Thou couldst love a wretch like me, and be the God Thou art, is darkness to my intellect but sunshine to my heart'. From the time Thomas Charles heard Daniel Rowland preach, he tells us, 'I have lived in a new heaven and a new earth . . . my mind was overwhelmed and overpowered with amazement. The truths exhibited to my view appeared too wonderfully gracious to be believed.'[1] Such a statement was equally made by people at Sandfields (Aberavon) and Westminster Chapel, and the preacher viewed it as nothing more than a testimony to the power of the Holy Spirit. Preachers are only as the kitchen maid in Naaman's house who had the answer that others did not know. Lloyd-Jones believed that modern preaching was weak because of a failure in handling 'the sword of the Spirit, which is the word of God' (*Eph.* 6:17); Scripture was not being 'rightly divided', and often because men thought evangelism would be more effective if it did not start where Scripture starts. 'The tragedy is that we do not believe in the power of the Holy Ghost as Paul did. Paul did not ask "will the Romans like this doctrine? I wonder whether, when they see that this is my message, they will stay away!" Paul knew that it all depended upon the power of the Holy Spirit.'[2]

The solution to the present predicament of the churches does not lie simply in a new understanding of preaching. There must be men and congregations raised up afresh by the Spirit of God. But in pleading for such blessings let us not forget the present wonder that we have the abiding Word of God in our hands.

Over a century ago there was more than one man by the name of Smith identified with Higher Criticism of the Bible. George Adam Smith we have mentioned above. Robertson Smith was no less

[1] D. E. Jenkins, *The Life of Thomas Charles of Bala* (Denbigh, 1910), vol. 1, p. 35.
[2] *Romans, Exposition of Chapter 1*, p. 330.

famous in the same school. But another Smith, which a declining Protestantism did not choose to hear, was Henry M. Smith of Columbia Theological Seminary, South Carolina. In 1884 he gave an address on 'The Old Testament in History; Or, Revelation and Criticism'. It concluded with words on the Bible well suited to close this introduction:

Here is a book which comes among men as a stranger, yet it is received with spontaneous gladness by every race and in every age. As soon as it is received, every heart is fired with zeal to propagate and perpetuate it. It has filled the world with love and strife. Other things grow old, but it lives in immortal youth. Through all the centuries it has survived alike its friends and its foes. Without a stain upon its garments, it rises above the thoughts of man in peerless majesty. And it stands today on the threshold of a career grander, perhaps, than all its wondrous history.

'All flesh is as grass, and all the glory of man as the flower of grass. The grass withereth, and the flower therof falleth away: but the word of the Lord endureth for ever. And this is the word which by the gospel is preached unto you' (*1 Pet.* 1:24, 25).[1]

IAIN H. MURRAY
Edinburgh, March 1995

[1] *Memorial Volume of the Semi-Centennial of the Theological Seminary at Columbia, South Carolina* (Columbia, S.C., 1884), p. 83.

PUBLISHER'S NOTE

The sermons are printed according to the biblical sequence of their texts, not in the order in which they were preached. All the undated sermons were preached during Dr Lloyd-Jones' first pastorate at Sandfields, Aberavon, South Wales (1927–38) and are taken from his original manuscripts. Westminster Chapel sermons are given as recorded in shorthand. Dr Lloyd-Jones gave no titles to his sermons and in each instance, therefore, we have supplied them.

I

The Only Explanation[1]

And they heard the voice of the LORD God walking in the garden in the cool of the day: and Adam and his wife hid themselves from the presence of the LORD God amongst the trees of the garden. And the LORD God called unto Adam, and said unto him, Where art thou?

Genesis 3:8–9

In this third chapter of the book of Genesis we find ourselves face to face with one of the most important chapters of the Bible. It is one of those pivotal chapters because the doctrine which is there taught is something which is an absolute essential to the understanding of the central message of this Book. The Bible is primarily the textbook of salvation; it is an account of God's way of saving men and women and this particular chapter is one which is an absolute necessity to an understanding of the whole biblical standpoint. More precisely, we can put it like this: the message of this third chapter of Genesis is the one above all others which tells us exactly why this world of ours is as it is tonight. It is the chapter which shows us why God's way of salvation has ever become necessary; it tells us what it was that went wrong with man and with the world and why the coming of the Son of God from heaven to earth became an absolute necessity. It is here, I say, that we are provided with the explanation.

Now this is a subject which should be of concern to every thoughtful person at this present time and it is, of course, one which is very frequently being discussed. The question is: Why are things as they are? What is the matter with our world? How have we come to this present position? Why are we in our present predicament? That is the question of all questions at the present time. The books, the journals and the articles are all dealing with

[1] Westminster Chapel, 17 January 1948.

it and we can listen to series of talks about it. It is the so-called problem of our time and it is a problem which if we take life and ourselves at all seriously we must inevitably face. Let us face this whole question as we study this chapter and especially this first recorded question that was ever put to a human being – 'Adam, where art thou?'.

This is not a theoretical question. I do not propose that we just have an interesting discussion or a monologue as you may call it. We are not met to discuss this matter in an abstract manner; we are none of us in a position to indulge in such luxuries. We all heard the other day of a young man at the age of twenty cycling along a road and suddenly the end comes. We are all in that position; and in the midst of life we are in death. Therefore, we are really discussing ourselves and what is to be our ultimate destiny. In other words, while it is very interesting to talk about the state of the world, we must remember that the world is nothing but a collection of men and women just like ourselves, and the world is as it is because individuals are as they are. We must beware of this fatal tendency to isolate this something called the 'world' and forget that the world is but ourselves.

There are two points of view on the subject before us. There is the position which is expounded in this Book which we call the Bible, and there are all the other views, and all the other views in a sense can be summed up as a general belief in some evolutionary process. I do not want to go into this in detail tonight because I am concerned with a positive exposition, but I say that anybody that does not accept the biblical explanation of the state of the world and society tonight will be found to be holding the belief that the world has somehow evolved – that there was once a primitive form of life which has gradually evolved itself; man is undergoing a process of evolution and development and every generation finds him a little bit higher up the scale than he was before. As man is higher than the animal, so he is better than the generation before; we look back, therefore, and we believe that this process is taking man on to an ultimate perfection.

I just put it like this in a hurried word in passing. But is there anyone who still seriously can maintain that the present facts and the present position justify us in saying that man today is better and more advanced than he has ever been? that he is better spiritually and morally? that he is a more perfect example of human being? Is there anyone facing the stark facts of today who would venture to put this forward? The tragedy is that we hold on to these ideas, these theories, in spite of the facts which confront us. We must rather, I say, turn to this explanation which the Bible gives of the present state of life. We can put in this form: it does not tell us everything in detail, but it does give us a key to the main problem and to an understanding of the essential situation. There are many things which are left unanswered. People are always asking, what is the origin of evil? And there is but one answer – We do not know. Someone may say, 'Who is this serpent? How did he become what he became?' You may say in reply that there was some kind of cosmic fall before the creation. All right, but still the question remains, How was even a cosmic fall possible? And there we answer, We do not know. We are face to face with a fact. We do not claim that the Bible gives an ultimate explanation of the origin of evil in a primary sense. No-one else can explain it. But it does give us an extraordinary explanation and one which I want to try to show you so fits the facts as to call for our most serious consideration. Let me summarise it like this:

The Bible tells us God made the world, he made man. He placed male and female in a position that can be described as paradise. There they lived and had communion with God. You get an idyllic picture. Then you come on and get this other picture which is provided in this third chapter. It tells us of life as it was and then shows us this picture of Adam and Eve hiding in their misery and wretchedness, trying to avoid God and get away from that Voice that followed them. It announces the curse that came upon the earth – that the woman should conceive in sorrow and pain and that the man should toil and eat in the sweat of his face – and we are told how thorns and thistles, disease and death came in. First life as God made it; then life as it has become. There is the whole answer, the whole explanation of the position which we are considering together.

But you notice the Bible goes beyond just painting the two pictures. It tells us *how* the first became the second. And there it introduces us to its doctrine of what is called sin. It tells us that because man did certain things he changed the whole situation, and that everything that you and I inherit tonight is because of that;

[3]

that the world is as it is tonight simply because of this self-same thing. The Bible's philosophy can be summed up under two main headings:

The first is that *man's troubles are in himself and not in his environment.* There you see is a fundamental postulate as far as the Bible is concerned. Now all those other views believe the exact opposite. They say that man himself is all right if only he were given a chance. That is why they are so interested in environment; they believe that if only conditions can be put right then mankind is going to be all right. Their essential belief is that the trouble is in man's environment. In the very beginning the Bible gives the lie direct to any such theories and ideas. It tells us that man started in a perfect environment; he had everything that can be desired; there was nothing lacking and yet it tells us that it was in that perfect paradise of a condition that man did something that turned his paradise into a wilderness. In its history the Bible constantly goes on illustrating this same theme. At times it seems almost ironical in its method of presenting it. We are given pictures of men who were the sons of most saintly fathers, who were taught the Word of God, who had everything that could be desired, but they turned out to be some of the worst characters that are depicted in these pages. The Bible says man's troubles are not in his conditions and circumstances, but in himself.

And the second heading is that *ultimately our troubles are due to a wrong relationship to God.* That is the great message of this chapter. Here I need not turn aside to point out that this is the big thing that is never faced in the modern world. If only the world realised this tonight, then, I say, we should have taken the first vital step in the right direction. Yet here we see it so plainly and clearly. It is because man went out of the right relationship with God that everything else began to go wrong.

This, then, is the biblical explanation of all our troubles. It says that they are all due to sin. It gives us that first tragic picture and its message is to tell us that the tragedy of the world is that man goes on repeating this mistake. Men and women, in spite of this revelation, still go on doing exactly and precisely what Adam and Eve did at the beginning. Man's tragedy is that he will not listen but turns a blind eye to history. The trouble of this story in Genesis chapter three is still being enacted.

[4]

Let us look at it in this way: there in that garden you see a man and a woman, miserable, unhappy, ashamed, realising that something vital has gone wrong and they hear the Voice, they hear God walking in the garden in the cool of the evening and he comes to them and asks 'Adam, where art thou?' At which they cower and hide. That in a sense is the epitome of the whole of the message of the Bible. Man is in his present state because of certain fundamental troubles. Here they are put very plainly before us. If we analyse what led Adam into his unhappy position, we shall discover what brings man into that position tonight. What are the reasons?

The first is surely this: *man's fatal belief that he knows what is best for himself.* Here is man, created by God, in a state of perfection and placed in perfect conditions and surroundings. Why did that not continue? Why does man find himself hiding amongst the trees, and having to earn his bread by the sweat of his brow and face pestilence and disease and death itself? What has gone wrong? The simple answer is that man believed that he knew better than God how to manage his own affairs. It is as simple as that. God put man in the garden and said, 'Now you just live life as I ask you to live it; I give you great liberty; but there is just this one prohibition.' God gave man law and told him that he would be happy and in communion with God, that he would reap the benefits of this glorious creation, he would never have to face difficulties or death – but you remember what happened. The temptation came to man in this form. It was put to him that God was thus limiting him, being unfair to him; that if he only believed it there was a much bigger kind of life available for him, and so he should disbelieve what God said and flout his law, and should take of the fruit of that particular tree and thereby he would obtain knowledge and information and he would become a god. There was a way of life superior to that which God had indicated! Man accepted the lie and the whole message of the Bible is just to tell us that misery, wretchedness and death and all the troubles of the world, individually and collectively, tonight result from that one thing – the disobedience and lawlessness of Adam and Eve, their refusal to live as God would have them live, and putting their own thoughts in the position of God's holy law.

That, my friend, sounds almost childish in its simplicity and yet

[5]

I ask you to ponder and consider whether that is not something which is most obvious in this world of ours tonight. Just think of the tremendous efforts that are being made individually, in gatherings, in groups, to discuss the social problem, the economic problem, the political problem; the whole world is asking what is the matter with the world; what can be done to put it right. I am not saying that men are not perfectly sincere but I am here to point out that in all the noise and talk and conference and discussion the one vital thing is never mentioned. The one thing that is never being considered is this: are all our troubles after all due to the fact that we are not living life as God told us to live it? Because we are not in the right relationship to God?

But, I am not here to discuss this problem in terms of the national or international situation, I am here to be urgent and serious in an individual sense and the question I put at this point is, therefore, just this: On what is your life based? Are you happy? Is all well? Are you free from any sense of shame? Can you say that you have not got a running sore in your soul? Are you not longing for something better? Do you not know within yourself that there is another kind of life? How otherwise do you explain the sense of shame? – of being shackled and fettered? Is there not something standing between you and a glorious life? – Do we not have a curious feeling within us that we were not meant for the kind of thing we are experiencing, but for something bigger – an inner cry for an ampler and diviner air?

Our trouble is we repeat this ancient error of Adam; instead of facing life in the light of this Book, we live according to man's ideas, we choose the philosophies of men which say that our troubles are in our environment. No, my trouble is that I have not been obeying the law of God. God has told me very plainly what he wants me to do in the Ten Commandments, in the moral law, in the Sermon on the Mount, in all the teaching of the Gospels and Epistles. It has been in the teaching of the church throughout the ages and the centuries, the call to live life in God's way. Now, I say, the question we should ask is, Am I doing my all, my everything, to live my life in God's way? For, according to the Bible, the initial cause of all our ills and troubles is this fatal idea that we know how to live life in a manner that is better than that which is indicated by God.

Let every man examine himself. When I face my working

philosophy of life – we have all got some sort of theory by which we live, some sort of an idea, even the most thoughtless person. Now, if I review my philosophy of life, this is the question: Can I say that I am basing my life solidly and squarely on what God has revealed as his idea for the life of man? It was because he ceased to do that that Adam found himself slinking away from God with that sense of shame and hiding amongst the trees.

The second reason for man's continuing troubles I can put in this form: it is *the refusal to face seriously the fact of judgment.* That, I think, is obvious from this story. You see God made the position so clear to man. Man is left without excuse at all. God said to him, 'You live in this garden; you can do all these things, *but* if you do the one thing prohibited judgment is certain.' As God had the right to do as the Creator of man, he placed him under law, made his announcement of judgment and, therefore, I say, man was without excuse at all. God has told man right from the beginning that he holds him responsible. God made man a responsible being because he gave him certain of his own qualities, made him able to understand the mind of God and for that reason he put him under law, he held him responsible and announced the fact of judgment. Why did man ever find himself in misery? How obvious is the answer! He did not take seriously the fact of judgment. The tempter came and said, 'You do not believe all that surely? Just listen to me and you will have a much better life. You need not be afraid of any consequences. God is only trying to frighten you. You do as I tell you, you will be perfectly happy and you will have this amazing knowledge and understanding; you will be like a god yourself.' Man believed it and the judgment descended and men and women have reaped the consequences ever since. But man goes on repeating his mistake; we get the same story later in the record of the Flood. There God began to warn the world, but the world ridiculed the message and thought it funny that there was going to be a judgment. Noah preached for over a hundred years, but man would not listen and so the judgment descended and the Flood came. Move on and you will see the same thing in Sodom and Gomorrah, although Lot pleaded with his contemporaries; judgment was announced and judgment came. It is the whole story of the Old Testament. God has announced judgment through his prophets and servants. He has said that 'the way of transgressors is hard' (*Prov.* 13:15). 'There is no peace, saith my God, to the wicked' (*Isa.* 57:21).

You are going to suffer if you do not listen to God. The children of Israel were told that as they entered Canaan but they refused to listen and judgment came. Read on further to the New Testament: John the Baptist went about preaching 'Repent or judgment will descend'. Jesus of Nazareth preached exactly the same message; for three years he warned the nation; he told them it was the last word. Remember the Parable of the Vineyard, how the owner of the vineyard sent his servants and they ill-treated them. Then, he said, I will send my one son; I will give them a last chance. 'They will reverence my son', but if they will not, then I will destroy them (*Mark* 12:1–9). How this Son warned them but the Jews would not listen. It was the old mistake. Then in A.D. 70 the Roman legionaries sacked everything; the nation was thrown out into the world and there she remains until this very night. That is the message of the Bible. You have got it, too, in your New Testament in the Book of Revelation. Believe in this, realise that judgment is a fact; listen before it is too late.

But, as I have said, it is all here in the third chapter of Genesis. This is a summary of the whole Bible for you and, put in individual and personal terms, it means something like this: God, though he is almighty and absolute and illimitable and infinite in power and majesty, knows us one by one. The next thing that is obvious is that God sees everything we do, he is omniscient; he is omnipresent. There is nothing we do but God sees it and knows all about it. Our every action is known to him. This Word of God, as the author of the letter to the Hebrews says, 'penetrates even to the dividing asunder of the joints and marrow' (*Heb.* 4:12). That is the One with whom we have to do. God is a discerner of the thoughts of the heart. Our every action is laid open to him.

'Surely nobody believes anything like that? My dear sir, you ought to have been preaching years ago! No-one believes that now.' I ask you, has God changed? Can you deny that he knows us one by one? Whether we believe it or not, this is the message of the Bible. A time is coming for certain in the life of every one of us when we shall suddenly hear a Voice, and this is what the Voice shall say, 'Adam, where art thou?' God, our Maker, will address us. The One who gave us our soul and put within us these amazing propensities that we possess. He will speak my name and your name and what he will say is this: 'What have you done with the life I gave you? What has happened to the soul I placed within you? Adam, I gave you these great possibilities – Adam, where art thou? What have you done with yourself?' It was because he did not take seriously this doctrine of judgment that Adam found himself in misery and wretchedness, hiding and thrown out of the garden to meet briars and thorns. My dear friend, this is pivotal, central; God is announcing judgment still.

Can you explain these World Wars one after another in any other terms? Why is our world as it is in spite of all our wisdom and culture? Why are we failing so tragically? It is God telling man, 'While you live apart from me you shall not be happy'. God is announcing judgment even through contemporary history. Oh the tragic folly of refusing something which was announced so long ago and confirmed so often through the centuries.

You know the final tragedy is due to the fact that man turns away from God, instead of turning to him in his trouble and misery. In his folly man has put his own ideas in the place of God's and thought nothing of this idea of judgment; but when he begins to awake to the knowledge that something is wrong – when he hears the voice of God – then his instinct is to get away from him. This is the greatest tragedy of all. When man fell, when he began to feel he had done wrong and was filled with this sense of unworthiness, why was it that he did not seek God and make a friend of him? If only he had gone to God! If only he had cried 'God, I realise my folly, I have sinned against thee; I acknowledge it, wilt thou pardon me?' But no, once he had sinned he went away from God and when God called him his instinct was to go still further. That is the ultimate tragedy of man, that in the depth of his need and misery and shame he avoids the only One who can really help him.

Who can put man and his world right? It is my privilege to stand here tonight and tell you that, though man is guilty of this triple folly, God had pity on him, God came after him and God called unto him, not only to condemn him but to speak to him and to give him the gracious promise that, though he had thus wronged himself and ruined the world in which he had been placed, God was going to come into it. God was going to enter into the fight with evil and was going to be a conqueror. The promise of salvation is announced – the serpent's head will be bruised! In his tenderness God clothed them in their nakedness and there gave an indication that the day would come when he would clothe them with the righteousness and the perfection of his own Son and receive them back to himself.

I say that this is the final tragedy – the folly of refusing to take the idea of judgment seriously. Here is the world tonight in its unhappiness – look at men and women; see how muddled and unhappy life has become. They are trying to find happiness in pleasure, they need something and the very thing they need is being offered and yet they turn away from God while he is speaking, from the only One who can bless.

Is there anyone, I wonder, who has been guilty of this tragic folly. If you are in this state of misery and unhappiness, I suggest that your trouble is that you will not listen to God. He is speaking to you. He has come after you. He has sent his Son to earth and he took your sin and bore it in his own body and bore it on Calvary's hill. He asks you to listen to him, to believe his message, to yield your life to him and he promises you that if you do so you will inherit greater blessings than your father Adam lost. Oh may God grant us grace to see our need that we must live our life as he dictates; and understanding that we know where we are going, to death and to judgment for certain, but, above all, that we shall hear the voice of God calling us to accept his free gift of salvation in Jesus Christ his Son.

2

Before and After Penuel:
The Evidence of True Conversion[1]

And Jacob was left alone; and there wrestled a man with him until the breaking of the day.

Genesis 32:24

This is one of the great, if not indeed one of the greatest dramatic stories to be found anywhere in the Bible. You cannot read this chapter without literally seeing the whole position. It takes little imagination to see Jacob, to watch him as he moves backwards and forwards making his arrangements and then, eventually, as he finds himself alone. Let me briefly give you some of the details of his life which led up to this incident. Esau and Jacob were the two sons of Isaac. Although twins, Esau was the first-born and they were two very different men. Jacob was the favourite of his mother and in her anxiety for his success she devised a scheme whereby he should obtain the blessing of the first-born from his father. You remember how Jacob disguised himself as his brother Esau and went into the presence of Isaac, his blind and aged father. He put certain hairy material on his hands so that the old man in touching him should imagine that it was the hairy Esau. So Jacob obtained the blessing and his brother Esau was filled with such a sense of anger and grievance that he had thoughts of killing his brother. Rebecca, the mother, realised this and suggested to Jacob that he had better escape. This is what Jacob did, going away to the country of his uncle Laban. In the chapters preceding this one we read of how there he worked for his uncle, was given two daughters as his wives, and how he prospered, even though again there were certain things in his conduct which we must condemn. However,

[1] Westminster Chapel, 20 April 1947.

there he is, a successful man with his wives, his children and his great possessions and the time has come when he feels they must leave Laban and go back to his own country. That is the point at which this thirty-second chapter begins. Jacob has left Laban and, with his wives and his possessions, he is now about to enter his own homeland. But he knows that Esau is there; he remembers exactly what he had done to Esau, he imagines Esau's feelings and here we find him full of a spirit of fear. He is concerned about his possessions; he is concerned about his wives and children and he does not know what to do. Still he tries to scheme and to plan, and to appease his brother he sends forward messengers. You remember the scheme as he works it out – it is clever, it is typical in a sense of Jacob. Here he is, how can he appease his brother?

The story goes on with its dramatic power to tell us how Jacob, for safety, divided his possessions and the people that were with him into bands and sent them ahead across the river. He is left for the time being with his wives and children and a small company. Then, after he has taken them forward, he returns to the river where we find him alone, and it is at that point that the extraordinary thing happens to him which we want to consider together this evening.

Here is Jacob wondering what is going to happen. He is a wealthy man but he does not know how to meet his brother Esau on the next day. He had already had a message that Esau was advancing in his direction with 400 armed men and he feels utterly defenceless. He foresees his goods being taken, himself, his wives and children being killed, and he is filled with a sense of terror and alarm. There we see him, everything has gone before over the river, and here he is alone – walking backwards and forwards, restless, unable to sleep, full of foreboding, wondering what is going to happen; then this amazing thing begins to take place which leads to this extraordinary result recorded in the last verses of the chapter. This is undoubtedly the turning point in the whole life story of Jacob – there can be no question about that – it was the point at which Jacob really became a man of God. Until this time Jacob, if you like, was a man who had been playing with religion. Oh yes, he believed in God and when in trouble and difficulty he always prayed to God, and yet it is perfectly clear that until this point he was only playing with religion. It was something external to him, something that was quite all right when it suited him. You remember when he first left his home he made a bargain with God – 'You bless me and then I will do this.' But from this point onwards everything is different; it is beyond any question the great central turning point in this man's strange and chequered life history. From this point onwards religion becomes real, he becomes a true man of God, never the same after the experience of the night before he met his brother Esau.

It is then a story which brings us face to face with the turning point in the life history of one of the most important of the Old Testament characters. I am calling your attention to it, however, for another reason: it gives us a perfect portrayal and delineation of the essence of the true experience of religion and of God which is known as conversion. In a sense it shows us what the Christian gospel is and what it does in an individual. We are living in days and times when it seems to me increasingly that the first thing we have to do is to examine ourselves. Many of our friends at the present hour are very concerned about the world that is right outside of the church and is not taking any interest in it. I do not want to criticise them but it seems to me that we must start with ourselves. To 'believe in God' is not enough as this story shows us. To pray to God when we need him is not enough. To have an interest in religion may be equally insufficient. The vital question is whether we have this true, central experience – are we like Jacob *before* this Penuel vision or Jacob *after* this Penuel vision? That is the question; in other words, the call that comes at this hour is a call to us to examine ourselves and our own belief and our own position. Have we had this vital experience which Jacob had on this occasion? Do we know something of this climactic change which makes a man for ever after different because of this meeting between him and God? Here, I say, is one of the classical biblical accounts of a vital experience of God. How often this self-same thing is recorded in other places in the Bible. You will find it in the form of direct statements, in teaching and exposition, and in wonderful illustration in the lives of men. Obviously this is a great subject and no-one in the space of one sermon can hope to deal with it exhaustively. All I want to do tonight is to look at this dramatic experience through which Jacob passed in a general manner. God willing, I hope to consider it in detail next week.

If you like you can divide the subject like this. The general nature of the Christian experience, and then secondly the detailed way in which that experience comes to pass and how it works itself out.

As we look at it tonight in general there are certain simple, elementary questions which we must ask. The great underlying central question is this. Have I had the true Christian experience? Do I conform to the New Testament picture and pattern of such a person? I imagine someone turning to me and saying, 'It is right to ask that question but what are the characteristics? How may I test myself; how am I to know whether my religion is something which is real, or whether it is not? How am I to know whether I am in the position of Jacob before Penuel or after Penuel?' Let me show you some of the characteristics of this vital experience.

The first point I am going to make is – *conversion is always an intensely personal experience* – 'And Jacob was left alone'. The first thing about this experience is that it always isolates us; it puts us apart and on our own, it makes us realise our own individuality. Now surely we all must agree that this is one of the most difficult things in life at this present time, and especially in this world as it is at this hour. Does it not seem to you that everything in life seems to be conspiring together to make us forget our individuality and our separate identity? How easy it is for man to become lost in his work, in his profession, in his occupation; how easy indeed for one to become lost in one's family, how easy to be lost in one's class; how easy to become lost in the world as a whole. It has become a fact that the world is thinking increasingly of the mass and the crowd – that was something that was true before the War, but it is something that has become greatly accentuated by the War. We read about masses of people, millions of people, and the world thinks in those terms. The individual is at a discount; everything is being organised into masses and groups, and everything becomes larger and larger. You see it in business, the small man is swallowed up in combines and chainstores; you find the same thing in the realm of politics and in industry where the individual workman is being lost in his trade union. This is not simply criticism, it is a fact that the individual relationship between employer and servant is not what it was – more is being handled by machinery, the whole of life in every department is being thought of in terms of the mass rather than of the individual. And when you begin to think of things like international relationships and atomic bombs the same thing becomes still more true. The individual is being made to feel that he matters very little – global war, world war, a bomb that can destroy so many thousands, perhaps millions – where is the individual? He does not seem to count at all. Everything is in terms of numbers.

There is nothing that is quite so inimical to this vital experience which we are discussing together tonight as just that outlook because it is the thing that is most inimical to true Christian experience. The first step in the direction of this experience is always that we come to a realisation of our own individuality. 'Jacob was left alone', then being left alone 'a man', God, began to wrestle with him. Now God has many ways of bringing us to this point. The one which we have in our text this evening is perhaps one of the most dramatic ways. Jacob had to be separated literally from his wives and children, especially perhaps from his goods and his possessions. Jacob's danger was to identify himself with those things – God separated him. This is something, I say, that God brings to pass in a variety of ways. Sometimes he does it by means of illness. A man may be going on living his life with his family, surrounded by his children, very interested in his business or his profession and he lives for these things. He never stops to ask, Who am I? have I a soul? what is going to happen to me after this life? He is lost and immersed in other concerns, then suddenly he is taken ill, God separates him from his business, God separates him from his possessions and from his interests. Perhaps he is taken to hospital, separated from his family, and there lying on a hospital bed he begins to realise that after all he is an individual and that he is absolutely alone. A hospital bed has been the means of bringing many a person to this experience or a sick bed in one's own house may do the same thing. I am simply illustrating the ways in which God brings this thing to pass. God sometimes has to come into our lives and give us a disappointment, he has to rob us of our money, he has to bring a crash in our business. Or we may be brought to the same point by a disappointment in a friendship, it may be disappointment in the still more tender realm of the human affections. You read the lives of the saints and you will find that it is in such ways that God has begun to speak to them. He has had to isolate them, to cut them off from the things in which they were losing themselves and their souls, and there in isolation they have stopped and realised that they are individuals and that they have to face certain questions for themselves.

That, after all, is the whole business of preaching. The first business of preaching is to bring us each and every one to a realisation that we are individuals; that is why all the talk in pulpits about social conditions, economic and political conditions, and the international situation, is in a sense doing violence to the preaching of this gospel. The gospel is always intensely personal in the first instance, it says you are an individual and you stand alone. Its first message is to remind us that though we are in the world, with its teeming masses, we stand out one by one. We are born alone. We must all die one by one – we do not go out of life in a crowd; death is something intensely individual. And then it reminds us that we are individuals in the sight of God and that God will make individual demands upon us. At the bar of God's judgment we shall not be seen in crowds but every man will be judged alone. The Bible tells us there is a record of every single individual and every work that you and I have ever done is set down, even 'every idle word' – everything we do and say is known to God and each man is individually responsible. 'And Jacob was left alone.'

Have you looked at yourself in isolation? Have you realised that you are an individual in this world and in this life before God? Oh I beseech you, my friend, get away from the mob and the mass, isolate yourself, hear the word of this gospel tonight, come and stand alone and recognise that you have an individual responsibility. The first mark of this gospel is always that it is intensely personal, it makes a man realise that he is responsible for his life in this world and not responsible for the life of everyone else. It brings home to him the fact that he is here today and gone tomorrow and that he must stand in judgment for himself.

But let me move on to my second point: *conversion is an experience which always brings us into a personal relationship with God.* I want to emphasise this because it is the great thing that is emphasised in this story. The essence of this vital experience is this: an individual comes into personal contact with God. We must not think of religion and Christianity simply as a matter of morals and of actions. Nor must we think of it merely as a matter of ideas or principles. Christianity is not a point of view; it is not just an attitude towards peace and war, education or industry. It is not primarily a message about what can be done for society – No, no, in the first instance it is this – a man coming to a personal encounter with God.

Now Jacob before this incident at Penuel had been in the other position. Jacob, like so many of us, had always conceived of God as a kind of agency that would give him blessings when he needed them, or as some great power somewhere there in heaven to whom he could turn and make requests when he needed strength and power. But then, after doing so, he went out and forgot all about God. This was all changed for ever on this dramatic night when he met God face to face and the essence of every conversion experience is this same personal encounter with God. The most hopeful sign that I see in the present religious scene, and especially among theological students, is that this idea is coming back into prominence. For far too long the church has been interested in a social gospel, religion was a matter of ethics, something to uplift and raise a man, it was a matter of abstract theology, but increasingly people are coming to see that a man's personal relationship to God is the very essence of the matter. In a sense this new interest started with the work of that famous Dane, Kierkegaard, who lived one hundred years ago. He was given to see this particular aspect very clearly and said that Christianity is not playing with religious ideas, it is a man meeting God and because he meets God he has to do something about it – it is a critical encounter. This has been made still more popular recently in a book bearing the interesting and significant title *I and Thou*. In other words the danger is to think of God as 'IT' somewhere in the heavens instead of the 'I and Thou' personal relationship. Another man puts it like this, real life is an encounter between persons. We must not live in the realm of ideas, we must realise this is a matter of a personal meeting with God. So that I would emphasise and stress that the second mark of this vital experience is that God no longer is just an abstract quantity in our philosophies, God is no longer a concept which we have to postulate to make our scheme complete – an idea far away and remote from us. Nor is God an agency who sometimes blesses us. God is a Person, God is real, God is Someone to whom we speak, whom we hear, with whom we have business, with whom we deal and between him and ourselves there is a living communication.

Jacob before Penuel believed in that remote, impersonal God, but at Penuel he met him – God came to him; Jacob was left alone and the 'man', that was God, talked with him, struggled with him, and Jacob was aware of the presence. Is God real to you, is God personal to you, is God a reality to you, is God a living God to you? I say that it is always the second mark of this experience that it brings us into a direct and immediate personal relationship with God.

Let me put it quite simply and bluntly: when you get on your knees in prayer, do you know that God is there? What is prayer to you, is it just the muttering of a few pious hopes and aspirations; do you talk about yourself and do you just ask about certain possibilities, or have you felt the presence of God, have you known that he is there, a living, real, holy person? Have you met God? God in Christ is a real, a living person to those who have passed through this experience.

The next thing must follow of necessity from what I have said. It is that *a man who has this experience always recognises it as the most important thing of all in his life.* I need not keep you, it is here on the very surface of this ancient story. Let me put it in a brief closing word. Here is this man Jacob, pacing backwards and forwards, full of worry and foreboding, full of anxiety and care, wondering what is going to happen, thinking about Esau and the danger to his goods and possessions, but as this experience began and proceeded Jacob forgot all about Esau, he forgot all about his cattle, his sheep and oxen, his wealth and his possessions, his wives and his children, he forgot everything except this Person, this amazing experience, this possibility of blessing which is held out to him. Was it not obvious and inevitable and is it not something that is always true of those who pass through this essential Christian experience? Jacob struggled for this blessing, he pleaded for it, he says, 'I will not let you go unless you bless me' – the morning is dawning and Esau may come, but what does it matter? 'I will not let you go; this is the thing of all things, if I lose everything, I must have this.' That is always the language of vital Christian experience. The man who is truly Christian is the man who has come to realise that God is the most important person in all his life. What is a Christian? I define him as the man who has come to realise he has a soul and that he has lost that soul in a spiritual sense. He is a man who realises he is guilty before God. He is a man who has come to see that what matters is the destiny of his soul. He was interested in other things, but he knows they will all disappear when the soul still goes on. He sees judgment to come, and because of all this, he now sees the most important thing of all – 'I need salvation, I need forgiveness, I need a new life, I need to be reconciled to God!' Is there anyone who can help? Yes, there is, and he turns to Christ and says, 'I will not let thee go, I must have this blessing.' For this he pleads, for this he cries – it is now the supreme interest in his life. May I again put my simple question. Is this the biggest thing in your life? If I ask tonight from this pulpit what is the one thing to which you would hold if everything else has to go, what would you say? Would you hold on to Christ at the expense and the cost of everything else? That is the mark of the Christian. He sees that it is Christ dying on the cross that alone can give him forgiveness of sin. He sees it is in Christ alone he is given a new life and a new nature and a new standing before God. He sees it is in Christ, who has conquered death and the grave, that he is given an eternal and glorious inheritance. He sees all that in Christ and he says, 'Though I am bereft of everything, as long as I have him all is well.' Is Christ supreme in our lives? Do we know that this is the most vital thing and would we gladly sacrifice everything else for the sake of this? That is what Jacob came to feel. It has always been the feeling of every true Christian. Man may trouble and distress me, man may persecute me and do all manner of things to me, yet, says the Christian, if Christ is with me all is well.

Lastly, this is *an experience that always leads to a permanent change.* I want to emphasise the permanence of the change. A true experience of God in Christ is not a mere emotional experience. People may have an emotional experience and profess conversion and yet not have a true experience of God in Christ at all. There are such things as psychological conversions. We are not here to advocate emotion. I say the mark of the genuine experience is its permanence. Jacob after Penuel was never the same again. He was lame, he had a mark upon him, and his name was changed from Jacob to Israel. As you read the story from this point onwards you will find that he behaved in an entirely different manner. Jacob, the old Jacob, was no more. Now he is a cripple in a sense but a new man and living a different life. This experience always leads to a permanent change. A man who has come to know God in Christ is a new man, he is given a new experience – the old man that he was is gone and the world knows that he is different. As anybody looked at Jacob, though lame for the rest of his life, they could see he was a different man. So anyone who has had this vital experience knows he is a different being; his old man has been crucified with Christ, he has got the marks upon him, and he has a new life. Jacob, the strong self-reliant Jacob, is gone and the crippled Jacob – Israel – relying upon God, halts 'upon his thigh'.

That is the last mark and therefore the last test of this vital experience – it leads to a permanent change. The man who has met God in Christ is no longer what he used to be, he is a new man and for him old things are passed away and behold all things are become new. My dear friends, have you been through this Penuel experience? Have you seen yourself in isolation and responsible before a holy God? Have you met God, is he real to you, do you know him? Is this knowledge of God in Christ the biggest thing, the central thing in your life? Can you say honestly, I am what I am by the grace of God? Are you aware of a new man in yourself, a new life, a new interest, a new power, a new being, something beyond yourself that you cannot understand, and have you said with Paul, 'I live, yet not I but Christ liveth in me and the life I now live in the flesh I live by the faith of the Son of God who loved me and gave himself for me.'

In the isolation has Christ come to you, have you met him, have you found him, have you confronted him, have you pleaded for the blessing he can give you? If you haven't until this night and until this moment, God grant that this may be your Penuel, that even now you may feel his presence and may know he is here! Emulate the example of Jacob, hold on to him, ask him to bless you, ask him to give you this experience and if you ask in faith believing, he will not say you nay, but he will give you the blessing and you will go on and forward as a post-Penuel man, knowing God in Jesus Christ.

3

Penuel: The Life-Changing Meeting[1]

And Jacob was left alone, and there wrestled a man with him until the breaking of the day.

Genesis 32:24

We were at pains to point out last Sunday night that this turning point in the life history and story of this patriarch, Jacob, is worthy of our consideration not only as a key whereby alone we can understand his subsequent history, but it is of special importance to us as it is a picture and a portrayal of what always constitutes the essence of the experience of conversion, or the coming, if you like, into a definite and real knowledge and experience of God. I need not remind you, I am sure, of the details of the story of Jacob – it is a well-known and familiar one. Jacob had done his brother, Esau, a very great wrong; by stealth, he had obtained the blessing from his father, Isaac, and because of that he had to flee the country. He went into a distant country where he found employment and married and became extremely prosperous. At this point in the story we find him leaving the country where he had been and coming back to his homeland. Of course, he was immediately in difficulty, the difficulty was how would Esau receive him? Esau, he knew, was angry and he expected terrible things from him and earlier in this chapter we read of Jacob's schemes and ideas as to how he could appease his brother. The account tells us how, after he had made all his preparations, he sent presents forward, later he sent his wives and children and he is left alone waiting and wondering. It was then that 'there wrestled a man with him until the breaking of the day', and some extraordinary things happened. That is the story in its essence.

Now last Sunday night we looked at it in a general way, as a

[1] Westminster Chapel, 27 April 1947.

portrayal of a man coming into a living experience of God in Christ. We made some general points – let me briefly remind you of them. We said that this story indicates first of all that this experience is a very personal one – it is intensely personal – 'Jacob was left alone' – a man has to be isolated before he can truly meet God; we meet him one by one. The second point was that it is a personal experience of God as a person – it is not taking up some general ideas about God and about religion, it is a personal encounter with God. That, in turn, led us to see that when a man comes to this he always sees it as the biggest and the most important thing in his life; he forgets everything else – so we said that a man can easily test whether he is a true Christian or not by asking whether he can say truthfully that his relationship to God is the most important thing in his mind and life. Our last point was that it is an experience which leads to a permanent change. A man who has met God is never the same again; he is altogether changed, he is not perfect but he is different – like Jacob, lame with this muscle in his thigh shortened – so the Christian is permanently marked, he is never the same man again.

These were the general features which we looked at last Sunday evening. I want to continue our consideration of this incident, bearing in mind that it is a perfect picture and representation of conversion, a man coming into a true Christian experience. I think we will all agree that there are certain things that strike us on the very surface of this whole matter. The first thing is that *it is an experience which is always surprising* – there is always a surprising element in man's conversion, in his coming to this definite knowledge of God in Christ. The story before us makes it perfectly plain and clear that all this happened to Jacob very suddenly and utterly unexpectedly. Jacob never imagined that that night was going to be what it actually turned out to be. He was going to meet Esau, thinking about the meeting and what he would say when his brother confronted him, when, in colloquial language, he had the shock of his life. Unexpectedly and suddenly the night was entirely different from what he had anticipated, and what happened to Jacob was altogether different from what he had ever imagined.

There is nothing that is so characteristic of the gospel as the way in which it always comes to the natural man as a complete surprise, for the trouble with us is that we will confront this matter with prejudice heavy upon us. We have all got some prejudice with respect to what a Christian is, or what constitutes the essence of Christianity. I am always mentioning this in this pulpit because I hear the question 'What is it that makes a man a Christian?' so repeatedly asked, and it is amazing to hear the replies that are given – born in a certain country, christened when a baby, immersed when at a certain age, a moral man, a philanthropist, an idealist – these are some of the definitions that are given. Now I say when a man really becomes a Christian, when he has this meeting with God, the first thing that always happens to him is that he is amazed and surprised and astounded. I do not hesitate to lay it down as being one of the basic tests of a true experience of God in Christ. I argue on the basis of the Bible that it is impossible for a man to be a Christian without being surprised at himself. The great instance of that, perhaps, is the Apostle Paul – you remember how he puts it – 'I live, yet not I, but Christ liveth in me' – that is Paul's way of saying that he does not understand himself any longer, he is surprised at himself, he looks at himself in amazement – Am I really this man, have I become this, has this happened to me?

We start with low conceptions of Christianity. We have got these human moral ideas and opinions with respect to the gospel, and when the real thing happens we are amazed and astounded. Conversion is always surprising, and often, as here with Jacob, it is the last thing that people expect to happen to them, but it does happen. You remember how it was once said 'Fools who came to scoff remained to pray'. Read the history of the revivals and you will see how often that happened. How many instances there have been of men who went to listen to the preachers with the sole purpose of disturbing the meeting, sometimes taking a rabble with them to make a noise, and suddenly in the meeting God met them and they were changed and converted and went home to their families proclaiming that they had become followers of this Messiah whom they had set out to persecute. And that is one of the most marvellous and glorious things about the gospel. It is what makes a meeting like this so different from a merely secular meeting, you never know what may happen here. Someone who has expected nothing may suddenly meet with God.

That leads me to the second general feature which is, that the gospel does something surprising for us, *because it is altogether the result of God's action.* Here again is a point which need not detain us. 'And Jacob was left alone and there wrestled a man with him until the breaking of the day.' What happened to Jacob that night was not the result of Jacob's action, it was God who came to Jacob – it was not Jacob who decided to spend the night in seeking God and trying to find God. Jacob was immersed in other things – it was God who came to Jacob and did certain things to him. The whole basis of the story is that Jacob found God as a result of the activity and the action of God himself. And let me make this perfectly plain and clear. The very first thing we have to say about the gospel of Jesus Christ is that it is essentially and primarily the action of God. What makes a man a Christian is not something that he does, it is something that God has done and God does.

This is obviously basic. If I believe that I, by my own efforts, can find God, I am violating the very basis of the gospel of Christ. The preaching of the gospel is not meant to be an appeal to men and women to do something that will make them Christian – it is an announcement, a proclamation to them about something that God has done and that will make them Christian. Salvation is solely and entirely the result of God's grace and God's amazing love. Now this, I say, once more is absolutely basic and vital and fundamental: it is the essence of the Christian gospel. Man has sinned against God and thereby all his miseries have come upon him, and he can do nothing about it; he can never do away with his sins, he can never make atonement for his transgressions, he can never by seeking find out God; he can decide to scale the heights and spend the rest of his life in meditation but he will never arrive at God. Is man then utterly hopeless? No, no, for this reason – man himself can do nothing but God, praised be his Name, has done everything. God has looked upon man in his sin and misery and shame and God has provided a way of salvation. 'God has sent forth his Son made of a woman, made under the law, to redeem them that are under the law' – the whole message of the gospel is to tell us this, that God sent his only-begotten Son, Jesus of Nazareth, the One who was born as a babe in Bethlehem, he sent him deliberately into this world because of our sins, he came and identified himself with the sin of mankind, he went to that cross of Calvary bearing the sins of man – God there 'made him to be sin for us who knew no sin that we might be made the righteousness of God in him.' That is the message! Quite apart from us, God there dealt with sin, he punished it, he dealt with its guilt and because of that he offers us pardon, he offers us forgiveness, he offers us salvation, a new life, everything we need. It is God's action. God, I say, came to Jacob and the very beginning and essence of my message is that God at the cross has done the work for you and for me, he died for our sins. And what he does in a meeting like this is to tell us about things like that through his Holy Spirit. We have come together as Jacob arrived at this particular place; we may have come with all sorts of ideas, of motives and thoughts, it doesn't matter, the whole point is this, that God knows, God speaks, God the Holy Spirit, reveals certain things to us. As he spoke there to Jacob and revealed certain things to Jacob, so he does by the Spirit through the preaching of the gospel,

Very well, that being the essence and the great characteristic of the gospel, what are the things that the gospel reveals to us? Let us look at them in the light of this story of Jacob. Here is this man Jacob standing there alone; his wives and children and possessions and everything gone forward – Jacob was left alone and then God came and revealed certain things to him. What does the gospel through the Spirit reveal to us? Let me give you them all together in order that you may remember them. First of all the gospel reveals to us that the problems to which we give so much of our time and attention are not the real and vital problems, or the ultimately important problems. That is the first thing. The second thing is it reveals the true problem and, thirdly, it shows us the blessing that God is offering us which astounds and amazes us and surpasses our highest hopes and imaginations.

Let me try to deal with these points hurriedly. The first thing the gospel reveals to us is that *the problems to which we give so much of our time and attention, and about which we worry and trouble so much, are not the vital problems* nor ultimately the important problems. I need not keep you by illustrating this point in the particular case of Jacob. As Jacob stood there alone, he had sent over his wives and children and all his possessions and his men and women servants to the other side of the river, Jacob said to himself, 'Well now of course there is only one problem to solve and that is Esau, if only I could solve the problem of Esau all is going to be well.' Esau is the one and only problem and so he schemed and planned how he would approach him – that is what makes this thirty-second chapter of the Book of Genesis so interesting from the mere standpoint of a story. Don't you see yourself in this man, Jacob? There he is and he is going back to his homeland – ah, but there is Esau – there is always something. What can Jacob do about him; watch the ingenuity – 'I know Esau pretty well', said Jacob to himself, 'if he isn't changed very much since I last saw him, I can buy him off. He likes animals that are well bred and well fed, I will divide my stock up into groups so that if he is angry with the first he may be satisfied with the second' – you see how he planned and thought. Let me go further, he probably prayed about it and prayed absolutely sincerely – 'Oh God have mercy upon me', and he reminded God of certain promises. Yes, men who are not Christian can pray very fervently when they think their goods and possessions are in danger of being lost. Jacob thought and schemed and prayed. There was only one problem to him and that was Esau and how he bothered and troubled and perplexed himself about him. But what really happened to Jacob that night was just this, God revealed to him that he wasn't considering the vital problem, the real problem was not Esau. That is the first thing the gospel does, it shows us that the things about which we trouble and agonise and plan and scheme so much are not the real and vital things at all.

The first message therefore of the gospel to this troubled world of ours tonight is that it is not facing and considering its real problem, Now, as Jacob knew that he was in trouble so the world tonight knows that it is in trouble. There was poor Jacob, alone, he does not lie down to sleep, he is so worried and troubled he cannot sleep, and any man today who thinks or reads at all is well aware of the fact that the world is very ill and seriously in trouble. But that is not the vital question – the vital question is, what is the trouble? The real trouble I suggest to you this evening is that the world is just repeating the action of Jacob so long ago. The problems which are exercising men's minds, and the ingenuity they show in bringing forth plans and schemes, are not the real problems and are not the most vital problems. What are the things the world is thinking about tonight? The world is thinking about things like this: it says, 'If only we could have some arrangement to banish war all would be well! How happily things were going until war came in 1914–1918 and then before the Second World War, if only we could get rid of these things . . .' So international relationships and conferences are planned, and measures to prevent war and to put an end to it; schemes to deal with the atomic bomb, with industrial problems and social problems – murders, thefts, immorality, the breakdown of marriage, the breakdown of morals and so on – these are the things about which the world is thinking. As Jacob stood there and thought and meditated upon Esau he could see nothing but Esau. So the world today gives a whole week to discussing the atomic bomb (you have never had a week given to the gospel!) and supposes its real problems are those you hear discussed on the wireless and read about constantly in newspapers, books and articles. It is very clear that the world is the same as Jacob in its methods of trying to deal with the problems. I suppose that it is literally true to say that the world has never been so busy trying to solve its problems and to put itself right as it is at this present hour. Indeed the world has never worked so hard in trying to solve its problems as in this century; think of the acts of Parliament, think of the new institutions, think of the fresh organisations, think of the multiplicity of educational arrangements and all the things designed for social amelioration, and you will see exactly what I mean. There is a breakdown in life and we are trying to deal with it. To me there is something very sad about the way in which the world is trying to solve these problems. It is all due to the fact that the world refuses to face the real and fundamental problem. We are always producing new institutions and organisations to try to solve the problems, and yet the world is miserable and unhappy and wretched, and of course what is true of the world at large is equally true of the individual. How many individuals are there in the world tonight who in their personal lives are just repeating this action of Jacob. There is many a person in the world who says, 'If only I had wealth all would be well, I have everything else, if only I had a little more money, then my world would be paradise' – that is their Esau. To another it is education, 'If only I had knowledge or educational opportunities or facilities then all would be well' – that is everything. To another it is a matter of relationships – it is this other person – 'It is only Esau', said Jacob to himself, 'if only I could put Esau right all is going to be well with me.' 'Ah,' says many a person tonight, 'I'm right, it is this other person – if only ...' That is their Esau. To another the one thing that is needed is a new environment, a new start, a new opportunity. There are many people crossing oceans today to go to another country, firmly believing if only they can make a start in some wonderful new land all is going to be well – there is their Esau. And another man says if only I could get rid of that one weakness – that is all it is – and he fights and strives and struggles to get rid of that one sin.

Now the first message of the gospel is to tell all such people that this problem which is engaging them so much is not the real problem, it is not vital. Jacob had to be shown that the problem of Esau was not the main problem.

That leads me to the second point. The business of the gospel is, by the Holy Spirit, *to reveal to us our real problem*. What is the real problem? Let me summarise it very hurriedly. Jacob, let us say this for him, did not take very long in seeing it once God appeared to him and began to deal with him; the moment Jacob saw his real problem, as I reminded you hurriedly last Sunday night, he forgot all about Esau; the moment Jacob had revealed to him the central thing, I say he forgot all about Esau and he clung to God. The real problem of man is his relationship to God. The first thing Jacob discovered there at Penuel was that his real problem, if I may put it with reverence, was not Esau, but God. You see this man's primary error was, 'How can I appease Esau?' but what God said was, 'My dear Jacob, what you need is not to be reconciled to Esau, but to be reconciled to me', and that, I say, is the essence of the modern difficulty and the modern trouble. We persist in looking at all these other problems of which I have been reminding you and in forgetting that the real, central cause of our ill is our wrong relationship to God. That is the very first statement of this gospel. It tells us that God has made man for himself and that God has placed certain laws within the nature and being of man and that man can only be happy in this world as long as he obeys those laws. The Bible tells us, in other words, that all personal problems and all general problems arise from that central source and that a man can search heaven and earth and do anything he likes but as long as he is in a wrong relationship to God he will never find peace and happiness, he will never find rest to his soul, he will never find that for which he longs. The problem of man in the first instance is not Esau – it is God himself. The gospel, I say, reminds us of that fact, that unless and until man is right with God at the centre, he cannot be right anywhere else. God not Esau!

Then the gospel goes on to show that as long as man has false ideas about that first point he has equally false views about himself. In other words, the second thing that was shown to Jacob there was not only that his problem was not Esau, he was made to see himself as he truly was. Now let me put it in this form. Jacob's constant trouble was to forget the man that God had intended him to be. Jacob had gone off into that other country, there he had done remarkably well and prospered, and his whole idea about himself was that he might return to his homeland and settle down in a position of affluence. He would have plenty, enjoy his life and his family, and become a marvellously successful man of the world. But God came to him and reminded him how utterly false all that was when put in the light of what God intended him to be. Jacob was a man who had received a birthright, he had received the blessing of God, and God had given him this blessing in order that through him he might do certain things. God here called Jacob back to a realisation of his true nature and of his true destiny, and that is what the gospel of Jesus Christ always does when it comes to man. It comes to man and asks him this question, Is the life you are living worthy of the man God intended and meant you to be? Is a life devoted only to this life, and world, big enough and good enough and worthy enough of what God intended? Man was made by God, in the image of God – man was meant for companionship with God, meant to be like Christ, man was given a spirit that linked him to God. And what is man like now? That is the question. The gospel comes to us and makes us see that by living a life apart from God and apart from Christ we are living a life which is a travesty of human nature and we are doing something that is utterly insulting to God. Man is meant to be a living soul in communion with God – the gospel makes us see that.

The next thing that it makes us see is *our real danger.* These are the problems – not the Esaus we put up. These are the problems – my relationship to God, my relationship to myself, yes, and my real danger. Now to Jacob of course the danger was this, that Esau might rob him of a certain amount of his goods, or that Esau might kill his wives and children, or indeed that Esau might go so far as to take the life of Jacob – that to Jacob was the danger. As we look and watch him as he paces backwards and forwards, he says, 'What is Esau going to do to me? I may lose this wonderful stock, that I bred in the land of Laban, I may lose it, it would be a terrible loss – I may lose my wives and children, I may lose my life, isn't this terrible ...' And he prays to God frantically. But what does God do? 'Jacob', says God, 'you haven't realised your greatest danger – your greatest danger is that you may lose your soul. Jacob', said God to him, 'these things about which you are worrying are things which of necessity sooner or later you are bound to lose. There is a day coming when you are going to die and, then you will have to lose your stock, you will have to leave your wives and children and all your possessions. There is a day coming when you will be on your death bed and you cannot take any of these things with you, but at that moment and hour you will still have your soul and you will have to render up an account to me of that soul. I have given you that soul, Jacob – your greatest danger at this moment is the loss of your soul and not being the man I want you to be, the man with the birthright blessing – that is the danger – the wrong relationship to me that leads to wrath and punishment and hell and destruction.'

And that is the message of God to man in the gospel of Jesus Christ tonight. There is the danger of the atomic bomb – I am not here to say that there is not a danger – but my dear friends, infinitely greater and more important than the danger of being killed perhaps in a few years with an atomic bomb is this danger that my ever-lasting and eternal soul may go to hell and spend itself there in misery and torment because I am wrong with God – that is my danger! Esau isn't the problem, the atomic bomb isn't the problem, industrial conditions are not the problem – No, no, you yourself are the problem ultimately, not Esau but God, not Esau but myself, not being what I am meant to be; not land and possessions and goods but the loss of my immortal soul and the jeopardising of my eternal future.

The gospel, I say, reveals to man that he worries and troubles about the wrong problem, it then goes on to show him the real problem, but thank God it does not stop at that. *It then reveals to man the blessings of life, possibilities infinitely greater and transcending everything that man has ever thought of or dreamed of or imagined.* Look at it in terms of Jacob. Jacob stands there and he says to himself, 'Now what about my future, if only I can appease Esau I will cross the river, I will settle down and be a wealthy and prosperous man – I will have the stock and the crop, I will have the wives and the children – that will be a wonderful life.' This is what he coveted. But when God met him there that night Jacob was given such a vision of blessing that he forgot all about Esau and his stock and crop and everything else. He saw God and he met God. God revealed to him the blessing that he had in store for him and Jacob said, 'I will not let thee go, I will let my animals go, I will let my wives and children go, I will let everything go but I will not let thee go and the blessing of God.' He had met the God who was offering him pardon for his failure, who assured him that he would place his hand upon him, who gave him there a vision of his own future as the father of a nation, the father ultimately of the Lord Jesus Christ who was to be the Saviour of the world. Jacob, I believe, was given a glimpse of that – out of his seed even the Messiah shall come – and he said 'I will not let thee go. What are earthly honours and goods and possessions when I see that through me and out of this nation will come Shiloh, the Deliverer' – that is the blessing – the new name, no longer Jacob but 'Israel'. And that is what the gospel says to every man who hears it by the power of the Holy Spirit. It offers us, let me say it again, pardon, forgiveness, assurance that God blots out our sins as a thick cloud and casts them behind him. Can you think of anything greater in this world tonight than that, having your conscience cleansed, being able to face and look at God and say, 'I am guilty but Christ suffered for my sin and I am free, pardoned and forgiven.' It means a new start in life, a new nature – the nature of God himself, being made a child of God. Oh how inadequate is language! We covet honours, we are like Jacob, we have an eye to the main chance, we scheme and plan – but this is what God offers you, he offers for you to be made a child of God. Can you imagine anything bigger or greater? He offers new power and strength and new might; he will enable us to conquer old sins and get rid of the things that have spoilt and ruined our past existence; he gives us righteousness and joy and peace; he removes the fear of death and the grave; he enables you to smile at death and the grave and say, 'I have gone through and beyond it in Christ, I have passed from death to life, through judgment to eternity.' And it gives us an everlasting hope which can never fade away. In other words, what the gospel tells us is something like this. It tells us that this world is ultimately going to be rid of sin. It tells us that Jesus of Nazareth, the Son of God, is coming back into this world; he is going to destroy all his enemies, Satan and sin and evil and all that is foul and ugly. It tells us that everything that is sinful and evil is going to be taken out of the world, even out of creation itself – that there is going to be 'a new heaven and a new earth in which dwelleth righteousness' and that those who are Christian are going to live in that world with Christ at their head, looking into the face of God and enjoying everlasting and eternal bliss. It offers that. That is why I said at the beginning that the gospel surprises us. It does not mean just pulling yourself together and trying to be a better man – No, no, it means that God will make you a child of his own; it means he will put his own nature into you, he will make you an heir of that bliss which I have tried to describe so inadequately; it means death will have no terror for you; you can look forward to that glorified existence. That is the blessing which he offers us. We have but to realise our need of him, the failure of our life, the danger to the soul and believe on the Lord Jesus Christ and those are the things we receive.

Is it possible that there is anyone in this congregation who, having heard these things, does not want to say with Jacob at this moment, 'I will not let thee go'. Are you a child of God? Do you know you are a child of God? Are you surprised at yourself? Are you aware of a new man in you? Have you lost the fear of death and the grave? Have you had victory over your former sin? Are you aware of a new power in your life? Can you look to that glorious era that is coming and say, 'I am going to be there'? Do these things come to you with reality? If not, cry out to him – 'I will not let thee go' –

> *Pass me not, O gentle Saviour,*
> *Hear my humble cry,*
> *While on others Thou art calling*
> *Do not pass me by.*

'I will not let Thee go'. If you say that to him honestly and sincerely, as he blessed Jacob of old he will bless you and you will be a new man and an heir of the wealth of God himself.

4

The Approach to the Gospel[1]

*And Moses said, I will now turn aside, and see this great sight, why
the bush is not burnt. And when the LORD saw that he turned aside
to see, God called unto him out of the midst of the bush, and said,
Moses, Moses. And he said, Here am I. And he said, Draw not nigh
hither: put off thy shoes from off thy feet, for the place whereon thou
standest is holy ground.*

Exodus 3:3–5

While I want to consider the entire incident with you, I place
special emphasis upon these three verses, because we cannot hope
to understand the whole passage and its great message without a
correct and true understanding of these words.

We have here one of the central incidents in Holy Writ, one
which has vital importance not only in connection with the
personal life of Moses but also in the life of the children of Israel
and the history of their deliverance from the bondage of Egypt and
of their being taken into possession of the promised land of Canaan.
It is one of those pivotal incidents and that is why references are
made to it so frequently in other parts of Scripture.

We are looking, then, at a narrative of history, and very vital
history, but I am concerned with it mainly because it is at the
same time a great type or lesson with regard to the whole matter of
salvation in and through our Lord and Saviour Jesus Christ. It can
never be pointed out too frequently that the great message of the
Old Testament, and the great message of the New Testament, are
really one. It is the same God who acts in both, and that is why the
Christian church was led of the Holy Spirit at the very beginning
to incorporate the Old Testament with the Gospels and the New
Testament Epistles. People have often wondered at that, indeed

[1] Westminster Chapel, 1 October 1950.

[33]

there are certain foolish people today who try to say that Christian people should not be interested any longer in the Old Testament. They say that it is Jewish and has nothing to do with us who possess the New Testament. But the early church, led by the Holy Spirit and by the wisdom that was given to her, saw the importance both of preserving the Old and of incorporating it with the New to form this one Book which we call the Bible. The reason for that is that it is the same God who acts in both and who acts in the same way in both. It is the same God, it is the same gracious purpose, it is essentially the same message. So I say that as we look at this great event in the life of Moses and of the children of Israel, we can learn some vital and important lessons with regard to the gospel of our Lord Jesus Christ. It puts one particular lesson before us in a peculiarly striking manner and it has to do with the question of our approach to the gospel. It seems to me that the difficulty which so many people have with regard to the Christian faith and gospel has to do with the whole question of their approach to the gospel. That is where many people go wrong, and I say that not only on the basis of my reading of the Scriptures but on the basis also of my experience in the ministry for some twenty-three years. The problem in the vast majority of cases lies further back than the gospel itself. It is the approach, the very attitude which is wrong and because that is wrong everything else must of necessity be wrong.

Now let me put it to you like this. Here in this passage you see Moses keeping the flock of Jethro his father-in-law, the priest of Midian. He had been a shepherd for some time, indeed for forty years, and he had been going on from day to day in the same humdrum, ordinary manner, taking the sheep from here to there, looking out for better pasture, and so on. The life of the shepherd has nothing very romantic or exciting about it. Here he was on this particular day, looking after the sheep as hitherto, and as he led the flock on this particular occasion to the back-side of the desert he came to the mountain of God, even to Horeb. Nothing very remarkable about that, probably they had exhausted pasture land somewhere else and here was a place where he felt his sheep could have adequate provision. He was just driving the sheep into position in the ordinary way when suddenly, unexpectedly, 'the angel of the Lord appeared to him in a flame of fire out of the midst of a bush: and he looked, and behold, the bush burned with fire, and the bush was not consumed. And Moses said, I will now turn aside, and see this great sight, why the bush is not burnt. And when the Lord saw that he turned aside to see, God called unto him out of the midst of the bush, and said, Moses, Moses. And he said, Here am I. And he said, Draw not nigh hither: put off thy shoes from off thy feet, for the place whereon thou standest is holy ground'. And then God delivered a great message to Moses, showing him how he was going to deliver the children of Israel from their cruel bondage and captivity in Egypt and bring them into the promised land of Canaan.

That is the story and it is a perfect illustration and picture of what happens in some shape or form to every man and woman who ever becomes a Christian. We are all like Moses here, going about our daily tasks and duties in this world, sharing the ordinary life of ordinary people. And thus we would have gone on and continued to go on were it not that something happens, something to disturb the even tenor of our ways. It may be one of a thousand and one things, but something happens which pulls us up and makes us begin to pay attention to 'religion' as we call it, to the Christian faith and to the Bible. Perhaps the unexpected comes in the form of an illness. There are many people who are Christians tonight, in a sense, because they had an illness. Once they went on heedlessly and thoughtlessly without any concern, and would apparently have gone on like that to the end, but they were taken ill. Suddenly lying on a sick bed they began to think and the result was they began to pay attention to these things and it ended in their conversion. Sometimes it is an accident, coming suddenly unawares and the whole of a man's life is changed. It may be a death, a bereavement, a sorrow, or some sort of trouble in business, an industrial depression or collapse. Indeed it may be world war. I say there are a thousand and one things which can pull people up and make them begin to think about these things exactly as Moses was arrested by the burning bush – a very ordinary afternoon but in the midst of the most mundane proceedings something happened. The unexpected may come suddenly or gradually (that does not matter at all); or perhaps in a meeting such as this, where we may have come quite hurriedly for one of many reasons, suddenly an arresting word is uttered and our attention is directed to the gospel and to the Word of God.

But, sadly, the truth is that that has happened to many people and yet it has not led to their conversion. They have been arrested, they have been made to think, they have been made to pause and ponder, they have paid attention to it, but all this never developed into full fruition. They have never really had an experience of salvation, they have never come to know God. So this is the question, what went wrong?

I am certain that the trouble with the vast majority of such people is their attitude towards what has happened which accounts for the failure. They have not understood the nature of their need, what they lack is the very lesson which is taught us in this famous incident. At first Moses does something which so many of us are prone to do. When he suddenly and unexpectedly sees the burning bush he says, 'I will now turn aside, and see this great sight, why the bush is not burnt', but God reprimanded him and gave him instructions. Now let me try to put the message in this form: if you and I are to know truly the blessings which the Christian gospel alone can give, we must approach it not in a spirit of curiosity but in a spirit of submission. Moses, you see, became curious – of course, it was a phenomenon, something unusual, something striking – 'I will turn aside and investigate', says Moses. He was but a man like the rest of us – something interesting, his curiosity roused and he is going to look at it in this spirit when the message comes to him.

Am I being unfair when I suggest that that is far too often the way in which people approach these matters? I believe it is true to say that there is in the world tonight a new kind of interest in these matters. It is not surprising after the two terrible wars through which we have passed – looking as we do out upon the modern world, seeing the failure and collapse of almost everything to which we had pinned our hopes – it is not surprising that men and women at last should be wistfully beginning to ask is there something in religion after all, if the Christian faith and the gospel is the answer. But oh, my friend, if you are in that position let me impress upon you the importance of facing and approaching these matters in the right way and manner. There is a wrong way of approach and we see it in many who are attracted by religion. They tell us that they find great pleasure in reading and discussing Christianity, and having arguments and debates about it. They assure us that they believe in investigating it and examining it. You are familiar with this type of person, generally intellectual and thoughtful; he comes and speaks that kind of language and says, 'You know I really am becoming very interested in this whole question'. How often am I told that by various people! They tell me that they find it tremendously interesting, they like listening to an occasional sermon, or some broadcast discussion of these religious beliefs. Perhaps they begin to read, discuss and have arguments and debates about it; they may even read books on theology or on what is called 'comparative religions', or perhaps it is the psychological approach and books on philosophy which they say fascinate them. Certainly they are interested – 'the burning bush' – 'I will turn aside and investigate and examine and have a look at this thing!'. There are some people who spend the whole of their lives approaching the Christian faith in that way, it is the great interest of their lives; they are always reading and talking about it and they do a tremendous lot with respect to it. They are still interested on their death bed but they know nothing, they have not experienced its power, they do not know it in such a way that when they come to die, they can die happy, triumphantly and gloriously. They are not able to say 'to die is gain' for it means to be 'with Christ which is far better'. No! they start investigating and they end in investigating. As the Scripture itself puts it, 'ever learning, and never able to come to the knowledge of the truth' (*2 Tim.* 3:7); supposed seekers after truth and reality who never seem to find it. What is the matter with them is that very often their approach is altogether and entirely wrong. Listen again, when Moses said, 'I will now turn aside and see this great sight, why the bush is not burnt' – a most amazing phenomenon in the humdrum life of a shepherd – and when we are confronted by the Christian faith, and say we will become interested, this is the message that comes to Moses and to us, 'God called to him out of the midst of the bush, and said ...' Give up your investigation, 'Draw not nigh hither; put off thy shoes from off thy feet for the place whereon thou standest is holy ground'. 'Moses', said God, out of the midst of the bush, 'drop that attitude, drop that attitude of investigation and examination, drop that objectivity, take your shoes off your feet, stay where you are and submit yourself'.

I start with this because it is the message of the Bible from beginning to end. If you are just an investigator, or an inspector, examining the Bible with that detached air, you will never know its message. If you think that God is someone who arouses your curiosity, upon whom you can speculate, you may go on investigating him but you will never *know* him except in wrath, you will remain outside his life. No!, the very beginning is this, 'take off thy shoes from off thy feet for the place whereon thou standest is holy ground'. That is something absolutely preliminary. Now I do not apologise for saying that. Our Lord said exactly the same thing to Nicodemus. Nicodemus, that great master and teacher of Israel, came to our Lord and, as it were, he was beginning to say, 'I am very interested, I have been listening to your sermons and I have seen your wonderful miracles, you seem to have gone a step further than me, now then' – but back came exactly the same answer, 'Verily, verily I say unto you, Except a man be born again, he cannot see the kingdom of God' (*John* 3:3). 'I cannot have a discussion with you', says our Lord, 'you have to go back, we are not equal, go down and take off your shoes, your whole attitude and approach is wrong' – the same message, it is everywhere here in this Book. Saul of Tarsus, afterwards the apostle Paul, tells us, 'I thought with myself that I ought to do many things contrary to the name of Jesus Christ' (*Acts* 26:9), and then Christ flashed upon him and struck him helpless and blind to the ground.

It is the same thing again.

Well, asks someone, why this attitude, why should I approach these things in a different manner from everything else in this world, why should I start with submitting myself?

Let me give you some of the answers to that question. The first is this; *this gospel which I am privileged to preach to you is primarily a matter of revelation.* It is not enquiry, it is not discovery. More or less everything else in life is enquiry and discovery, that is why we drop into that habit, and think it should apply here. Is that not the argument of the modern man; he says all truth is discovered in science and nature as the result of investigation, why not here? The answer is that here you start with revelation not investigation, a man by searching cannot 'find out God' (*Job* 11:7). No! The whole message of the burning bush is that when Moses was probably thinking about none of these things that afternoon but only of his sheep and where he could find the best pasture, suddenly God appears, God comes into the bush with the burning flame.

It is always that, I have no message unless this is revelation from God. This Christian faith is not philosophy, it is not what men think of God and life and the world; it is God revealing himself, God coming to us and telling us things, it is revelation. That is the reason we must not come in the spirit of investigation and examination; here is revelation to which we must look and listen.

The whole story of the Bible, from beginning to end, is of God coming in, God breaking in. He made the world at the beginning and man sinned and went wrong. What is the next step? God came into the garden in the cool of the day, God broke in. God spoke – that is revelation, that is the beginning and it has continued like that ever since. God speaking to Noah telling him what to do, God calling out Abraham. In all this great history you see the activity of God everywhere – Judges, Kings, the Prophets – God the whole time. I say it is the essence of the message of the gospel, 'when the fulness of the time was come, God sent forth his own Son, made of a woman, made under the law'. Revelation! God acted and God revealing unto us his gracious purpose. Now electricity was not discovered like that. It was discovered by much thought, investigation and enquiry and everything else in life is like that. But here is a different order of truth, unique and separate and distinct. It is God speaking and telling us something, revealing and manifesting himself to us. That is the first reason to show why we must approach the Christian faith in an entirely different way.

The second reason is this: that *the revelation given is marvellous and wonderful*; indeed, it is miraculous and supernatural. Moses was quite right when he said, 'I will now turn aside, and see this great sight, why the bush is not burnt. This thing is a miracle, it is something I cannot fathom' – though he did not realise how right he was. You and I have to start by realising that the gospel of Jesus Christ starts with the supernatural. It is absolutely unique and unexplainable, beyond the understanding and the comprehension of the greatest men and of all mankind put together. Yes, I say that in 1950, the gospel of Jesus Christ is miraculous. It starts by telling us it is beyond the grasp of man's mind; it is God and God acting. Very well then, my friend, is it not rather a waste of time for you to start 'investigating' and 'examining' it? Do you not see why these poor people, after perhaps eighty years of investigation, are as far away at the end as they were at the beginning. No man who wants to trust to his own understanding and says, 'I must be able to grasp it', will ever be anything more than an investigator. He will remain unsaved. By definition man's mind is natural at its best and highest and cannot understand the supernatural.

But let us hurry to the next point which is still more important. The third reason for taking the shoes from off our feet is that *the whole point and purpose of the Christian gospel is to bring us to meet God*. That was the blunder of Moses – Moses forgot that central thing; he thought it was only a phenomenon, a burning bush, perhaps even a supernatural phenomenon. Instead he found it was meeting a Person, not a flame, and that is why he had to take his shoes from off his feet. He was meeting God and the whole purpose of the Christian faith is to bring us to a personal encounter and a personal meeting with God. A personal knowledge of God – that is the central business of the Christian faith and its wondrous offer of salvation!

Let me put it like this negatively: We must not even be concerned with truths about God. The business of the gospel is not to bring us to a knowledge of things 'about God', it is to bring us to a knowledge of God himself. So many think that the business of the gospel is to bring us into a knowledge of truths about life, how to live. They say, 'I want to know how to live a better life, let us turn to the gospel for instruction and guidance'. It may help at certain points but that is not the central business, its central business is to bring us to know God. Let me go further and say, the business of the Christian faith is not to give us a knowledge of theology. You can have a great knowledge of theology and still not know God. I am the last man to decry theology, one of the greatest troubles is the lack of a knowledge of theology, but I say you may have a knowledge of theology and still be a stranger to the love of God. There are many who go through this world arguing about theology and who may be staunch defenders of the faith, yet they do not know God and are outside salvation. No, it is not that, neither is this Christian gospel concerned with ideas, with maxims on morality and ethics. Neither is it, I say, a question of concepts, of philosophy – no, no, it is meeting God, it is coming into the presence of God and knowing that you are dealing with him directly and personally. And let me add one more to my list of negatives. The business of men who approach the Christian faith and its message is not even to be

interested in a phenomenon such as experience. There are many
people today who are interested in experience, I have often had to
speak and deal with them. They say: 'I have not the slightest use for
theology and philosophy but I am interested in experience. I have
seen a great change in somebody else's life – what can I do to get an
experience?' The Bible is not interested in experience primarily, it
is interested in the fact that you and I should come to know God.
That is an experience, thank God it is, but while you are looking at
and are interested in experience and are intrigued by the difference
between psychology and spiritual experience and go no further, you
will never come to know him. That is the wrong way of looking at
the burning bush. 'Put off thy shoes from off thy feet' – you must
not be interested in experience, you must be interested in getting to
know God. The central business of this Book is to bring us to such
knowledge.

The last reason for taking our shoes off and approaching in an
attitude of submission is *because of what the God whom we thus
meet has to say to us*. What is the revelation that he gives to us? The
first thing is, it is a revelation of his own holiness. That is always the
first thing you find out about God, God is holy, 'take off thy shoes
from off thy feet because the place whereon thou standest is holy
ground'. If you have not started with the holiness of God, you have
never known him. I can put that very briefly in this form: read the
pages of the four Gospels and watch our Lord Jesus Christ, the very
Son of God himself. Have you noticed how he speaks of God as
'Holy Father'? There is nothing that so alarms and frightens me as
I listen to people discussing these matters, as the glib way in which
they talk about God. God, they say, ought to do this or that and
they express their opinions. Do you realise what you are saying, my
friend, do you realise that this God is a consuming fire, a holy God,
'the Father of lights, with whom is no variableness neither shadow
of turning'. I beseech you be careful how you use the very name of
God. I can understand the ancient Jews and their fear of using the
Name. They were afraid to use the Name in a sense because of
the holiness of God, but you and I have heard Christian people in
prayer talk about 'dear Father'. The Son of God did not address
him as 'dear Father'; he addressed him as 'Holy Father' – 'take off
thy shoes from off thy feet, for the place whereon thou standest is
holy ground'. God has revealed himself as a holy God. That is the

meaning of the Ten Commandments; be careful, I say, how you speak and how you express your opinion, for you are in the hands of this God.

But thank God I can add something else. He wants us to listen to his message and having revealed his holiness to us he goes on to reveal his love and mercy and compassion. 'The Lord said, I have surely seen the affliction of my people which are in Egypt, and have heard their cry by reason of their taskmasters; for I know their sorrows' (*Exod.* 3:7). O blessed Word! My dear friend, the problem confronting you is not an intellectual one, it is the problem of yourself – the life, the bondage you are in to sin and Satan. The problem over Christianity is not intellectual, it is a fatal tendency of man to think that. Here is the way you must begin; you are slaves of sin and you know it; you are slaves of your bad temper, your jealousy and your dishonesty in various forms and that is your problem. Your problem is not to understand God or understand the miracles, it is the problem of somehow being delivered and emancipated out of the things that really bring you down and make a failure of you and of your life. Thank God for a message which tells us – if we but listen to it, if we but take off our shoes and with reverence pay attention – 'I have surely seen the affliction of my people which are in Egypt, and have heard their cry, I know their sorrows'. That is what God is saying to you if you give up examining, investigating and trying to understand him. Listen to him and tonight you will hear him saying, 'I know your sorrows, I know your unhappiness and failure, I know all about you, I am a God of love and mercy and compassion'. And then he goes on to say a final thing in verse 8: 'I am come down to deliver them out of the hand of the Egyptians, and to bring them up out of that land unto a good land and a large, unto a land flowing with milk and honey'. What a perfect statement that is – 'I am come down to deliver'. Did I not start by telling you the gospel is to be found in the Old Testament? That is the whole story of the New Testament. Jesus of Nazareth is none other than the blessed second Person of the Holy Trinity. God the Son came down from heaven. Why? Because he had seen your affliction and mine, because he knew our wretchedness, because he saw our sin and shame and failure. He has come down, he came to deliver, and the only way to deliver was to take your sins and mine and bear them in his own holy, spotless, sinless body on the Cross on

Calvary's hill. There he did it, he has paid the ransom, he has made the atonement, God is satisfied, the law is satisfied, hell and Satan are defeated and Egypt has been conquered. The Red Sea – the way to God and new life – is open. There is forgiveness of sins, reconciliation to God, being born again, new strength and power and an everlasting and blessed hope of entering into the heavenly kingdom and enjoying its spiritual milk and honey throughout the countless ages of eternity. That is the message.

While you remain in this detached so-called objective attitude of investigation and enquiry, and are merely interested in religion, you will never know it, you will remain a slave to sin and you will be in darkness and go to perdition. But if only you stop, if only you listen, if only you take off your shoes and give up your pride of intellect and all these other things and humble yourself as a little child and listen to the message concerning the Lord Jesus Christ, the Son of God who came from heaven to earth, he will make a new person of you. He will deliver you from the bondage of sin and Satan and evil, and take you by the hand at the last to present you to God faultless and perfect and to usher you into that eternal bliss. My dear friend, have you met God? Do you know God? Are you ready to meet God? Have you heard God's Word to you? Have you heard God telling you, 'I know your sorrows, and I have done this about it, I have sent my Son to deliver you, to set you free'. Are you free – has Christ delivered you, do you know your sins are forgiven, have you received life anew? You have but to listen to and believe this simple message, to tell God that you accept it, and that you are trusting yourself and your whole life to him, and then you will know it and experience it as a blessed reality. If you have not already done so, take off thy shoes from off thy feet and listen and believe.

5
False Safety

Then the five men departed, and came to Laish, and saw the people that were therein, how they dwelt careless, after the manner of the Zidonians, quiet and secure; and there was no magistrate in the land, that might put them to shame in anything; and they were far from the Zidonians, and had no business with any man . . . And there was no deliverer, because it was far from Zidon, and they had no business with any man; and it was in the valley that lieth by Beth-rehob. And they built a city, and dwelt therein.

Judges 18:7, 28

In these two verses we have the beginning and the end of the story of these Zidonians. It is a remarkable account and what strikes me most of all about it is its modernity. The story is this. A number of the people of Zidon had wandered off on their own as colonists anxious to find a place in which they could settle and live their own lives in their own way. What made them do this we are not told. It may have been that they were anxious to avoid the responsibilities of life at Zidon in the matter of taxes. It may have been that they felt they were constantly in danger of being called upon to go to war to protect and defend their city. Perhaps they felt that their district had become overcrowded and, therefore, that it made life difficult. Or it may have been that they thought that if they could get to a more uncultivated district it would mean greater returns for less work on their part – a district which was so blessed and so fruitful in a natural respect that they would have to do scarcely any work at all but just gather in the fruit. We cannot tell exactly what the notions were that urged and guided these people but the account itself suggests strongly that the last was probably the reason. Whatever the reason, these people had gone off on their own and found just the right kind of place for which they were looking. There they settled their colony and called it Laish.

Of their mode of life after they had settled at Laish we are told the following facts. They were peaceable and peace loving, they all behaved themselves so well that there was no need of a magistrate in the land in order to keep law and order. Each man looked after his own work and business and did not interfere with anyone else. There were no internal troubles in the colony. Also, we are told that they 'dwelt careless, quiet and secure' which just means that they had taken no measures at all to defend their country. They made no provision whatsoever against any possible attacks from the outside. In that respect they were indeed 'careless'. Nor were they concerned to note who entered their area and made observations. As they were peace-loving themselves they assumed that all others would be the same. They had no thought of attacking their neighbours or anyone near them and they assumed that all others were animated by precisely the same feelings. They 'dwelt careless, quiet and secure'.

The other important point about the life of these new colonists was that they were 'far from the Zidonians' – 'their own people' – and had no business 'with any man'. They had cut themselves right off from their own country. They lived their own lives amongst themselves and for themselves and had nothing to do with anyone else. The richness of their region was such that there was no need for them to trade. They were self-supporting in every respect and were able to provide and produce all the commodities of which they had need. Furthermore, the district in which they had settled seems to have been off 'the beaten track' and unknown to most others. So their life was one of isolation and complete independence. There they lived and enjoyed life in this apparently ideal and idyllic manner. And so they would have continued to live were it not that some of the Danites, being anxious to find more room for themselves, began to explore and eventually came upon these people.

Our chapter tells us that the five spies found this land of Laish, observed its mode of life and went back and reported to their fellows. Then how six hundred men with weapons of war went up and smote these colonists with the edge of the sword, burned the city with extreme ease, and settled there. 'With extreme ease' I say because the account tells us 'that there was no deliverer because it was far from Zidon and they had no business with any man.'

Such is the story of these Zidonian colonists, and I call your attention to it not merely because it is worthy of consideration in and of itself but rather because it is a perfect picture of the life story of a large number of men and women in a religious sense at this present time. There is nothing in connection with the whole realm of religion which is quite so important as the need for us to realise that there are a large number of ways in which men and women may defy God and sin against him. If I may presume to criticise our own immediate fathers and grandfathers I would say that their essential error and weakness was that they always tended to identify sin with certain obvious open acts of sin and failed to see the real subtlety of sin, and the most deadly form of all which it was tending to assume in their very own generation. They formed organisations to fight this and that particular sin as if that alone mattered, not realising that many of the people who belonged to these organisations, and who seemed to be most zealous as members within them, were being assailed by, and were actually succumbing to, a form of sin which is infinitely more dangerous and deadly: namely, the sin of irreligion and a gradual departure from God altogether.

That the fathers failed to observe this is not surprising because the whole process is so insidious. It is so much easier for us after the event to see it happening. And indeed the fact is that there are so many today who do not see it. The danger still exists of identifying sin and defiance of God with certain well-defined external manifestations of that attitude. Everyone is clear about the irreligion of the Soviet Union, with its leaving of religion altogether and its open defiance of God and blasphemy. Most people are also clear about the gradual substitution of a form of paganism and race-worship for the Christian religion in a country like Nazi Germany. The persecution and the imprisoning of pastors, etc., draws attention to it and all seem to be well aware of it. Likewise, all people can see that the activities of the various atheistical and so-called free-thought societies, and some of the other cults, are definitely anti-God and sinful. In the same way also, those who fall to the grosser and more obvious sins of the flesh habitually are clear to all as being godless people. Those who speak openly and plainly against God and who blaspheme his name without the slightest hesitation and those who by their riotous living proclaim the same thing are recognised by all as being irreligious. But there is another type of person who is guilty of precisely the same thing – a type which, I fear, includes a larger number of people at the present time than all the other types put together – and this type, the Zidonian type, is generally ignored by us. Let us look at it.

As these colonists had started life in Zidon, so the Zidonian type of religious person has also made a very definite start. They were brought up in a religious tradition and from their earliest days they heard about God and about his Son Jesus Christ. They were taught certain truths, such as that God was not only Creator but also Judge and Lord, that he demanded worship and homage, and indicated to mankind the type of life he would have it live. They were told further that all mankind had sinned, had failed and stood condemned before God without a plea and without a hope, but that God in his infinite love had actually sent his only-begotten Son into the world to live and die and rise again in order to make a way of salvation and in order that God might reconcile the world to himself. They heard all that at the beginning and were brought up in that atmosphere and in a tradition which impressed this upon their minds.

Furthermore, there was a voice within themselves which agreed with it all and attested it all. That was the kind of life in which they started and which they felt within themselves to be right. The call was to worship God, to believe that reconciliation to him was only possible in Jesus Christ, and to live a life along the lines laid down in the ten commandments and especially in the Sermon on the Mount and the New Testament. That was the beginning. But exactly like the people in our story they gradually contracted out of this and wandered away to form and to live a new kind of life of their own making. The reasons which prompted them to do this we shall see later as we come to analyse this kind of life. They are of exactly the same type as the Zidonian colonists. They have wandered away from God, have turned their backs upon him and have shut themselves and their lives within certain confines they have mapped out for themselves. They mean to live their own lives in their own way without any communication with God or any reference to his holy laws.

Now there are two points concerning this type of person that I want to stress, two general points before we come to the more detailed criticism and consideration. The first is that this kind of person never opposes religion and God openly. They never say a word against him, they are never guilty of open blasphemy and in their lives they do not seem to be irreligious. They just ignore God and shut him right out of their lives. Their antagonism and opposition is not active but passive. The Zidonians did not attack their own people and their own country. They just left it and had nothing further whatsoever to do with it. We hear a great deal today of the violent attacks on religion in various places, the onslaught of the sceptics are quickly repeated in the daily newspapers, but we never hear a word about the large masses who have quietly turned their backs upon God and are living a thoroughly irreligious life!

The second matter I am anxious to impress upon you is that the religious situation with which we are dealing is very much more subtle than that depicted in our story. In the story the people actually left Zidon, but in the religious application actual physical removal is not essential. All the irreligious people are not outside the church and never have been. We can see that in the case of the Church of Rome, but we are not always alive to it in Protestantism and Nonconformity and in our own midst. The type of person I am describing does not of necessity stay away altogether from a place of worship. That is not the point I am making. It is not departure from organised Christianity that we are considering but departure from God and from a truly religious life. If you would know whether you belong to the Zidonian type or not irrespective of church membership, etc., face and answer the following questions:

Do you know God? Do you have regular communion with him? Is your life ordered and controlled by his laws and by his holy will? Are you still in touch with him? Can you find him when in need and in trouble? Or, to put it all in one question, is your life a God-controlled life or are you living your own life in your own way independently of him? I am not asking whether you openly deny God in words or renounce him in specific statements to that effect. My question is, are you denying him in your life? Is it his way or your way? These questions, I think, make it abundantly clear that the life of cleavage is not that of mere chapel or church attendance but something much deeper – Zidonian colonists are to be found inside the church as well as outside.

That then is the kind of life and the kind of person we are considering. What have we to say of it? At once we can say many of the things, if not all, that are said about the people in this chapter. Such people seem very nice and harmless. All they desire is to be allowed to live their own lives in their own way. They do not desire to interfere with the life of anyone else and all they ask is that they be treated in the same way. They dislike people who interfere with them and they dislike the type of religion that interferes with them. They have no objection to platitudes and to sentimental idealism. They have no objection to religion as long as it is general and does not become personal and make demands of them.

They never break the law and never cause trouble. They are almost invariably highly respectable, even in their sins – no magistrates are needed in their case either. Their life seems to be easy and carefree, apparently highly successful and most happy. Nothing seems to trouble and to worry them. Everything seems to go easily and smoothly. They go to work or to business and return home and have their pleasures and enjoy themselves in their own way and so it goes on from year to year. The family life seems happy and they have their friends and their social round. But I need not elaborate; you all know this type of life which is one of the commonest types of life to be seen in this country at the present moment. What of it?

It is decent and respectable, self-contained and apparently perfectly happy. What can be wrong with such a type of life? We suggest the following considerations:

1.   The first thing we say of it is that *it is an essentially selfish type of life*. This is very clear, of course, in the case of the people in the actual story. We have already considered the motives that led these Zidonians to leave their home district and settle at Laish. They were altogether selfish. They considered no one but themselves and having found a place which suited them, they settled down in it and cut off communications with the outside world. They had what they desired and nothing else troubled them. Their case reminds us that selfishness does not always take the aggressive, 'Mussolini' form, in which a man desires what he can get for himself irrespective of other people's wishes. Selfishness does not always take the form of greed and is not always 'grabbing'. There is another

type of selfishness, the type which shows itself by its lack of concern about the lot of others.

It is that type of selfishness which is quite happy as long as it itself is all right and well-cared for, no matter what may be the state and condition of others. These colonists had all they desired. They cared not at all about anyone else. This is always one of the first results of irreligion and there is nothing which is so plainly to be seen in the modern world as just this very type of selfishness.

It is to be seen in the international situation and the way in which feeling is determined almost exclusively and entirely by what is best for each particular country. Each country tends to consider itself alone. Thus we have economic nationalism and the failure of countries to commit themselves to the defence of justice and matters of principle.

But it is a feature which is evident in the whole of life, personal and individual as well as national. Every man is out for himself and for his own family and lot. Listen to men talking to each other, yes, men in every class and walk of life. What are they after? What do they covet? The maximum of wealth and ease and the minimum amount of effort and responsibility. Happiness and ease and comfort have become the goals for the vast majority of people. The so-called 'good time' is the thing of which people speak most frequently. Every man is out for himself and for what he can get. Principles are not only ignored and forgotten but actually sold, and life is ever-increasingly assessed in terms of money and possessions. Little is heard of duty and service and the whole responsibility of life and living, and many who appear to take an interest in the common welfare are often suspected, and that rightly, of having a thoroughly selfish and personal ulterior motive.

Is not this a perfectly true picture of life today? And is it not one which has become increasingly more and more evident during the progress of this century? What is the cause of it? We have already given the answer. It is the departure from God and from the way of life he has set down for us. For God commands us to think of our neighbour, indeed to love him as ourself. God calls upon us to start by 'denying ourselves' and to yield ourselves to him. He teaches us that we are not really owners of any possessions but mere stewards, not even owners of our own children or of our own very lives. He tells us that happiness is not to be the ultimate goal but truth and righteousness, that we are to seek first not the various things that are to be obtained in life but 'the kingdom of God and his righteousness and that then all these things will be added unto us' (*Matt.* 6:33). His word is that only those who 'hunger and thirst after righteousness' shall be filled and be really made blessed. Christ, far from telling us to contract out of life and just settle down nicely and snugly somewhere where we can enjoy ourselves to our heart's content in a state of ease, counsels us rather to take up our cross and to follow him. 'Whosoever will save his life', he adds, 'shall lose it: and whosoever will lose his life for my sake shall find it' (*Matt.* 16:24, 25). And all the teaching of the New Testament is everywhere the same. Listen to Paul for instance, referring to the same principle in writing in 1 Corinthians 8 in the matter of meat offered to idols. 'Don't consider yourselves', says Paul in effect to the more enlightened church members, 'remember the weaker brother also'. 'Conscience, I say, not thine own, but of the other' (*1 Cor.* 10:29), says Paul.

As you read the lives of the saints there is nothing which strikes you so much as the way in which they denied themselves to give their all for the sake of others. Such persons are the greatest benefactors the world has ever known and their lives are the most beautiful lives that have ever been lived, the supreme point of beauty being their utter selflessness. It is because they cannot endure doctrine of this kind that men and women really turn away from religion. It is because of the selfishness of their hearts, their love of ease and comfort, their desire to look after themselves first and last and always, that they have turned their backs upon God and wandered away from his laws and 'settled down' to enjoy life in their own place and in their own way in this present evil world. Yes, and it is as they have done so that life has become increasingly materialistic, selfish, ugly and harsh. Just contrast for a moment in your mind the type of life that appeals to so many today with the life of any one of the saints. How selfish, how ugly, how hideous!

Then compare that selfish life with the life of Jesus of Nazareth, the Son of God. And especially as he hangs nailed to that cross which he in no way deserved and to which he went solely and entirely for the sake of others – for you and for me. Can you look at that and realise what it means and still continue to think of nothing but yourself and your own happiness?

Oh! the selfishness, the shame, the ugliness, the foulness of the godless life, however respectable and quiet it may be.

2.   I had also intended to draw your attention to *the smallness of this kind of life*. For there is surely nothing which strikes us so much as the way in which this kind of life is circumscribed and small and petty. These Zidonian colonists lived their own little life. They cut themselves off from Zidon and also from all other people. There is nothing which is more pathetic about the godless life than its smallness. We have already seen that really in considering its selfishness, but there are also many other ways in which the small-ness of the irreligious life appears. But we have no time this evening. The fact itself is surely clear to all who have followed so far and who really have eyes to see. We must move on to the other aspects of this kind of life which are perfectly illustrated in this story.

3.   We observe that *this is a very short-sighted type of life*. Its whole view of life is hopelessly inadequate. We read of these Zidonian colonists at the beginning that they were leading a 'quiet and secure' life and that they 'dwelt carelessly'. Everything seems to be perfectly happy and serene. There is nothing to trouble them and they trouble about nothing. They give no thought at all to the question of defence against possible attacks, they make no provision whatsoever for all kinds of possible eventualities. They refuse to think about such things and if anyone ever mentions them they would just silence him and tell him not to be ridiculous. Indeed they would regard him as some unkind spoil-sport who is always going out of his way to look for trouble. Were they not perfectly happy? Very well, let them enjoy the happiness without going forward to meet difficulties, 'they dwelt careless'. Now there we have a perfect description of an attitude towards life which I would impress upon you is short-sighted, utterly useless and hopeless as a philosophy of life. Indeed the truth about it is just that it is not a philosophy at all, it represents the complete absence of a philosophy. The whole basis of this type of life is just the refusal to think, the readiness to trust that all will be well and the belittlement

of everything that seems to point in the opposite direction. These Zidonians seemed to be 'quiet and secure'. But they did not analyse that security and realise that it was solely and entirely dependent upon the fact that hitherto no one outside of their territory had thought of attacking them. They see and think of security and quietness only and never trouble to consider and to analyse the basis of that security. They go on saying that all is well. The fact that they are sitting on a volcano is of no concern to them as long as the volcano is not in a state of eruption. They do not trouble even to cater for possible eventualities.

As long as they are happy and secure they care for nothing else and think of nothing else and trouble about nothing. 'They dwelt careless'. Yes! and because of that they took no notice of five men who approached one day and spied out their country. Perhaps they did not even see them. If they did, they took no notice and did nothing about them.

They just went on as they were, heedless and careless, until one day an army suddenly descended upon them and they were utterly helpless and powerless to defend themselves.

Let me ask a number of simple questions: Have you a scheme of life, a philosophy of life? Do you look forward and look ahead? Have you considered and envisaged all the possibilities of life, yes, all the inevitable certainties? What is the basis of your life? Are you content just to live from moment to moment, from hand to mouth, content merely as long as you have no present troubles and difficulties? Have you thought deeply and thoroughly about life? Do you face the problems right through or do you just shelve them and push them to one side saying that life is too short for that sort of thing? Or do you perhaps refuse to consider them, feeling that all consideration is vain and futile, that troubles will come soon enough and that therefore the thing to do in the meantime is just to enjoy yourself as much as you can and get the maximum out of life while it lasts? At the moment, you may be dwelling 'quiet and secure'. There may be no cloud at all in your sky. Everything may be perfectly bright and happy as it was with these Zidonian colonists for such a long time. Are you content with that? Are you just resting in that and hoping that it will continue and remain? Are you dwelling careless also? Have you seen the spies that have entered your country? No, I know that they have done no harm as yet and have left everything quite undisturbed. They have only come to look around and have now gone back to report to their main army which will soon advance upon you. But have you seen them? Have you made provision for what they will certainly bring to pass sooner or later? All is well now, but where will you be and what will be your position if adversity overtakes you? What have you got with which to face poverty or illness, pain and suffering, disappointment and disillusionment? What if you meet with treachery on the part of someone you have trusted and in whom you have confided? What about bereavement and sorrow, and death itself? Are you in training for these things? Have you a defence ready for the time of attack? Have you power with which to resist? Have you any reserves on which you can fall back?

Am I merely being unpleasant and ghoulish? Is all this but morbid imagining? These are the ordinary common facts of life. To refuse to face them and to be prepared for them is not only to court disaster but also to manifest the sheer lack of intelligence, the utter philosophical bankruptcy of all who live in a fool's paradise. These spies have entered and have prospected the land. Awake! Rouse yourself! Shake off this dull sloth and carelessness! Prepare along the only lines that can succeed as laid down in the gospel of our Lord and Saviour Jesus Christ.

4.   For if you do not, the last characteristic of life to which we would refer tonight will also become evident in your life as it did in the life of the Zidonian colonists, namely, its *suicidal nature.* Let me explain what I mean by that. These people were not only careless in that they did not think and made no preparations for their own defence, but, further, they had cut themselves off from Zidon and had even cut themselves off from all other people so that there was no hope even of getting anyone to send a message to Zidon. These are the words, listen to them, 'And there was no deliverer, because it was far from Zidon, and they had no business with any man.' They had wandered off and had isolated themselves by cutting off all means of communication with others. How wonderful it was at first! Here they were, 'dwelling careless', 'quiet and secure' – nothing to worry or to trouble them, free from all the duties and responsibilities of life, just living for themselves and enjoying themselves to their heart's content. Often they laughed at those still left

in Zidon and pitied them for their lack of courage and initiative and their lack of spirit of adventure. This is life, not that old way in Zidon. This new life was the life! How wonderful! But suddenly a powerful army, six hundred men appointed with weapons of war appears, their swords flashing in the sun, and it descends upon their city intent upon its conquest and destruction. At once they see their hopeless plight. They have nothing with which to defend themselves and there is no one whose aid they can invoke. 'If only we were nearer to Zidon', they say, 'if only we could send someone there.' But these were vain and useless regrets. They were too far from Zidon and there was no neighbour who would go for them as they had dealings with none. How they wished that they had kept up communications. But now it was too late and they were destroyed and their city burnt. They had removed their only hope of deliverance deliberately, had cut off their own retreat, had voluntarily broken the one means of communication by which they could have obtained help and relief. Their isolation of themselves from Zidon was the direct cause of their death, their policy was ultimately suicidal.

The life which turns away from God, and ignores his law and way of life, at first and for a long time appears to be very wonderful and highly successful. It seems to be *the* life and those who live it often deride and pity those who still strive to walk the narrow path and the narrow way. You can cut off your contact with God and turn your back upon him and go your way and apparently all will be well. But we have already asked you to face certain eventualities. Are you strong enough to meet them? Of course you are not. Well, have you anyone on whom you can fall back? Is there any deliverer to whom you can turn and for whom you can send? Have you lines of communication open? Like many others, when in trouble you turn to God in prayer, but can you find him? Does he not seem to be far away and too distant? Can you find 'grace to help in time of need'? And do you not find when you then turn to him that you are a coward and that you have been a cad as well as a fool?

But we have not finished. Not only do disappointment and accident and sickness and pain and bereavement and death itself come. There is another enemy even more rebellious and more deadly. How do you meet an accusing conscience? How do you reply to the thundering onslaught of a holy law? What will you have to say at the day of judgment? That you shut yourself off into a little life and compartment of your own has no effect whatsoever upon the eternal fact and verities. By hiding yourself you do not do away with God, by refusing to think you do not change eternal realities. By adopting modern theories and ideas which suit your fancy and accord with your desires and sinful instincts you do not abrogate eternal decrees. You fool none but yourself, 'Be not deceived, God is not mocked'. Where are you? Is there any way of escape? Is there no deliverer?

In the case of the Zidonian colonists there was none and they were utterly destroyed but, thanks be to God, we have something further to say, a glorious gospel to unfold. You and I, all of us, are by nature in the position of these people. We have turned away from God, have spurned the voice divine, have broken the means of communication and face to face with the final test of life and, above all, face to face with the truth of God and eternity, we are lost and helpless. In our agony we try to save ourselves but find we cannot. We try to reach out for God and to find him, but we are 'too far' away. We have lost our way and the very road itself seems to have been destroyed.

There is no way back that we can find. But, wonder of wonders, God himself provides a way and opens a new means of communication. Right into the sinful iniquitous colony into which mankind has turned this world, God sent his only-begotten Son. While they 'dwelt careless', and at ease and thoughtlessly, God planned and then executed his plan – that glorious plan of redemption whereby through the death of his Son for our sins he can forgive us and reconcile us to himself, the plan by which he also restores us to communion with himself and which makes him 'our refuge and our strength, a very present help in time of trouble' (*Psa.* 46:1). Here is a plan of salvation which conquers all our enemies, answers all our foes, and gives us ultimate complete deliverance.

Are you in touch with this deliverer, Jesus of Nazareth, the Son of God? The spies have come! But so has he! Have you seen him? Do you know him? Are you linked to him! He is here tonight offering himself and his salvation to you. Yield yourself to him! Listen to him! Follow him! Obey him! The way to God and to heaven are open in him in spite of all your sin and shame. He came, he lived, he died, he rose again for you. Give yourself to him and begin to sing:

> *A Sovereign Protector I have;*
> *Unseen, yet forever at hand,*
> *Unchangeably faithful to save,*
> *Almighty to rule and command,*
>
> *He smiles, and my comforts abound,*
> *His grace as the dew shall descend.*
> *And walls of salvation surround*
> *The soul He delights to defend.*

6

When the Gods Fall[1]

And the Philistines took the ark of God, and brought it from Eben-ezer unto Ashdod.

When the Philistines took the ark of God, they brought it into the house of Dagon and set it by Dagon.

And when they of Ashdod arose early on the morrow morning, behold, Dagon was fallen upon his face to the earth before the ark of the LORD. And they took Dagon, and set him in his place again.

And when they arose early on the morrow morning, behold, Dagon was fallen upon his face to the ground before the ark of the LORD; and the head of Dagon and both the palms of his hands were cut off upon the threshold; only the stump of Dagon was left to him.

1 Samuel 5:1–4

These verses come as a kind of sequel or epilogue to the incident that is recorded in the previous chapter. It is an account of a period in the history of the children of Israel which is one of the saddest in their long and chequered history. Owing to their forgetting of God, and their religious declension, they had declined politically and even in a military sense, and they had been conquered by their old and traditional enemies, the Philistines. But the account tells us that, after a certain length of time, the Israelites begun to feel that they should like to rid themselves of this Philistine yoke. So they gathered an army together and challenged the Philistines to battle. When the two armies met, the children of Israel were defeated.

Then they met together, and held a council of war to discover, if possible, the cause of their defeat. There, somebody seems to have suggested this. He said: 'Our defeat was due to the fact that, in our hurry, we rushed off to attack the Philistines, without taking with us the ark of the Lord'. You see, they regarded the ark as a kind of

[1] International Congress for Reformed Faith and Action, France, 1953.

mascot. If you took it with you, you would probably have good luck, you would succeed. If you went without it, the probability was that you would be defeated. So this spokesman said: 'That is the cause of the trouble. We went without the ark of the Lord. Let us gather together another army, and, this time, let us take the ark with us. If we only do that we are bound to succeed and we will conquer the Philistines.'

This is what the Israelites proceeded to do. They gathered another army, took the ark with them, and went up and challenged the Philistines. But you remember what happened. They were not only defeated; their army was completely routed. Not only that; the Philistines captured the ark of the covenant of the Lord and took it away with them.

Now these four verses that we are going to look at tell us what happened after that. And this is what we are told. The Philistines, when they captured the ark of the Lord, did not destroy it. They said: 'After all, it is very valuable. It has brought great success many times to these Israelites, and the day may come when it may be a very great help to us.' So they decided that they would take the ark of the Lord and put it in the temple of their own god, Dagon. They paid a kind of compliment to the God of Israel, who, they thought, was in this box, this ark. So they took the ark and put it in the temple of Dagon, and put it by the side of Dagon, on the shelf. Then, having done that, they began to celebrate their great victory, and they seemed to have every reason for doing so. They had conquered their traditional enemies, they had routed their army, but, above all, they had captured the God of their enemies. There he was, in their own temple. Why, the world was perfect. There was nothing to do but to give themselves to a perpetual round of rejoicings and of celebrations. So they began to do so.

But then we read this extraordinary history. The next morning the keeper of the temple of Dagon, making a kind of routine round and not expecting to find anything wrong, to his astonishment and amazement found that their god Dagon had fallen to the ground immediately beneath the ark of the Lord. He could not understand this. It was unexpected. However, he said, accidents will happen in the best ordered societies. It is all right. So we are told that he took Dagon again, and placed him back on the shelf, by the side of the ark of the Lord. And he and the rest of the people proceeded once more to their victory celebrations and to their great rejoicings.

However, we are told that the next morning this man went once more into the temple, and to his consternation, he found not only that Dagon had fallen to the ground, immediately beneath the ark of the Lord, but this time both the hands of Dagon and his head were cut off upon the threshold. Nothing was left of Dagon, except his stump!

Now that is the story. Someone may be tempted to ask: 'What has that Old Testament story to do with us? What has it to say to us? What is its relevance to our position and condition today?'

Well, for myself, I see in that story a very great and important and vital lesson for the Christian church at this present hour. For what, after all, is this story? Surely, it is nothing but an account of religion in a state of declension. It is religion and the God of the Christians apparently defeated and routed by the enemy. That is the picture. It is God, and God's cause, apparently completely routed and almost, as it were, destroyed, by the great traditional enemy. The enemy is triumphant all along the line, and is rejoicing. That is the picture.

I need not, in a learned congress like this, take up any time in applying the picture in detail. But it is interesting to notice that it is a description and an account of the present situation down almost to the smallest and minutest detail. The church of God has been confronted by the attack of the Philistines in a very fierce and cruel manner for over a long hundred years. The form which the Philistines take is not always the same. Sometimes, it is a purely military form, as it was in those days of long ago in the history of the children of Israel. But it is not always that form. The Philistines can assume many guises; they can appear in quite a variety of forms.

During the past hundred years or so, the Philistines attacking the church of God, and God himself and his Christ, have taken the following forms.

First and foremost, in respect to their assaults, I would place intellectual knowledge and understanding. We are all familiar with the fact that one of the greatest attacks that has been made upon the church and upon the Bible, and upon the whole cause of God, has been the attack that has come from philosophy. For over a hundred years now people have been tending to put revelation on one side, and to put philosophy in its place. They no longer believe in the inspired, uniquely inspired and inerrant Word of God. They believe in human thought, human reason, human understanding, human speculation. This tremendous attack has come along the line of philosophy.

But it has not been confined to that. There is the attack of the Philistines in the form of science. It is very nearly a hundred years now since Charles Darwin published his book, *The Origin of Species,* in 1859. To the average person, that book not only attacked the Bible, it shook and destroyed, once and for ever, the whole basis and foundation of the Christian faith. The average man takes the view that biological knowledge has really made the faith look ridiculous. The Bible has been demolished.

The Philistine attack has also taken a social and political form. The idea became current that man, and his lot in this world, could be made perfect by means of social legislation, by acts of Parliament, by the mitigation of wrongs and the amelioration of suffering. All that was necessary was that we should educate people and, if we did so, they would soon banish war. They would begin to love one another, and would make a paradise of this world. The story would be, 'and they all lived happily ever afterwards'.

Thus, the Philistines have made this onslaught upon God's people, upon God himself, and upon his cause. And, let us be quite frank and honest, if we look at this situation, on the surface we might very well come to the conclusion that the modern Philistines have been as successful as their ancient prototypes. Indeed, our contemporaries believe that the modern Philistine really has demolished the church and the Christian cause. The enemy seems to be triumphant all along the line: the secularisation of the whole of life seems to be almost complete. The enemy seems to be universally triumphant.

The comparison does not end there, however, for it is clear that the modern Philistine is virtually identical with the ancient Philistine. He repeats the actions of the ancient Philistine down into details. Let me show you what I mean.

I pointed out to you how those old Philistines, when they captured the ark of the Lord, did not destroy it. They said: 'No, we will put it into the temple of Dagon, so that if ever we find we can use it, we can take it down from the shelf, and employ it; and then, when we have used it, put it back again.' They said: 'You never know when it will become useful.' They relegated it to the background but they did not destroy it altogether. They just put it there, where they could take it and use it, and put it back again as they chose to do so.

I suggest that the modern Philistines have done precisely the same thing. Modern man has really ceased to believe in God and in religion. And yet, you notice, he has not altogether finished with it. No. In most countries he tends to do today what those ancient Philistines did. He makes use of religion when it suits his purpose to do so and when he feels inclined to do so. Most people, at any rate in Great Britain, who never go near a place of worship on Sunday, still like to be married in church; they like to have their children christened, though they never go to a place of worship themselves; and they like to have a religious service at a funeral. And if you should happen to be fighting a great war, and your army suffers a number of defeats, well then, the government calls for a so-called 'national day of prayer'. Or if you happen to be crowning a Queen or a King you must have a religious service. Though they no longer believe in it, they believe in keeping it somewhere in the background, where they can take it down and use it and employ it when it suits them, and then put it back when they no longer need it. They pay it a kind of lip-service, a general respect, without really believing in it, without truly worshipping God.

That, I am suggesting, is the position at this present hour. That has been the position more or less, speaking generally, during this present century. There are the Philistines, apparently universally successful, and God's cause and God's church seem to be in a state of abject defeat and misery.

Now the great question is, What has this incident to tell us at such a time and in such a situation?

Well, thank God, it has a great deal to tell us.

Before I come to the positive exposition of this message, let me ask one question in passing: Why is it, do you think, that Israel ever suffered that defeat ? Why is it that God's people should ever thus be defeated by the Philistines and apparently routed? That is a most important question. It is one of the most urgent questions facing the church today. If you are content to receive the answer that is given by the great religious denominations in practically every country, you will believe that the cause of the defeat of Israel is to be found in the strength, the power, and the prowess of the Philistines. That is the explanation we are given. 'Brethren,' they say, 'we must not be down-hearted. The Christian church today is facing an enemy such as our fathers scarcely ever had to face. Our fathers did not have to face the competition of a world highly organised for pleasure and for secular pursuits. Our fathers did not have to compete with the motor-car; they did not have to compete with the cinema, with the radio and with television, and all these other things that today are attracting the people away from God's house.' That is the cause of the trouble. And on top of all this, they add, 'the modern man is educated, he has been to school and to the university'. We are confronted by this powerful enemy; and the suggestion is that the church has been defeated, and appears to be in a state of defeat today, because of the power and the ability of the Philistines.

But I want to suggest to you that this is a completely false explanation. It was false in the time of the Old Testament, and it is equally false today. Go back, and read the story of the children of Israel, and you will find invariably that when they were defeated, it was never due to the strength of the enemy, it was always due to their own internal weakness. When the children of Israel were in the right relationship to God they always conquered their enemies. But the moment they forgot God and became indolent and slack in their religion, and trusted to themselves and their own powers, they were always defeated. It was never the strength of the Philistines that mattered, it was always the strength or the weakness of Israel. A few chapters later on in this first book of Samuel, you will find that just two men, Jonathan and his armour-bearer, defeated a great army of Philistines. Yes, two men. The same strength in the Philistines, yes, but the variation was in the strength of Israel.

The same is true today. When Israel was defeated, she was always defeated because God allowed her to be defeated. She turned her back upon God, she would not obey God, and she would not rely upon God and his power. And whenever she refused to do so, God left her to herself, just to show her and to teach her that she was his people, and that without him, she could do nothing.

I am profoundly convinced that the same is the only true

explanation of the state of the Christian church today. The tragedy is that most of the branches of the Christian church fail to recognise this. They think that it is the state of the world that accounts for their condition. They attribute their failure to hold the people to the motor-car, the radio, the cinema, television and other things that keep people from the house of God. 'Our fathers and fore-fathers', they say, 'never had to face such a powerful enemy. The world has never been so strong and so highly organised in its opposition to God and his church.'

But that is entirely false. The world has always been opposed to the church and men have always found ways and means of entertaining themselves and of finding reasons for not attending God's house. The forms which the pleasures and amusements take change from age to age, but the natural man's enmity towards God never varies.

There is no variation in the world: the world is always opposed to us. Where is the variation, then? I am suggesting that the variation is in the Christian church herself, and that the church is in her present weak and powerless condition because she has repeated the mistake of the children of Israel of old. We have been trusting to ourselves and our own abilities and powers and our own understanding. And I believe that God has, as it were, abandoned us to ourselves in order that he may teach us this vital and all-important lesson. The Christian church has forgotten that she is the church of God, and that, without him, she can do nothing. She has been trusting to learning and to knowledge, to understanding, and to organisation. She has multiplied her institutions. She has organisations for young people, for middle-aged and old people, sisterhoods, brotherhoods, cultural organisations. She has believed that she, herself, by her own power, can perpetuate her own life. She has forgotten prayer. She has forgotten her complete depend-ence upon God. And I believe that the true explanation therefore of the present situation is that God is teaching us this vital and all-important lesson. He is calling us back to himself, and to a dependence upon his power. And I am certain that I am right when I say that until we come to the end of our own self-reliance (it does not matter what form it takes), until the church is crushed to her knees, and has come to the end of her own power and ability, and looks to God for his power and the might of the Holy Spirit – until then I am certain that the declension will continue and even increase. When the church of God is in a state of eclipse and of apparent defeat, it is always because she has forgotten who she is, has forgotten her reliance upon God and has been trusting, in her folly, to her own ability and her own prowess. That, to me, is the most important lesson of all.

But, thank God, this incident gives us also a certain amount of comfort. I can put that to you briefly by asking a question: What does God do at such a time in the history of his church? Well, this old story answers that question. The first thing God always does, at such a time, is that *he breaks into and irrupts into our plans and arrangements, and upsets them.* Look at the old story. Look at those Philistines. They had conquered their enemies, they had routed their army, they had captured their God. And, as I said, they thought that the world was perfect, and that nothing could ever go wrong again. But, just as they are congratulating themselves, and believing that they have made a perfect world for themselves, things begin to go wrong. This man goes into the temple of Dagon and finds Dagon on the floor! He is upset. Something has gone wrong. He picks up Dagon and puts him back in his place. 'It is all right', he says, 'carry on'. But Dagon falls again, and, finally, is destroyed.

I see in that old picture a perfect description and delineation of what has been happening in this twentieth century. I wonder whether you have looked at the history of the twentieth century in that particular manner? There was the world at the end of the nineteenth century, full of confidence and of optimism, believing that man, as the result of his knowledge and of his development and of his evolution and advance, was really on the verge of entering a kind of Paradise. The twentieth century was to be the greatest century of all history. War was to be banished, there was to be universal peace because man was now too intelligent to fight. We were entering upon the perfect phase of human history. And God was, as I say, relegated to the shelf.

But what happened? Well, we had not gone very far into this present century before things began to go wrong. Many of us, indeed most of us, in this conference remember a day in 1911 when we read in our newspapers of what was called the Morocco crisis. There seemed to be the possibility of a war over Morocco, as between England and France on one side, and Germany on the other. But we said, 'Impossible! It cannot happen in the twentieth century.' And the crisis passed. Dagon had fallen. We put him up again, and on we went.

Then there was a day in 1912 when the whole world was staggered to read in its newspaper of the sinking of a very remarkable ship in the Atlantic. It was claimed to be unique and was called the Titanic. It was said to be the ultimate achievement of science. It was described as an unsinkable ship. Man had so advanced and developed that he had built a ship which nothing whatsoever could possibly sink. The Unsinkable Ship! And there was that unsinkable ship steaming across the Atlantic on a Sunday afternoon, with the band playing its jazz music, and the people enjoying themselves, celebrating this ultimate achievement of science. Then messages begun to come in to say that there were icebergs about. But what is an iceberg to an unsinkable ship! It was something to be ignored, to be laughed at. The ship went steaming ahead. Suddenly there was that terrible thud: the ship had struck an iceberg. And soon she sank with a terrible loss of life. Our whole world was shaken again. Dagon had fallen once more. 'But it is all right', we said. 'Accidents must happen now and again. Put Dagon back. Let us carry on, and enter into this Paradise.' And on we went.

In August 1914 the war that was said to be impossible for modern, cultured, enlightened men actually began. 'It is all right', we were told, 'there certainly is a war, but it is the war-to-end-war. This is the last war. It will introduce the era of the common man, the perfect democracy.' Eventually the war ended, and we were told that, at last, we really could begin to enjoy ourselves. Everything seemed to be perfect.

But it did not last very long. Dagon kept on falling: strikes, industrial problems and difficulties came. And then we began to hear of certain new philosophies, Fascism and so on, which seemed to be taking man back again into the jungle. It seemed incredible but Dagon was falling constantly. Our perfect world, our paradise, was being upset. But we could not believe it. On we came to the 1930s and the preparations for another war. But still mankind in general said: 'It cannot happen, it is impossible. You cannot have two world wars within a quarter of a century. It cannot take place. It will not happen.' But, nevertheless, the war came in September 1939. But again we were told: 'Yes, Dagon has fallen. But it is all just due to one man, and so long as we get rid of him, then we really will have perfect peace.' When victory finally came, the world was again looking forward to the promised perfect paradise and bliss. The twentieth century had come at last!

But you remember that we had not even gone beyond August 1945 before we came down one morning and looked at our newspapers, and saw that something which was called an atomic bomb had been dropped in Japan. The whole world began to shake and to quake again, and it has been quaking ever since! The peace never seems to come. The paradise can never be entered. Though we think all is perfect, Dagon keeps on falling. Things will go wrong. That is what has been happening.

To me there is but one explanation of it all: the God who kept on throwing Dagon to the floor in his own temple is disturbing our life. He will not allow men to enjoy life apart from himself. He has told us: 'There is no peace, saith my God, to the wicked.' He breaks in upon us; he interrupts us; he irrupts into our plans. He shakes us, he disturbs us, he upsets us.

And what I am saying is not only true of nations, it is equally true of individuals. I have known many a man who has laughed at God and at religion, and has claimed that he is able to make a perfect life for himself without God at all. I have seen him apparently successful with his wife and his children, his profession or his business, and everything seemed to be perfect. But suddenly that man gets the first stab of angina. He gets that awful pain that brings him face to face with death, and his world begins to shake. His plans are upset. Everything seems to go wrong. It is the same explanation still.

Let me hurry, however, to the second thing that God does at such a time: *he always humbles and humiliates our gods*. That was what he did in the temple of Dagon. The god of the Philistines was Dagon, and they worshipped him. And what the God who was apparently defeated and captured did, was to humble and to humiliate, and finally to destroy Dagon. There, again, is something, surely, that we all ought to be able to see very clearly in the story of this twentieth century. I see nothing in this century except evidence of God humbling and humiliating our gods. What has he been doing? Let us look at it like this. What are the gods that we have worshipped? I have reminded you of some of them. The god of education. Do not misunderstand me. I believe in education, I thank God for it. I think it is the right of every child that is born into this world. Yes. But you must not make a god, even of education. And mankind has made a god of knowledge and of education. But what is the result? Well, in Great Britain, one of our major problems (and I believe it is equally true of every other country) is what we call juvenile delinquency. It is on the increase. Our children, who are better educated than children have ever been, in a sense have become a greater problem than they have ever been. Education does not solve the problem.

Not only that, there is this terrible problem of drunkenness, which I believe is an acute problem in this country of France as well as other countries. The problems of drunkenness, of immorality, of infidelity, of separations and of divorce, the break-down of marriage and the sacred things of life – all in the educated democracy of which we boast in all our countries! Man believed that education would solve his problems. He made a god of education, and his god is being humbled before his very eyes.

Likewise with the god of politics, and with the belief in the ability of men, by means of legislation, to solve their problems. With all our politics, and our international conferences, and all our other efforts and arrangements, we obviously and clearly are failing to solve the problems of mankind on the national or on the international level. And our politicians, whom we tended almost to worship in the last century, have become discredited in the eyes of the masses of the people.

And the same is true of that other god, science. This god science that so many have worshipped is in a sense our greatest problem at this present hour.

But ultimately I suppose that the supreme god that man has worshipped for the last hundred years is man himself. Man has been worshipping himself. That is why he has said that God was unnecessary. He has made an image of himself, and has bowed down before it. And what has happened?

This twentieth century has taught us the truth about man. What is man? Well, look at Belsen and Buchenwald; look into the concentration camps in Russia today; look at men dropping bombs upon innocent women and children and blasting them to destruction. That is man. Look at a man entering into another man's married life and home, and deliberately wrecking it. That is man. The newspapers are daily displaying to us the humiliation of the god man. He is being cast to the ground, humbled and humiliated before his own worshippers. That is the second thing.

The last thing I would mention is that God in that temple of Dagon was not only interfering and upsetting the arrangements in this way, and humbling their god. He was, by doing this, *announcing and pronouncing judgment*. He was warning the Philistines that he could not be dealt with in that manner. He was manifesting his power. He was showing them what he was proposing to do. He was pronouncing judgment upon the Philistines and upon the Israelites at the same time.

I need not keep you with this. Surely, if there is one thing that ought to be clearer to all mankind in this century than anything else, it is that God is pronouncing judgment upon mankind. There is no other adequate explanation of the two world wars but just that. What I see in the two world wars I would put in this form: it is God turning to men and to the world and saying: 'You claimed that you could make a perfect world without me. You claimed that you had so outgrown me that you could carry on without me. You have said that I am unnecessary. You have relegated me to heaven and I have allowed you to see what you are, and what you make of life when you try to live without me. I am allowing you to reap the consequences of your own sin. I am showing you that sin is always followed by destruction; and that these two wars are but pictures and illustrations, in the field of history, of the final judgment of man, by my only-begotten Son, the Lord Jesus Christ.' As the Flood was a prediction of the final judgment, and as the end of Sodom and Gomorrah contained a similar prophecy, so all the judgments in Scripture point to this Last Judgment. Everything that is happening in this century is, in the same way, pointing to the judgment of God upon rebellious man, and announcing the final destruction of all who do not submit to him.

Very well, in the light of all that, what is the message that you and I have to preach in this modern world and to the modern man?

Our message to him must be this message of judgment. We must tell him that God is still the same God, the God who confronted the children of Israel with Mount Ebal and Mount Gerizim, the God who said that he either blesses or else curses. We must proclaim that if man in this world wants to know blessing, and to be blessed of God, then he must recognize and believe these things that God revealed so long ago in the temple of Dagon. God is the *living* God. The mistake that was made by the Israelites, and the Philistines, was to think that God was someone who could be carried about in an ark, in a box. That was their conception of God. The Israelites had forgotten all about him: they rushed to battle against the Philistines without taking the ark. 'Ha!', they said, 'That was the mistake! If only we carry God with us, we are going to succeed.' God was someone whom they could handle. And the Philistines, obviously, thought the same thing.

But what God taught them there, in the temple of Dagon, was this. That he is a living God. He is not a God that can be carried about by men. He is the God in whose hand man is: the living God, the Almighty, the Eternal, the All-powerful God. When you think him defeated, then he is active; when you think you have him captive, he knocks down your god. He is a God who cannot be restrained; illimitable, absolute, eternal – the living God.

Oh yes, but it is equally important to remember that he is the *only* God. The Philistines thought that they were paying him a compliment by putting him on the shelf by the side of Dagon. They said: 'He is a god amongst gods. He is like our god Dagon. We will put him by the side of Dagon.' They thought he was one amongst the gods. But he demonstrated to them in the very temple of Dagon that he is the only God. He would not share the shelf with Dagon or with any other god. He wants the entire place to himself. And if you put any god by the side of the living God, he will throw it down, he will silence it. He is the only God.

It does not matter what god you try to put by the side of him, he will not tolerate it. He is a jealous God, he is a totalitarian God, he is an absolute God. 'Thou shalt have no other gods beside me', he says. And if you make other gods he will destroy them. If you make a god of Fascism or Nazism or Communism or any other political creed he will most certainly destroy it. If you make your country or your love of your country or your race or nationality your god, it will receive the same fate. If you put your wife by the side of God in your life as your god, do not be surprised if things go wrong. If you put your husband, if you put your children, if you put your knowledge, if you put anything by the side of God in your life, he will destroy it. He calls upon us to love him 'with all our hearts, and all our souls, and all our minds, and all our strength'. He wants to be on the throne of our life. He wants to be at the centre of our being. He wants our entire allegiance. He will not share our love with anybody or anything. He is the only God, as well as the living God.

And, finally, he has taught us that he is to be *approached in the way he indicates*. Read the Old Testament story, and you will find that the Israelites and the Philistines suffered and were punished when they handled this ark of God in the wrong way. It had to be handled in God's way. Now that also is equally true today. If we would really be blessed of God and know him, well then, we must go to him in the way that he himself has appointed. And there is but one way. It is to go through him who has said: 'I am the way, the truth, and the life; no man cometh unto the Father, but by me.' There is but one way to enter into the holiest of all: it is by the blood of Jesus. There is no way to God, and to be blessed of God, except that we recognize ourselves as helpless, hopeless, damned sinners who have nothing to recommend us, and who must go as supplicants and paupers to God, pleading nothing but the death of his only-begotten Son for our sins, and his rising again for our justification.

My friends, to us is committed this glorious message. Our God is not defeated. He is still on the throne, and he will destroy his every enemy.

But let us especially learn this vital lesson for ourselves. If we would be blessed by him in our individual lives and in our churches, we must not rely upon ourselves, upon our knowledge and understanding, upon our philosophy, upon our arguments, upon our institutions. We must go to him in our helplessness and receive the fullness of his Holy Spirit. And it is only as we are em-powered by the Holy Spirit that we can meet, and challenge, and preach this message to the modern man in such a way as to convict him of his sin, and to bring him to repentance and contrition and to cause him to turn to the Lord Jesus Christ, who alone is able to save.

May God grant us the understanding necessary to a realisation of this our utter dependence upon the demonstration and power of the Spirit of God.

7

What is Sin?

And David said unto Nathan, I have sinned against the LORD. And Nathan said unto David, The LORD also hath put away thy sin; thou shalt not die.

2 Samuel 12:13

I call your attention to this story which is such a dark and terrible blot on the whole history of King David in order that I may consider with you the deep nature of the whole problem of sin. My reason for doing so is not that I have suddenly become an iconoclast or a devotee of the modern biographical method which believes in 'debunking' the heroes of the past and concentrating only on that which is unfavourable in the record of men. Neither do I set out upon an examination of this story because I desire to emphasise the exact details of the account as such and thereby to pander to the modern interest in, and craving for, pornographic literature. Nor do I do so because I delight in being odd and unusual in choosing a theme that is not often considered and which, as a principle, most people would prefer not to consider. I can say honestly that I dislike considering this question of sin and that I dearly wish that it was never necessary to consider it at all. If only we could always be talking about nothing but the love of God and other themes that are delightful and enjoyable! Oh, that there were no other themes at all and no other side to be even considered. But alas, such is not the case. Indeed, one can go further and say that there is not much point in trying to consider the theme of God's love until one has first of all considered the question of sin.

We have to deal with the problem of sin for one reason only – because it is a fact. But it is vitally important that we should realise the exact nature of the fact. And that is why I intend to consider this story which throws so much light upon the deep nature of sin.

The details of this particular case do not matter to us in and of themselves – their value and their importance lie in the principles which they illustrate.

The difficulties which men seem to experience today with the biblical doctrine of salvation are to be traced, it seems to me, to two main causes. The first is that the approach tends to be far too detached and theoretical and almost entirely divorced from actual experience and the facts of life. One of the greatest enemies of true religion is the fact that religion is so interesting. I mean interesting from the standpoint of thought and philosophy; interesting, therefore, as a mere matter of speculation and as a subject for debate and discussion. Religious discussions always have been popular and are still popular. Men delight in expressing their views on God and what he is and what he should do. In the same way they enjoy taking up the various possible sides and points of view with respect to the great doctrines which have been enunciated by the church from time to time. But how detached are these discussions generally speaking! The questions are debated as if they were as abstract as the problems of Euclid. And this is true not only of those who take the heterodox point of view but also very frequently of those who defend the orthodox statements of the church. Doctrine is essential for reasons which we cannot consider here tonight, but there are times when I dearly wish that it could be utterly abolished. Its formulations and definitions are so liable to instruct us in a purely intellectual and philosophical manner and thereby to conceal the great and terrible truth that is behind them. We forget that whatever side is right, it is a matter of vital concern to us – one which may make an eternal difference to us. If only at the beginning of their argument, debates and discussions someone could get up and say: 'Gentlemen, remember that though we cannot see him, God can see us and that though we cannot hear him with the natural ear, he can and does hear us. Remember, further, that his eye is upon us here and now and his ear open to our words. And then recollect that we are but creatures of time and that he is eternal. Above all bear in mind as you speak, his return, and the fact that at any moment, we know not when, we may find ourselves standing before him as our judge. You may now begin'! If only someone said that what a difference it would make! Or if, short of that, someone were always to remind us of what we are and what lives we have lived, like David on this occasion, I think we would be a little more careful in our expressions of opinion! Remember, in other words, that in all these apparently abstract and theoretical discussions on religion you are, in reality, discussing yourself even as David was with Nathan.

The second main difficulty in a sense arises out of the first and is, at the same time, a little more particular. It is the utter failure to realise the true nature of the problem with which religion is concerned, or, in a word, the failure to realise the true and the deep nature of sin. It is not my desire on this occasion to consider the various modern ideas with respect to sin. It is sufficient for our immediate purpose that we should say that they all, in some way or another, do not view it deeply and profoundly. They all regard it lightly and are thoroughly optimistic, therefore, as to its treatment. Regarding it as they do as a mere weakness, or some mere negative phase in the history of mankind, or as something which is to be explained entirely in terms of culture or lack of culture, its eradication is to them obviously a matter merely of training and of time. They cannot see any need or necessity, therefore, for the kind of salvation taught in the Bible, a salvation demanding an atoning sacrifice and which is so pessimistic with regard to man as to use a term like regeneration with respect to his nature.

If the problem is simple, the solution also will be simple and there is a sense in which it is utterly impossible for a man who has not seen the nature of sin to believe in and to accept the gospel offer of salvation. For to him the latter seems extravagant. The modern man not only does not see sin as it is from the standpoint of God, he fails also to see it as it is from man's standpoint. He not only does not know God, he does not even know himself. The trouble is that we all by nature refuse to face honestly the problem of ourselves and our own inner nature. We argue about our ideal selves instead of our actual selves. We refuse to face the naked truth of our own hearts as they are. If only we faced the truth about ourselves we should soon be right on the question of sin, we would soon realise its terrible and awful nature, and above all, its terrible force and power. And it is in order that we may be helped and aided to do so that I call your attention to this incident.

King David stands out as one of the greatest, if not *the* greatest man in the Old Testament. There are to be seen in him all the signs of true greatness. Not only that, he is one of those loveable characters whom we not only admire but love. He was, moreover, a good man, a religious man, a devout man. But perhaps the most outstanding trait in his character was his essential nobility. There is surely nothing grander anywhere in literature than David's loyalty and faithfulness to King Saul. In spite of insults and abuses, in spite of jealousy and indeed treachery, in spite of Saul's repeated attempts upon his life and his continual hounding of him from place to place, David still speaks of him in terms of real respect and affection and as one anxious to serve him. On two occasions Saul's life was in David's hands and most people would say that, in view of what Saul had done to him and in view of what David knew of the future, he would have been fully justified in killing him. But David does not do so, though he is encouraged to do so by everyone. And when a man comes to him informing him of Saul's death and trusting that the news will please David, he is surprised to find that David is overwhelmed with sadness. That it means David's own promotion to the throne and the kingdom meant nothing to him.

But the true nobility and generosity of David's character shines out most gloriously in his treatment of the descendants of Saul. How solicitous he is of their welfare and how anxious to honour them. And how ready is he under all kinds of circumstances to forgive. Here then is a good, godly, noble soul – a real king in the highest sense of the term and yet, it is the very selfsame man who is capable of the cowardly, dastardly, unutterably selfish and despicable action which is recorded here in this and the previous chapter! It is really almost unbelievable and yet it is an actual fact. The man who was characterised above all else by nobility becomes a knave and a cur, the loyal soul becomes a traitor, the man who was so ready to forgive and to bear insults becomes a murderer. Many superficial people today think of David solely in terms of this story – his name, to them, is a byword and an example of the low moral state of that world of long ago which they regard as being so primitive in comparison with the world of today. But that view is based either upon ignorance or on wilful distortion of the facts. David was the man we have described him to be. This is the one great blot on his escutcheon. But the terrible and terrifying thing is not only that it is there, but that such a thing is really possible at all in such a man! How do you account for it? How do you explain it? What is it that happens to a man like that and makes him capable of an action that is so utterly contradictory of all that he really represents? Is it a mere weakness, mere lack of knowledge, temporary forgetfulness of better things or some other phenomenon? How utterly trivial all that seems as an explanation. It is something deep, profound, terrible – a mighty power. Yes, and it is in you and in me. It does not always take the same form, but it is always there and it is always the same in its nature. Consider yourself and your own experience. Face for a moment the struggles that go on within your own heart. Conjure up the vain thoughts and desires that grip you and control you from time to time. Would you like to state them all in public? Would you like the world to know all about you? If only we started there in our religious discussions instead of arguing theoretically about 'atonement' and 'regeneration' and the various other doctrines! When a man really knows himself and thereby knows something of the nature and the problem of sin he doesn't want to argue about the doctrines of grace, he just thanks God for them and accepts them with his whole soul and heart and mind.

In order that we all may do so, if we have not already done so, let us consider together what we are told concerning sin in this terrible story. I would concentrate your attention upon it by emphasising the following clearly defined principles.

1.   *The first is that sin, far from being a mere weakness or negation, is actually an overpowering and blinding force which defeats even the strongest human nature.* It is failure to realise this that constitutes the very essence of the modern religious confusion. Sin as a power, as a force, is not appreciated and understood as it should be. Even the so-called new psychology, which has certainly ridiculed the old humanistic optimism about man and his nature, fails to bring out this truth as it tends to explain it away in terms of material and biological reactions. It does not see that sin is a force and a power quite apart from man himself and quite apart from the various factors that operate upon man. And yet that is the whole horror of sin. It is such a power, that, taking hold of us, it can manipulate us at will and make us believe as it chooses, upsetting all our former calculations and resolutions. That is what is shown so clearly in this story and I would like you to consider it as follows:

(a) The power of sin is seen clearly in the way in which it entirely sweeps aside all other interests and considerations for the time being. Look at that here in the case of David. This one desire of his, this one lust and sin entirely grips him and at the expense of everything else which we saw to be so true of him. It initially makes an entirely different man of him. Nowhere in the story is that fact put quite so clearly as in 2 Samuel 11:21. That subtle man Joab was not only a great warrior and general but also shows himself to be a psychologist and a man who knows something about the power of sin. He sends a man to David with a report of the battle. Things had not gone well and Joab had made something of a mistake. He knew that David as a general would be annoyed at that so he instructed the messenger what to say when he observes that David's anger has risen. All he has to say is 'Thy servant Uriah the Hittite is dead also.' Normally David would be most anxious and concerned about the success of his troops, the defeat of the enemy and the honour of the name of Israel. But under the grip of sin all these things do not count and become quite unimportant. David sees and desires one thing only and as long as that is gratified and granted he cares not what the price nor the cost may be. This one thing sweeps aside pride of country and race, pride of military achievement and all else – it is a consuming passion.

Now this is only one illustration of that which is always true of sin. Think of a man in a temper and rage – think of yourself in that condition. He says and does things which he will never do normally and which he bitterly regrets afterwards. Even while he is saying them there is a warning and a restraining voice within but it scarcely counts at all. This terrible power within is gripping and driving him and he is helpless. He does not care at the moment how much he may hurt nor what the consequences may be – the one thing he desires is to do and say that which grips him at the moment. Jealousy and envy, malice and bitterness all work in the same way. How they entirely monopolise and consume us. The jealous person can see nothing but the object of his or her envy. The fact that he is doing well himself is not sufficient for him and does not satisfy him. It is the other object that matters. Though he may have everything a man desires it will not satisfy him if he desires that which someone else has. And under the terrible grip and power of this passion some of the most terrible things that happen in life take place. A jealous person is, in a sense, a demented person – a maniac. Or think again how a wrong, whether imagined or real can grip us. The desire for revenge is waiting for the opportunity to retaliate and to pay back! But think also of the way in which men risk their reputation, their character, their honour and sometimes even their life and health for the sake of gratifying some desire. A man may love his wife and children very dearly, but if he is unfortunately the slave of the lust for drink they will be pushed aside. A man may be proud of his ancestral home and his possessions, but if he becomes the slave of the gambling mania he will stake them all. But I need not continue. It explains a case like this of David, it alone explains the terrible downfall of many a noble man from many a high position, it explains everything in our own present position of which we are ashamed. Sin sweeps all other interests aside and entirely controls us.

(b) But we can state that in a slightly different manner by observing that sin paralyses our better judgement. That is why it leads to all the results we have just been considering and that is also why all optimistic views about the treatment of sin by education, etc., are so puerile and pathetic. David and his son Solomon are two of the wisest and sanest men in the Old Testament. Yet they both are guilty of sin and that of a marked type. But the same is true of all the great, learned and wise men of the world. It is one thing to draw up an ethical code or to be familiar with one, the difficulty lies in putting it into practice. In a sense, every sin we have ever committed is a sin against our own better judgment and is always the result of a battle between conscience and this terrible force and power. And how subtle it is in its argument, how clever at twisting and perverting what we know to be the real truth. And that is why remorse always follows sin and leaves us without any excuse whatever. After the sin – anger and temper, spitefulness or cruelty, lust or craving or whatever – it may be we simply cannot understand ourselves or explain to ourselves how it was that we came to do such a thing. There seems to be nothing in its favour and everything is against it. Yet we did it! Why? There is only one explanation. This power called sin paralysed us and blinded us, mastered and overpowered us. A knowledge of right and wrong does not preserve from sin. 'By the law is the knowledge of sin'

(*Rom.* 3:20) and not its cure. 'For the good that I would I do not: but the evil which I would not, that I do' (*Rom.* 7:19). That is the confession of a man of ability, knowledge and culture, a man who was an expert in the law, a Pharisee of the Pharisees – Saul of Tarsus. Knowledge is excellent, but it is a hopeless shield and protection against 'the fiery dart of the evil one' (*Eph.* 6:16).

2. *The second general principle to which I would draw your attention is to the effect that sin is utterly indefensible and merits punishment.* We have already touched upon that in our last statement, but the real value of 2 Samuel chapter 12 is that it brings out this truth in a particularly clear and incontrovertible manner. It takes away every plea and excuse that can ever be offered for sin and shows that the knowledge we possess already takes the ground from beneath our feet as we attempt to defend ourselves in terms of development and evolution.

(a) First of all it shows us that man himself utterly condemns sin and says that it is deserving of the severest punishment. That is the real master-stroke in the interview between Nathan the prophet and David – he makes David deliver an impartial and disinterested verdict on himself and his own action. The whole difficulty with the question of sin is that we scarcely ever regard it in that way and manner. We are always on the defensive and our views are coloured by our actions and by the consequences that we fear will follow any opinion we may chance to deliver. We are always out to defend ourselves and it is remarkable how clever we all are at explaining away what we have done. We are equally able to satisfy ourselves and to persuade ourselves that all is well and that, therefore, we deserve no punishment at all.

But we are not quite as clever as we imagine ourselves to be and we are constantly condemning ourselves in what we say about others. Nathan stated the case to David (*2 Sam.* 12:1–4) and David without the slightest hesitation – and not recognising himself – delivers the true verdict. He sees how terrible the sin is and is definite that it must be punished very severely. He says that it is utterly without excuse, that it can be defended on no grounds what-ever, that it is utterly abominable. He had never said that to himself about his own worst actions because of the instinct of self-defence and self-preservation. But here he takes the ground from under his own feet and has to admit that his sin is utterly indefensible and that it and he merit punishment. Paul, you may remember, in the second chapter of his epistle to the Romans, points out precisely the same thing where in dealing with the position of Gentiles who are not under the law he says that they 'show the work of the law written in their hearts, their conscience also bearing witness, and their thoughts the meanwhile accusing or else excusing one another' (*Rom.* 2:15). What he means by that is that the opinions which these people express on one another and their actions is proof positive that they know what is right and what is wrong. Take the personal element out and the desire for self-protection and self-justification, and then, as David admits here in no uncertain terms, sin is without defence and merits punishment.

(b) But still more vital and important is to see that God, who has the right and power, also says the same thing about sin: 'But the thing that David had done displeased the Lord' (*2 Sam.* 11:27). The first great revelation in the Bible is that God is a holy God. He hates sin and utterly abominates it. His wrath and his holy anger are roused against it. He has stated clearly that there are no excuses for it and that it shall be punished. Had you realised all that? Had you realised that sin is utterly indefensible? Let me adopt the method of Nathan for a moment and thereby get you to deliver your verdict on sin. Listen to the following cases carefully, remembering that you are to act as judge.

(i) What do you think of a man who betrays a solemn and a sacred trust and charge? Think of a man to whom has been committed the care and the guarding of something which is very valuable belonging to another. The person who gave it to him trusted him by doing so and thereby expressed his trust in him and his faith in him. But the man, instead of guarding it and taking care of it, misappropriated it, sells it and uses the proceeds to please himself and to satisfy his own craving and desire for pleasure. Though the thing did not belong to him and though the owner paid him that very great compliment by making him the steward, that is how he behaved. He betrays the sacred charge and trust. What do you think of him? What have you to say about him? Can you suggest some defence for the man and his actions? Can you say anything by way of mitigation of his crime and offence? Is there any defence for such an action? What does such a man deserve? What does the law of the land say of such a man? What would any judge say about him? What do you say about him? Admit that the action is utterly indefensible.

(ii) Then consider another case. Here is a man who is face to face with a marvellous and wonderful opportunity, what we call a golden opportunity. He has been left some money or he has been left a business or by some pure bit of coincidence he has been introduced to someone who gives him a grand post and sets him on the ladder which eventually may reach to wonderful success and promotion. Without the man doing anything at all, this extraordinary opportunity has come his way. All he needs to do is to realise that, to take full advantage of it and, with application and determination, to do all he can to improve the opportunity and to reap the full benefit. But alas, instead of doing so, this particular man regards it all quite lightly, plays with it for a while and then, either on account of laziness or sheer perverseness or something else, neglects it altogether and allows it to come to nothing. Quite deliberately he squanders the golden opportunity. He objects to the amount of work he is called upon to do. He wants to be enjoying himself with his friends. He resents the amount of discipline that is necessary. Though it is shown him clearly that, given this amazing opportunity, a little application on his part now will lead to astounding and unbelievable results in the future he does not care at all. He prefers to enjoy himself now. He deliberately throws away his great chance and opportunity and at the end finds himself penniless and helpless. What of him? What have you to say about him? Are you ready to defend him and to justify him? Can you say anything in his favour? Does he deserve anything but misery, wretchedness, failure and punishment? And what of the man who does that kind of thing several times?

(iii) Then take one other case. Think of a man who has been shown a great kindness by another and who has been trusted in a most magnanimous manner. A man, if you like, who has been charged with the care of valuables in the way in which I described in our first hypothetical case. Let us assume that, when the valuables were lost, the owner forgave the man to whom they were committed in spite of his treachery, refrained from punishing him, gave him a free pardon and far from taking his office of stewardship from him not only gave him another chance, but actually gave him promotion and went out of his way to be kind to him. But the man, instead of appreciating all this, just takes what advantages he can out of it and for the rest just insults the generous benefactor. His whole attitude to him is one of ingratitude and failure to appreciate the graciousness of the action. He is scarcely ever in his presence. He is even insulting and tries to claim that somehow or another he has been wronged and regards the one who has showered so much love and goodness upon him as an enemy. What do you think of such a person? What have you to say of a man who is utterly ungrateful and who ignores and insults a generous giver and his gifts? Have you anything to say of him save that he is an unutterable cad who deserves not only the loss and the forfeiting of all that he has been given but also in addition the most severe and rigorous punishment? Consider these three cases! Deliver your verdict! Face them quite impartially and disinterestedly. There can be but one result. The three are utterly indefensible in their actions and in themselves and they richly deserve to be severely punished. There can be no doubt at all about it.

But wait a moment! These three cases are parables of what is true of all men who are not Christians and believers in the gospel of our Lord and Saviour Jesus Christ. The soul is God's gift to men, indeed life itself is God's gift to men. We were not meant to use it for ourselves and for our own gratification. God has given us this treasure that we may guard it and preserve it, handle it in the way that he desires and at the end give an account to him of our stewardship. No man has a right to live as he likes and to handle God's image as he pleases. Sin is robbery and misappropriation; man has become a rebel who uses God's property for his own ends. You condemned the man who did that kind of thing. What have you done with your soul? What have you made of the life which God has given to you for a while? Consider what you are doing – your sins are under your own condemnation let alone that of God.

But consider also the man who throws away and squanders a golden opportunity. What a fool he is and how utterly we all condemned such a man and said that he deserved to lose all and to be in a state of misery. But had you realised that there you might have been condemning yourself. God in Christ offers you a new life, a life of power and of victory over sin, a life of blessing, of peace and joy. And after the world he offers to give you a free entry into heaven, to make of you a king with all the joys of everlasting bliss. There it is all offered you. Everything that the saints have known and experienced. Have you accepted it? Have you clutched at it with both hands and made the most of it? You feel it demands too much, that its discipline is too severe. You enjoy the way of the world and the life of the world. You prefer to hold on to certain things which can only last a few years and which never really satisfy. Is it possible? Recall what your verdict was on the type of man who did that, 'He deserved what he got' you cried. Yes, you are right. And the man who refuses God's offer of salvation and eternal life will of necessity go to hell and eternal misery with no one to blame but himself.

But after all the third case was the climax – the case of the cad who rejected the gracious loving action. But that is the precise position of all who are not Christians. Jesus of Nazareth, the Son of God, came down to earth to dwell. God in his infinite love sent him and he came. He came to die for our sins and to open the door of heaven for us. He suffered in life and endured the cruel death all for you. In him God offers you pardon for all your past sins whatever they may have been and all the other blessings to which I have referred. Have you ever thanked him for doing so? Have you ever shown your appreciation and gratitude by taking his Name upon you and by doing your all and your utmost to please him in all things and in every way? You remember what you thought and said of the man who did not do so. And again you were right. There is no need to argue about these things. The man who rejects the offer of God's eternal love deserves nothing and can expect nothing but the damnation of hell. There is no excuse. You have condemned yourself. Sin is utterly indefensible and merits punishment.

3.   And but for one thing that would be the fate of all, for *all have sinned: we have all robbed God, we have all spurned the voice divine and rejected his offer, we have all requited his eternal love with enmity and obstinacy.* And were we all consigned to perdition we could not complain, for we all must say with David to Nathan, 'I have sinned against the Lord'. But blessed be the Name of God, for

the reply still comes back and in an infinitely more glorious way than it could come from the lips of Nathan – 'The Lord also hath put away thy sin; thou shalt not die' (*2 Sam.* 12:13). Yes, he has put it away by putting it on the holy, spotless shoulders of his only begotten Son. 'He hath made him to be sin for us, who knew no sin' (*2 Cor.* 5:21). We shall not die because he has died for us and accomplished a perfect atonement on our behalf. And because of that death we can have life anew, life more abundantly, life which is life indeed. We can receive his life and his nature, and by the power which that gives we can overcome the terrible force called sin just as he did in the days of his flesh. The problem of life is sin – sin in its guilt, its power, its pollution. And the only solution is Christ and him crucified. He cancels the guilt, breaks the power, renews the nature. 'Thanks be unto God for his unspeakable gift.'

8

Biblical Psychology

And Adonijah and all the guests that were with him heard it as they had made an end of eating. And when Joab heard the sound of the trumpet, he said, Wherefore is this noise of the city being in an uproar?

1 Kings 1:41

Those of you who are at all interested in literary matters and who, even if you do not actually read any modern books and productions, are nevertheless sufficiently interested in them at least to read the reviews and criticisms of them which are offered to us by the daily papers, will have learned that among the many revolutionary changes in methods and expression which are so obvious in the world there is none which is perhaps quite so striking as the change which has taken place in the mode and style of writing biographies. The poets have always more or less exercised the right to vary the method or the metre; poetic licence is not something new or ultra-modern. But until comparatively recently there was scarcely, if any, variation at all in the style and method of writing biographies. There was a definite fixed type, modelled perhaps on Boswell's *Life of Johnson* and others similar to it. And that method consisted in first stating, in as elegant and attractive a manner as the writer could command, the main, and sometimes even some of the ordinary and apparently trivial facts, in the life of the man or the subject. A biography was in reality a 'life' of the person, in other words, it just collected together and stated everything about him that seemed to matter. It told of his birth, his parents, his behaviour as a child, his school, etc., right down until his last words, his death, his burial and perhaps a kind of epilogue in which his influence after his death was hurriedly indicated.

That was the old idea of writing a biography. But within the last twenty years there has been a great change and the new type of biography is something very different from all that. The mere recital of facts, incidents and details which characterised the old style is derided, ridiculed and condemned not only on the grounds of being incomplete and insufficient, but also of being misleading. The feeling is that the facts which have been collected and recorded, if they are to be truly appreciated and if they are to be of any value to us, must also be examined and analysed. Hence the modern biography is not merely a recital of facts but is above all else an attempt at a psychological analysis of these facts. The modern biographer does not stop at stating the facts, he is anxious to explain them. He is not content to state that such and such a thing happened. What interests him is why it happened. A modern historian of this school once put the whole thing perfectly when he said, 'the really important thing is not when did Columbus discover America but rather *why* did Columbus discover America'. The modern biographer, in other words, is as interested in the background as in the foreground. To him it is the play and interplay of the various forces and factors that go to produce the man and his action that really matter, and believing, as they do, that by the application of certain psychological principles and tests the very foundation of life and action can be laid bare, they produce in the end what they call 'a study' rather than a biography of their subject. They try to work out a philosophy of his life by means of a careful analysis of the various hidden springs and motives of his actions. The modern biography is really a psychological study. The way in which they justify this is to say that such a method alone is of any real and permanent value. If we are to profit by the study of these men's lives, they say, we must not approach the facts as if they were something which just happened. We must realise that they are the result of certain conditions and certain factors, to which the man reacted in a right way or in a wrong way. And the result of such study will be that when we find ourselves in like circumstances or face to face with similar conditions we, profiting by what we have read, will know exactly what to do. We shall avoid the pitfalls and the wrong reaction and do merely that which is right. By this method we are reminded that our hero was, after all, a man like ourselves and subject to the same laws and conditions, and that therefore we may learn a good deal from him instead of merely admiring him and wondering at him at a distance.

Now all this, which the world regards as so new and so modern, and of which it is so proud, is something with which those who really understand their Bibles have been familiar, in principle at any rate, for a very long time. For I suggest to you that it is the only key to a real understanding of the Old Testament in particular and especially of its historical and narrative portions. And it is precisely because this is forgotten that so many people tend to go astray when they are reading the historical books of the Old Testament. They feel that these books cannot be divinely inspired simply on account of certain incidents and details which they record. For the fact is that the Old Testament tells us everywhere that the history which it records is, in a sense, nothing but an illustration and a demonstration of a fundamental law which it is out to teach and to impress upon our minds. Clearly therefore, if we fail to grasp this we will not be able to interpret the history accurately and to learn the lesson which it would teach us. In other words, there is a very definite plan behind the Old Testament and its various writings, exactly as there is a plan in these modern psychological biographies. The Old Testament starts out with the statement of a certain law which it claims governs and controls the whole of life. Obedience to this law, it tells us, will lead to certain results and the breaking of the law, in a like manner, leads to the opposite and the contrary result. Time and time again the law is repeated and impressed upon us, and each time the statement of the law is accompanied by a clear indication of the blessing or the curse which follows obedience or disobedience respectively.

The whole point of the historical portions of Scripture, with all these accounts and biographies of kings, princes, generals and great men, is just to illustrate the law and to show how perfectly it works out in practice. The history is not given to us merely as history but in order that we may see God's plan and God's law in action. All this is seen to perfection in occasional psalms where the psalmist consciously and deliberately reviews the history of his people in the light of this principle. The Bible is not interested in mere facts as such and is never content merely with relating the facts. Its whole object is that we should grasp their meaning and really understand their deeper significance. Facts and history are but illustrations of the fundamental principle: even kings and princes do not matter except from the standpoint of their relationship to God.

We thus see that the Bible definitely and assuredly does that which is characteristic of the modern type of biography and history. The one big point of difference, of course, is just the nature of the psychology itself. And it is a vital difference. What strikes us at once as we compare the two is the simplicity and the clarity of the biblical method as contrasted with the other. In the secular sphere all sorts of motives and influences and factors are considered and invoked and there are many rival schools with their rival theories and ideas, all of which are designed to explain the same set of facts – often in utter and complete contradiction to each other. But the biblical psychology is simple. It recognises but one factor, it is concerned about one influence alone. It says that the key to all the many varied problems is to be found in one fact alone and that the fact of sin. Its psychology is deeper and more profound than that which is fashionable at the present time and also more accurate. Indeed it treats with utter contempt what are regarded as the basic principles of the modern method of analysis. It is utterly contemptuous for instance of the heredity factor of which one hears so much. Where it considers a person and his history it indeed seems to go out of its way to make sport and fun of this. It shows us how the most saintly father can produce an utterly useless and profligate son and how, on the other hand, a ne'er-do-well father can produce a son who is characterised above all else by his zeal for the house of God and reforming activities. Cain and Abel came from the same parents, as did Jacob and Esau. There is nothing that so baffles the investigator who thinks that most things can be explained by the heredity factor as the various genealogical tables and trees in which the Bible delights!

The environmental factor is treated in precisely the same way. The best and most ideal environment can lead to the most catastrophic results. At the very beginning we are reminded that the Fall took place in Eden, in paradise of all places. Then the great man Abraham, the friend of God, the father of the Jewish race, came out of a heathen tribe. And on I could go showing you how the best and most careful upbringing fails to keep a man straight and how at other times children brought up in the midst of idolatry and wrong-doing have become saints, even as brothers and sisters in the same environment behave in an entirely different way.

Again the self-same thing can be demonstrated when the factors of training and education, intellect and natural powers, wealth, etc., are considered. Able men are shown to be as fallible and as frail as others – even a Solomon dies under a cloud. But I imagine someone trying to answer all this by saying that all along I have been considering merely external factors. 'What about temperament?' says the critic. The answer is still the same. Some of the wildest and worst men by nature turn out to be the best men. Face the Bible and its records merely from the standpoint of modern ideas and modern psychological methods and it remains a hopeless jumble of discordant facts which cannot be harmonised and which baffles all attempts at classification and order. But approach it in the light of the psychology which the Bible itself suggests to you, face it with the key called sin and you will find every door opening and the tangled skein suddenly unravelling itself. Take any case you like, the key always works; what is more, it always works in precisely the same way. Life according to the Bible is never as complicated as it appears to be. Look at the facts alone and it appears to be hopelessly complicated, but the explanation is simple. The cause of all troubles is sin and the effect of sin is to produce complications. The Bible, like God, is no respecter of persons. Crowns and robes and even mitres do not succeed in concealing the man which is behind all and the sin which is in the man.

Now that is the biblical case and we are interested in it and alert to it this evening not merely that we may approach this particular story of Adonijah as if it were a detective story of which we possess the clue, but rather for the further and vital reason that we know that life is still the same and that the factors of which we talk and boast so much are as irrelevant and as unimportant as the various other factors we have considered already. Life is still the same and sin still remains the same. The law of God is eternal. 'Heaven and earth may pass away, but my words shall not pass away' (*Matt.* 24:35). That is still the position. Cause and effect still remain and still work themselves out along the same old lines. Obedience and disobedience are still the only two possibilities and the blessing and the curse that have been ordained to follow them respectively have not been abrogated or in any way modified by the passage of the years. What explains the story of this man Adonijah is precisely the same thing as explains the lives of hundreds of people at this present time. His story can be read just as a story and then there is

nothing to gain from it and no profit at all. The lives of many
people today just appear to be strange and odd and inexplicable, but
when you consider it all in the light of what the Bible teaches about
sin, the whole thing becomes perfectly plain. Let us approach this
story then in that way, keeping our eyes especially upon the
infallible psychological key which, as I shall show you, is provided
for us in the narrative itself. God grant that as we do so many may
see themselves and their error in this man and his life, and that,
further, they may be led to avail themselves of the only true
solution and remedy.

1. We must start at the beginning where the story starts and there
we discover that we are at once given the key to the understanding
of all that happened. Listen to these words of 1 Kings 1:5: 'Then
Adonijah the son of Haggith exalted himself, saying, I will be king'.
In other words, *we must start with a consideration of the nature of sin.*
Obviously we cannot deal with this exhaustively but we can at least
note the main thing about it, the thing that always characterises
it, the thing that is really responsible for it. The word 'exalted'
expresses that perfectly. Sin is pride, arrogance, self-conceit. And it
always leads to rebellion. You see it clearly in the case of this man
Adonijah. He felt that he ought to be king, that he had a right to be
king. His father had become an old man and was more or less
incompetent and clearly Solomon was a favourite of his and likely,
therefore, to be named as successor. Now to Adonijah all that was
quite wrong. He felt that he was the best man in every respect to fill
the office of king. What did it matter what his father said or
thought, he knew what he was doing. He had the ability and the
right. He wanted the thing, he desired it. He would govern the
country in his way and do so very much better than anybody else.
And how wonderful it would be to be king, seated upon the throne
with the crown on his head! No longer merely the king's son who
had to obey but the supreme and foremost person in the land with
everyone doing obeisance to him, everyone hanging on to his every
word, and the people even shouting 'God save the king'. How
wonderful! So we are told that 'he prepared him chariots and
horsemen and fifty men to run before him'. What a perfect picture
of the nature of sin. 'He exalted himself, saying, I will be king.'
What a mixture of pride, self-will and arrogance all culminating in

rebellion! And ah, how much easier it is to see this in terms of earthly kings and rebellions, than in terms of the rebellion of every sinner and every soul that is born into this world against the king of heaven!

Why is it thought wonderful and clever to dismiss religion and to have nothing to do with a place of worship? Why do most young men who reach the adolescent age think that that is a manly thing to do? Why does the self-styled 'man of the world' who has given up religion, and who has turned his back upon it, always look down upon and despise those who still are religious? Why the feeling of superiority? If man merely ceased to be interested in religion and just said nothing at all about it, in a sense I would understand that. But that is precisely what they never do. They will and must persist in talking about it and in trying to ridicule it. Why the feeling, why the heat, why the bitterness? What is the difficulty? We do not have to look very far before we discover the answer. We have but to listen to what men say, we have but to listen to our own natural thoughts and feelings. And if we do so we shall find that it is precisely the same thing as in the case of Adonijah and indeed, as in the case of Satan at the very beginning. It is still the same old feeling of pride and rebellion, still the same tendency to ask the question 'And has God said?' and 'why has God said?' Adonijah felt that he was being kept down and kept under, that he lacked freedom. That is precisely why men and women object to religion at the present time. They have a feeling that religion binds and fetters us and stands between us and the object of our desire. There are certain things that we like and that we are anxious to do. But there is the law of God standing in the way and prohibiting the very thing. The Bible, the teaching of the church, the lives of saints stand between us and the things that appeal most to our natural hearts. Of course, we do not put it in such terms to ourselves. Like Adonijah we always try to conduct the argument on a higher plane and represent it as being something reasonable and intellectual. He persuaded himself that he really had the good of the country at heart and that he was setting himself up as king merely because he was the best man to rule the country. Most rebels succeed in persuading themselves of that and thus it comes to pass that one might well imagine that the difficulty with religion is a purely intellectual one and that those who reject it are really the custodians and guardians of truth.

But let us be honest. The very feeling and passions which always characterise the language and the discussion, the blasphemy which is always so characteristic a feature of the attitude and mentality, remind us that the real seat of trouble is much lower down. It is just this idea of having your own way, this modern craving for what is called 'moral freedom' or 'self-expression', the right to live our own lives in our own way and as we think best and most fitting. It is this hatred of religion and the very name of God because they stand between us and all our pet theories and ideas, and especially because they thunder at us those infuriating words, 'Thou shalt not'! How ridiculous it is, we say. Why should we be held up and hemmed in in that way? Why be chained and fettered by all these old sanctions? If there is a God what right has he to interfere in our lives in this way and upset everything and stand between us and our most coveted schemes and desires? We want to live our lives in our way. Very well, we will live our lives in our own way. Let God think what he may, let religion go on raising its vetoes and its prohibitions and its laws, let father and mother and society and all else record their opinions as they choose, I am determined to do what I like and what I think! Yes, 'Adonijah exalted himself, saying I will be king.' It is no mere accident or coincidence that those who believe in what they call free-thought almost inevitably at the same time believe also in free-love and many other forms of licence. It is not merely a matter of chance that as a nation becomes more ungodly and more irreligious that at the same time it also becomes more immoral and loose living. The cause of sin, the cause of all our troubles is just pride and self-will, our rebellion against the will of God and our determination to go in our own way and not in his!

2.   But in 1 Kings 1:7 we are reminded of something else which is also invariably true in this connection, which is that *one never lacks encouragement when one proceeds in this manner,* for there we are told 'And he conferred with Joab the son of Zeruiah, and with Abiathar the priest; and they following Adonijah helped him'. Let us get the full impact of that verse. Joab was a great and a mighty man, one of the greatest soldiers of the time and a man who had remained faithful to David at the time of the rebellion of Absalom. As for Abiathar he was actually one of the two chief priests and also a man who had been faithful to David at that critical time in his

history. Adonijah consulted with them and they, agreeing with him and encouraging him, followed him. Had he not had this encouragement he might not have proceeded any further but, given this, obviously there was nothing to stop him. He desired to do this thing and then people agreed with him and assured him that he was right. And they were very great people! I need scarcely explain what I mean. It is all such a perfect picture. No man sins alone. No man is isolated in his rebellion against God. He can always quote great and inspiring and impressive names for support. He can say that practically all the novelists of the day agree with him and that high society is absolutely solid on his side. He has but to look at the way in which the so-called great people of the land spend their Sabbaths, and listen to the gossip about their private lives and behaviour to have full confirmation of all he believes and all he wants to do. Sometimes he gets great shocks. Even the Joabs, men who had always been loyal and true and whom one might have thought could be trusted implicitly in that respect, turn out to be really on the other side. Why, even Abiathar agrees! Yes, even priests and those who hold high and responsible positions in the church of God often support the rebel and by their speeches and sermons which the daily press is always so ready to report fully, seem to be doing their utmost to deny the power of God and the miraculous and to undermine completely the gospel which tells of the death of the Son of God in order to 'purify unto himself a peculiar people, zealous of good works' (*Titus* 2:14).

Decide to turn your back on God and live life according to your own ideas and the world will help you. Its Joabs and its Abiathars will be on your side. You will be popular. If you are going to be guided by the opinions of men rather than by your conscience and by the Word of God there can be no doubt at all as to the result. The world encourages all men to go wrong. Society is so organised and so run that it is well nigh impossible for a man to keep and to go straight. In its thought and philosophy, in its flattery of us, in its encouragement of us to shake off all the old nonsense about religion and to express ourselves and to be manly, in its suggestions and suggestiveness, in its pleasure and its entertainments, and above all by its example, it does all it can to encourage us to defy God and to proceed on our own chosen way. Truly did Paul write to the Corinthians, 'For ye see your calling, brethren, how that not many wise men after the flesh, not many mighty, not many noble, are called' (1 Cor. 1:26). Yes, Joab and Abiathar agreed with and helped Adonijah!

3.   Let us now move to verse nine where we read, 'And Adonijah slew sheep and oxen and fat cattle by the stone of Zoheleth, which is by En-rogel, and called all his brethren the king's sons, and all the men of Judah the king's servants'. What does that mean? Simply another well-known principle, which is that *the life of sin against God, the rebellion against the Almighty, always appears for a while to be highly successful.* We are told in verse six that 'his father had not displeased him at any time in saying Why hast thou done so?' Adonijah flushed with success, with support, proceeds to give a great dinner, a great feast. How foolish he was to have hesitated for a moment about all this. Why, all was well! How ridiculously conscientious and scrupulous he had been in examining himself concerning this matter of setting himself up as king! Why, the thing was obviously right and the success was greater than he had ever imagined! It was simply wonderful! What a fool he had been ever to have delayed so long!

There is no greater fallacy than to imagine that the moment a man sins he will immediately have his punishment. That, as some of you know, was one of the great problems of the people of the Old Testament. They could see the ungodly succeeding and prospering while God's people often had a very hard and difficult time. And they could not understand it. It was a problem to them. But it should not have been. Sin appears to be highly successful always and many a man has spoken to himself as Adonijah did. At first he is fearful and hesitant to turn his back upon God and upon religion. He is afraid of the consequences. He played and toyed with the idea of sin. He liked it, he desired it. But what would happen if he actually did it? Ah, that held him back. But the critical day arrived and at last he did it. And wonder of wonders, instead of some terrible calamity leading to his end, nothing untoward happened at all. Instead things appeared to be going remarkably and amazingly well. Never had he been so happy. Doing all he desired to do and yet succeeding and prospering in the world. The banquet ordered and the friends invited. How foolish, how childish, how super-stitious, how old-fashioned to have been held back so long by fear of

God and fear of punishment and fear of retribution. This free life is simply wonderful. No chapel-going on Sunday. No longer any fear of doing the things we want to do on that day. No longer the miserable argument and constant wrangle with conscience over certain things. Freedom, enjoyment, manliness, yes, success and prosperity! All is well! Can the pleasures of sin be enjoyed? Of course they can. Look at history, look at the world tonight! Look at Adonijah at his feast in verse nine.

4.   But we must hurry on as *the story does not end there.* The next verse in which we find Adonijah is verse forty-one, the particular verse which I choose as the text for this sermon. I have asked the question whether the pleasures of sin can be enjoyed and I have answered it by saying 'of course they can'. But here we are reminded of the answer that Moses gave to that question according to the writer of the epistle to the Hebrews who tells us that Moses chose 'rather to suffer affliction with the people of God, than to enjoy the pleasures of sin for a season' (*Heb.* 11:25). Here it is put thus: 'And Adonijah and all the guests that were with him heard it [the piping with the pipes and the rejoicing of the people with great joy at the anointing of Solomon as king] as they had made an end of eating'. There they were at the feast. And oh, how they had enjoyed themselves. The food was perfect; the company and the society brilliant and scintillating; the speakers had all excelled themselves; and the music had been superb. 'Long live king Adonijah.' 'Undoubtedly the finest man they could possibly have found.' 'The glories of David will soon be nothing in comparison with those of Adonijah. Long live the king.' Such were the shouts that constantly punctuated the proceedings. Never had Adonijah been so happy. At last a king! And surrounded by such wonderful friends who had just been saying in their speeches that they would risk all, their very lives for such a great and a wonderful man. And the proceedings were just ending, and they were on the point of parting from each other, when suddenly there is another sound. 'What is it?' 'Oh, nothing!' But there it is again. 'What is it? What can it be? Why is the city in uproar? What means this?' 'It is but the echo of the people cheering Adonijah?' But no, it does not sound like that. And it is advancing towards the banqueting hall! What can it be? Look at the faces of these men and observe their consternation and their

fear. Then the people come in and bear the news of the anointing of Solomon – just 'as they had made an end of eating'. Oh, how true of sin always everywhere. 'The pleasures of sin', yes, but only 'for a season'. The season may vary considerably in its length and its duration but it is always only a season and it always ends. Sometimes it ends very quickly and there is more or less immediate tragedy. But sometimes it goes on and on and seems to be quite endless. The man goes on defying God and rebelling against him, breaking all his laws and nothing seems to happen. 'Ah,' he says, 'all is well, soul! Take thine ease. Eat, drink and be merry.' Then suddenly comes that shout that always disturbs the end of the ungodly and sinful life. 'Thou fool, this night thy soul shall be required of thee' (*Luke* 12:20).

Yes, it can go on and on and you may think that all is well and you are perfectly safe and secure. But the end must come and the last word will always be God's. While Adonijah and his friends are feasting, Solomon and David are preparing. While you are enjoying your life of sin, time is running on, the end is drawing nearer, and the laws of God remain immutable. All may be well at the moment, you may be surrounded by success and apparent happiness. You may feel that all is perfect and that you have never been quite so happy. But what means that odd ache or pain? Oh, it is nothing, I can simply shake it off. But it seems to increase! What is it? Carry on! Go ahead! Forget about it! But it shouts yet louder and louder. The inevitable must happen. The end must come sooner or later. God grant that you may hear that shout of God before it is too late! Do you not even hear it now? Do what you will you cannot escape from God. Go where you will you will never escape from his presence. Do you not hear that shout outside? Of course you do, that is why you are here this evening. The procession of God is drawing nearer. You have heard some strange noise and intimation, you have felt that all is not well. Listen to it. It gets louder and louder, it is drawing nearer and nearer. And what is more you are powerless to prevent it. Are you not a little unhappy? Are you not beginning to ask questions about your life? Are you not a little uncertain about it all? Hearken to that noise! It is God advancing and calling you to judgment. It is the first intimation of the last trump, of the dread day when the trumpet shall sound and the dead shall rise to judgment and you in their midst. 'The pleasures of sin'! 'For a season'! 'And Adonijah and all the guests that were with him heard it as they had made an end of eating.'

5. Then there followed *the scene of consternation and confusion* which is so vividly described in verses forty-two to forty-nine. The only one I desire to underline is verse forty-nine where we are told, 'And all the guests that were with Adonijah were afraid, and rose up, and went every man his way'. I emphasise that verse again simply because of the truth which it contains and which is always the case with the sinful life. The very people who had agreed with him and who had supported him and who had encouraged him to go forward and praised him and promised him so much, at the moment of crisis and difficulty all get up, walk out and leave him. When they are needed most they are useless. The modern ideas and theories of life may be wonderful while we have health but how utterly useless they are when we are ill, and especially when we are in desperate trouble and face to face with death. Would you like to face eternity on a novel by H. G. Wells and Co.? Do you think you will be comforted and helped and consoled on your sick-bed or on your death-bed by the things to which you give your time, your money and your attention and all your enthusiasm? What has the public house to offer to a dying man who is in terror of his soul? What has sport to offer? What has jazz and dancing and the cinema and gambling and all these things? Yes, business and money and the smart society circle? What have they to give you when you need them most and are desperate? Like the friends of Adonijah, they suddenly desert you and leave you. Fair-weather friends and traitors. Can you be so foolish as to continue to listen to them and to rely upon them? As they have served all others before you so they will serve you. Look at the miserable, wretched man, Adonijah. Behold his terror and his alarm and his fear. Watch him as he runs to the altar and then clings to the horns. Is there not something debased about it all? False in its inception and conception, sin always inevitably works itself out along the very path that we have been considering until it ends in terror, alarm, wretchedness and hopelessness. What is wrong in itself and in its very essence must lead to trouble. As James puts it, 'Lust when it hath conceived bringeth forth sin, and sin when it is finished, bringeth forth death' (*Jas.* 1:15).

6.   What can be done? Is there any hope? Such is the divine plan behind these records that even that question is indicated clearly in this Old Testament story in verses fifty-one to fifty-three. Solomon hears of Adonijah's fear and terror and his plea for his life and 'Solomon said, If he will show himself a worthy man, there shall not an hair of him fall to the earth: but if wickedness shall be found in him, he shall die. So king Solomon sent, and they brought him down from the altar. And he came and bowed himself to king Solomon: and Solomon said unto him, Go to thine house.' In spite of his rebellion and all the trouble he has given, Solomon is prepared to pardon him and forgive him on condition that he acknowledges his wrong and promises to be faithful and loyal in the future. He sends for him and tells him this and when Adonijah bows before him, and owns his allegiance, all is well and he goes home pardoned. What a feeble shadow all that is of what God does with the sinner. In spite of all we have been and all we may have done. In spite of all our rebellion, disobedience, arrogance, pride and lust, God is prepared to forgive us and forget all if he is but satisfied that we are truly sorry and repent. He has no pleasure in the death of the ungodly.

Solomon sent his servant to fetch Adonijah. God, Oh infinite condescension and love, sent his only begotten Son to fetch us. He sent him to that cruel death and shame on Calvary's cross. You can be eternally forgiven. All your sins can be blotted out and not only will you be restored to your old position as Adonijah was, you will be promoted to sonship and God will make you an heir of eternity. That is the offer. But the conditions of Solomon to Adonijah still remain. You must show yourself a worthy man.

Here is an opportunity for you. You are in the presence of God and Jesus Christ. Are you genuine? Then bow to him as Adonijah bowed to King Solomon. Acknowledge God and do so publicly. Be a worthy man. Forsake your sin and the way of the world. Turn from it. Turn to God and acknowledge him and confess him. Cast yourself upon his mercy in Jesus Christ. Give yourself entirely to him! He is ready and waiting to receive you. He will give you

A joy that hath no ending,
A love that cannot cease.

'He will never leave you nor forsake you' (*Heb.* 13:5) whatever may happen to you. Cast yourself upon his love, the love of which Horatius Bonar could sing:

> *It blesses now, and shall for ever bless*
> *It saves me now, and shall for ever save*
> *It holds me up in days of helplessness,*
> *It bears me safely o'er each swelling wave.*

There is the offer. You have but to acknowledge your sin and rebellion, to bow yourself before him. And when you do so he will not say as Solomon said, 'Go to thine house' but rather, 'Come unto me' – 'Come, ye blessed of my Father, inherit the kingdom prepared for you from the foundation of the world' (*Matt.* 25:34).

9

Making Use of God

At that time Abijah the son of Jeroboam fell sick.

1 Kings 14:1

The story of Jeroboam the son of Nebat is one which no one who is at all interested in the Old Testament or in religion in general can afford to ignore. Indeed, it is not too much to say that one simply cannot understand the books of Kings and Chronicles at all and realise their teaching without first grasping the meaning and the significance of this man's story. And that is so because it is a story to which constant reference is made. The whole record of many of the kings is partly summed up in these oft-repeated words 'he walked and caused Israel to walk in the way of Jeroboam the son of Nebat', as if to say, 'you know exactly what that means'. We cannot understand the case of any one of these men then without knowing what this particular sin of Jeroboam was.

To discern what it was we have but to turn to the twelfth chapter of the book of Kings and then we will find that it amounts to this. Owing to the folly of Rehoboam, the son of Solomon, the children of Israel had become divided into two nations which we afterwards know as Israel and Judah, or the Northern and the Southern kingdoms. Ten of the tribes which had been ruled and governed by Saul, David and Solomon rebelled and constituted themselves as the Northern kingdom. Jeroboam the son of Nebat was their leader and when they broke away he became their king. He therefore is the first king of the separate kingdom of Israel. He built a place called Shechem and dwelt there. But at once he found himself confronted by a difficulty. The people had always gone up to Jerusalem to the temple to worship God and naturally were still anxious to do so. Jeroboam saw very clearly that if that position were continued it would probably mean that he would ultimately lose his hold on the people and therefore also his kingdom. His method of preventing this was to make two golden calves, one of which he placed in Bethel and the other in Dan. He then told the people that it was quite unnecessary that they should go up to Jerusalem to worship God, that it was 'too much' for them to do so, the journey being too far. In a few words, he built a kind of temple, ordained priests, appointed certain special feast days, and urged that the people should do more or less exactly with respect to their calves of gold what they had formerly done in Jerusalem. That was 'the sin of Jeroboam the son of Nebat who made the children of Israel to sin' to which such frequent reference is made in the Old Testament.

But I always find that the incident which is recorded here in 1 Kings chapter 14 is still more interesting and certainly very much more illuminating and helpful in the understanding of the man's character. Indeed it is only in the light of this incident concerning the illness of Jeroboam's child that we can really understand the other incident to which such frequent reference is made. For it is here we really see the man's attitude towards religion. The two incidents must be taken together before we can obtain the full and the complete view of him.

There are many things about this second incident which attract us and which in and of themselves are worthy of our consideration. From the mere standpoint of drama and human interest it is a superb story. The first short verse, 'At that time Abijah the son of Jeroboam fell sick', is a masterpiece, its very economy is thrilling and pregnant with the suggestion of drama. And on the human plane how interesting it is and how pathetic. What a strange creature man is, what a mixture of contradictory and discordant qualities. There is a tender spirit in all men, even the hardest and the most cruel. Jeroboam the son of Nebat was a strange and terrible man, indeed a violent man in whom you would never expect to find the slightest suspicion of tenderness. But here it is revealed. He was a good father, he loved his little boy Abijah. And because of the boy's illness he does something that he would never otherwise have done. How tempting it is to stop with that thought purely on the human level and to try to analyse the case of men who belong to this type – hard-hearted men of the world, unscrupulous and relentless who often do not hesitate to ruin men and even at times to take their very lives, who nevertheless show amazing compassion to children or their wives, or sometimes to a dog or a horse. Is it not a certain proof of the doctrine of the Fall? We must not, however, be detained by such thoughts as we have something of much greater importance to consider.

What we desire to note is that the matter of the illness of Abijah is essential and must be taken into consideration with the other matters to which we have already referred if we would truly understand Jeroboam's position with respect to religion. In a word, his attitude was that religion is precisely a matter of convenience. Jeroboam made the two golden calves not because he had ceased to believe in God but because he saw that religion was likely to cause him to lose his crown and his kingdom. The sin of Jeroboam is not the sin of becoming an atheist and giving up belief in God but rather the sin of a man who believes in God but who deliberately modifies and changes God's commandments in order to suit his own conscience. Jeroboam did not cease to be religious; what he did was to manipulate God's religion to suit his own plan and purpose. He did not tell the people that God was not God and that they need not worship him; what he said was that God could be worshipped perfectly through their golden calves and that therefore it was quite unnecessary to go to Jerusalem. Later on the children of Israel became idolatrous, but that is entirely different from 'the sin of Jeroboam the son of Nebat'. No! Jeroboam's sin is the sin of ignoring God's special commandment as to how he is to be worshipped and of substituting his own ideas for these. God's way did not suit Jeroboam. And yet when the little boy is taken ill he turns to God's way. In his agony, in the crisis, he sends to the prophet and does the right thing. Normally he really does not need God, at least so he thinks; but in the crisis he does and therefore turns to him. God and religion are purely a matter of convenience to him. What a strange man, what a peculiar type of being! And yet, how common a type!

Jeroboam is just *the* perfect biblical illustration of thousands of people who are alive today and who are to be found, alas, not only outside the church, but also within. All sinners do not sin in exactly and precisely the same way. Here we have a distinct and definite type. Here are people who believe in God and who desire his salvation. They always turn to him in times of trouble. They read the Bible at times and are familiar with certain of its contents. They believe anything it has to say about love and mercy and kindness and compassion. They accept readily its teaching on forgiveness and pardon. They desire to go to heaven and hope to go to him and nothing pleases them more than a gospel which tells them that they can get there because of God's amazing love. They weep with joy when they hear it and they can never hear it too frequently. Yes! they accept fully everything that the Bible has to say on these great themes but at the same time they persistently avoid and ignore all that the Bible has to say about truth, righteousness and holiness. They enjoy and are prepared to accept all that the gospel gives, but they dislike all that it demands. They want religion and believe in religion, but in their way and according to their own ideas, so they go to the Bible and extract from it everything that suits them but utterly reject the rest. When they are reminded of the Sermon on the Mount and of the ethical demands of the gospel, when they are informed that the Christian is to be holy as God is holy, when they are called upon to come out of the way of the world, and be separated and to avoid the very appearance of evil, they not only dislike it but actively resent it, and do not hesitate to doubt and to dismiss such teaching as being the mere expression of the narrowness of that particular type of preacher or of person. Like Jeroboam the son of Nebat they worship God, or at least they imagine they do so, in their own way and not in his. And what is still worse about the modern representative of this type, they defend all this in terms of 'the love of God'. They go to God for what he alone can give – for love and mercy and kindness and compassion, for help in trouble – but they turn away from him when he commands. They always drop on their knees in prayer and remember God when things go wrong, but forget all about him and even stifle his activity within them through the conscience when all is well. Such is the type of person portrayed here in this story of Jeroboam, yes, not only portrayed but also unmasked and exposed. Let us observe the following points.

1. *First, observe the insult to God that is involved and implied in this position.* I call your attention to this first of all because it constitutes the most terrible aspect of this whole question. If men but realised what this position is in the sight of God, if they but saw the consequences of the action in terms of God, they simply could not

continue with it for a moment longer. It is not for us to attempt to discriminate as between sin and sin and to try to apportion the relative and respective amounts of guilt involved in different sins, but as far as we can see, it seems clear that the position of the atheist who disobeys God is very much less heinous than that of the kind of person we are discussing who professes belief in God but who simply uses him to serve and to suit some small selfish personal end. Here then is not only disobedience and rebellion but furthermore a direct insult. We can examine this insult along two main lines:

(a) There is very especially an insult to the goodness of God involved in this attitude. For it is an attitude which shows clearly that it is not really interested in God as a person at all, it is simply interested in what he does and can do. It does not desire him, but simply desires his help. It has no interest in the Giver but only in the gifts which he can give. This is a point which really needs no demonstration. It ought to be perfectly obvious merely on the basis of human experience. Do we not all know something about this ourselves? Which of these persons hurts you and insults you the more, the one who openly says that he disagrees with you and dislikes you or the one who affects much liking for you and interest in you, who protests that he is on your side, but who ultimately reveals clearly that he is not really interested in you at all, he is simply out to use you for his own ends and for his own purposes? If there is one thing that a man worthy of the name resents it is just that very thing. Read your history books and biographies for testimony along this line, consult the annals of the various political parties for your evidence. The man who uses a party or a theory or teaching merely to advance his own ends is always regarded as a cad. He is the worst type of hypocrite. He really is not interested in the cause or the teaching at all. All he sees is that if he supports that cause it will help him to further some private object that he has in view. And then, having attained to the position or object, he ceases to be loyal to the teaching. History condemns such men without measure and pronounces its censure upon their meanness of soul and pettiness of character. But what of the man who does that not merely with a party but with a person? Truth is sacred but a human personality is infinitely more sacred. Truth is impersonal and cannot be hurt, but personality is sensitive and can be deeply wounded. Words fail us when we try to find an epithet to describe the mean cad of a person who can stoop so low as to use another's personality to advance his own selfish ends. And obviously as the greatness and importance of that personality increase, the offence becomes correspondingly greater. Treachery against a king is punishable by death. What then of the person who treats God thus? There is no need to elaborate or to argue. To turn to God only when you need him, to regard him as someone whom you can use to serve your own ends is to offer to him the greatest insult that can ever be offered.

(b) But it is an insult also to his holiness. This is the spirit of the matter that needs to be stressed most of all at this present time when men are prone, as we have seen, to defend their attitude in terms of the love of God. Their case is that the love of God covers everything. They refuse the moral and ethical teaching, they regard as narrow what God in his Word most clearly commands and orders; they accept the gospel teaching as regards salvation, they say, but ignore all else. Now if the position of such people was that they fully accepted the whole teaching but failed in practice, and bemoaned and regretted that failure, there would be no insult involved at all. They would recognise the holiness of God and their very regret at their failure and their repentance on account of it would be a recognition of that holiness.

But such is not the position with so many today. They do not recognise that teaching. They dislike it and refuse to acknowledge it. They are actually opposed to it. The case with them is not that they fail to live up to it but that they refuse to acknowledge it. They desire and want salvation but it is to be in their own way. Here then is a definite and specific insult to the holiness of God, for what they really believe is that God can save them and is prepared to save them without making them holy. They picture God as one who is content merely to forgive us our sins and who is not concerned to deliver us from our sins and to make us positively holy. In other words, they imagine that God regards sin as lightly as they do themselves, that it is something which does not matter in the sight of God, that it is not utterly abhorrent and detestable in his eyes. And furthermore they imply that God does not really mean what he says in the law and in his various commandments and ordinances. Indeed their view of the whole plan of salvation is that the love of God is virtually something which makes it possible for them to continue in a life of sin without having to fear punishment on account of it. They play the love of God against the holiness of God. To do that is not merely to insult the holiness of God but actually to imply an essential immoral contradiction in the very character of God.

Had it occurred to you that all that is involved in the attitude which picks and chooses what it desires in religion, the attitude which is prepared to make full use of the love of God but which entirely and utterly ignores his righteousness and his holiness? Consider this and ask yourself the following questions: On what grounds have you the right to say that one part of God's statement is correct and important and the other unimportant? Are you God's judge, that you can say what matters and what does not matter? Are you the master and he the puppet that you can handle him and use him just as you will and when and where? It were indeed better for you to say that you do not believe in God at all than to say that you believe in God and then proceed to insult him by accepting only that part of his divine revelation which suits you and pleases you, and rejecting that which condemns you and commands you to be holy even as he is holy.

2. *But let us consider also the self-deception that is involved in this position.* This is perhaps the most striking feature of this type of person as it is illustrated in the case of Jeroboam the son of Nebat. It is really almost inconceivable that we should be capable of such self-deception but such is nevertheless the case. How remarkable it is that men who generally are calculating, wise and astute should be capable of such childish failure to apply logic and to think clearly. But that is precisely the effect of sin upon us. Let us look at this self-deception along two main lines:

(a) There is nothing which is quite so clear about the case of Jeroboam as the fact that he really knew the whole time that what he was doing was wrong. As I have already shown, he did not cease to believe in God when he set up this alternative system of religion. All he did was to say that the new system was the full equivalent of the old and that it would be equally effective if practised by the people. And he persuaded the people that such was the case, but he never persuaded himself. He knew all along that the whole thing was a hollow sham and utterly useless. He kept on with it in spite of

that because it suited his other purpose. But when the little boy
Abijah is taken ill, he shows very clearly where he really stands.
He does not go to Dan or Bethel, he does not consult either of the
golden calves or offer his sacrifices and incense to them. Why?
Because he knows that they cannot help. Instead he sends his wife
to the prophet of God, the man who had predicted to him that he
would be made king, the man who belonged to the same God as
that other prophet who one day had afflicted him with leprosy and
had then miraculously healed it (*1 Kings* 13:4–6).

Jeroboam knew that the system of religion he had created was
utterly useless and valueless and that the other was the only true
and the only real religion. 'In that case', asks someone, 'how is it
that he could have commanded men as he did?' Well may the
question be asked. And there is but one answer. In spite of knowing
in his heart of hearts what was true and right he deliberately does
what is wrong and persuades himself that all will be well. The
crisis, the desperate need shows clearly what his real attitude is but,
while all went well, he persuaded himself that all was right and
stifled his conscience and argued with the voice divine that was
within him. How typical that is of all who are in a like position.
There is no need to argue about this. All that is necessary is that we
should listen to the voice of our conscience within us. There we are
told what is right, what is right to do and what we ought to be. The
conscience assures us that all we are told in the Bible is right, that
God is holy and that his commandments must be obeyed. We know
these things for certain. When we are honest and listen to the
inward monitor we know precisely and exactly the difference
between good and evil, right and wrong, moral and immoral. We
know exactly, we know for certain. But then we proceed to do what
Jeroboam did. All that which we know so certainly and definitely
does not suit us, does not agree with our plan. We desire to do
something else which is opposed to this. And we desire it so much
that we eventually do it and invent for ourselves this new type of
religion. Thus we proceed to prove and to demonstrate that this
new religion is right. We argue and debate. We say that the other is
too much and that this is quite sufficient. We wax eloquent and
turn down all the arguments and reasons to the contrary. We argue
against our conscience and the light within, we persuade ourselves
that we are right and surround our lives and our mode of action

with a kind of intellectual and philosophical justification. We pit our minds against our consciences, our own ideas with respect to what we think is right against our own sure, certain knowledge of what is right. And as long as life goes smoothly and there are no problems, all is well. While we are healthy and strong and young the system seems perfect. Now and again the conscience twinges and struggles but we silence it and argue it down. And then, Abijah is taken ill. Or we ourselves are taken ill and we cannot avoid the fact that we knew all along that we were living in a state of self-deception. When the Titanic struck the iceberg, the band began to play 'Nearer my God to thee'. When we cease to be merely clever, in the great crises of life we all know the truth of God. Listen to that voice within you that is greater and deeper than your intellect, pay heed to the inward direction and monitor which will teach you, not the theories of men which sound so wonderful, but the very truths of God himself. Cease to fool yourself as Jeroboam fooled himself. Look at the golden calves that you have set up in the place of God, compare what you advocate and defend with what the Bible teaches, contrast the life you lead with that of the saints. Be honest! What is there to be said really for the ungodly life? Examine it exactly as it is without all its trimmings and fineries. What has it to give to the soul? Above all examine it in the light of eternity. Instead of attacking the godly life in terms of narrowness try to discern what really there is to be said in favour of and in defence of the other life. The ceremony and ritual of our own arguments delude us and deceive us, but however ornate the decorations may be a golden calf remains a golden calf and will prove itself to be such when you need it most of all.

(b) But there is another element in the self-deception which is still more tragic and inexplicable when regarded purely in an objective manner. And that is the way in which it deceives itself about its own cleverness. You remember the story. Abijah is taken ill, Jeroboam realises the uselessness of his spurious religion and is anxious for help. So he decides to send his wife to the prophet. He does not go himself for reasons which we shall consider in a moment – he sends his wife. So he gets her to disguise herself as a poor woman and to take with her a present! He feared what would happen if the prophet recognised his wife and what the prophet would say to her. So disguise is essential! He will fool the prophet and at the same time obtain from him precisely and exactly what he needs. Without the prophet knowing who she is, Jeroboam's wife is to obtain the knowledge and the help desired. How clever! How subtle! What a perfect scheme! How perfectly planned! How typical of sin and of the sinner! How clever Jeroboam thought himself to be. But his cleverness was based upon ignorance and failure to think clearly and as the story proceeds to unfold the only person he succeeds in deceiving is himself! I say that it is all due to failure to think clearly and to think in a straight way. All this cunning, caution and astuteness is really based on pride and self-confidence which invariably paralyses one's thinking powers. Jeroboam no doubt thought that he was being clever and was congratulating himself on the result of the project before his wife even left the house. If only he had thought for a moment he would have seen how utterly preposterous the whole scheme was.

This is how Jeroboam should have enquired. This prophet Ahijah to whom he sent his wife was actually the man who had predicted to him that he would be king of Israel and that was while Solomon was still alive. Here there was a man who could see into the future and who had access to knowledge hid from the eyes of ordinary men. Here is a man who is not dependent upon mere sight and touch and ordinary human means of gaining information. Here is a man who, by the power of God, can read the future and foretell its events. This was miraculous power. And yet Jeroboam thinks that he can deceive him by just a little paint and powder and the wearing of old clothes! The fool. And how terribly and tremendously is the point brought out here. When Jeroboam's wife reaches Ahijah the prophet has actually become blind. In a sense there was no need for the disguise at all for the old man had lost his sight. And yet as the wife of Jeroboam approached his room this is what happened: 'And it was so, when Ahijah heard the sound of her feet as she came at the door, that he said, Come in, thou wife of Jeroboam; why feignest thou thyself to be another? for I am sent to thee with heavy tidings' (*1 Kings* 14:6). In spite of her disguise, yes, in spite of his own blindness he sees her and tells her all about herself and the position at home. How does he do it? The answer is given in the previous verse: 'And the Lord said unto Ahijah . . .'

Need I apply all this? What fools we are! And how clever we think we are! We persuade ourselves that we can play fast and loose with God's laws, and live our lives as we think fit. And then in the time of crisis we put on an anxious face, and shed our hypocritical tears, we don our mask of sanctimoniousness and holiness and take a little present to God and ask his help. And we really believe that it will work. We persuade ourselves that we can go on in our own way right through our lives and then just turn to God at the end when we need him very badly. How we imagine that we can fool God, not remembering that 'the Word of God is quick, and powerful, and sharper than any two-edged sword, piercing even to the dividing asunder of soul and spirit, and of the joints and marrow, and is a discerner of the thoughts and intents of the heart. Neither is there any creature that is not manifest in his sight: but all things are naked and opened unto the eyes of him with whom we have to do' (*Heb.* 4:12–13). If we did not say that we believe in God and never turned to him the position would be different. But we say we do believe. We confess him to be the Almighty, the Absolute. And yet we think we can deceive him! Dear friend, see the utter folly of this. Reason it out carefully and quietly as Jeroboam failed to do. Fool yourself no longer. God is the Almighty and he knows all about you.

3.   *I plead with you to do this because of the inevitable end to which Jeroboam's course of action always leads.* I have emphasised his self-deception but in that very state there was surely also an element of shame. When the illness became serious then Jeroboam was brought face to face with what he had done. He saw the utter use-lessness of his course of action and must have despised himself. And partly on account of that shame and also partly on account of his fear of facing the man of God, and his fear of hearing what he would have to say to him, he sends his wife instead of going himself to the prophet. Miserable man! And you know the end. His wife returns with that terrible message of disaster and woe (*1 Kings* 14:7-16), Abijah dies and all is lost.

Have you not known something of this already? In trouble and distress you have turned to God. Have you not felt yourself to be an utter cad? Has not a voice within you whispered 'You miserable coward who have gone your own way in your proud defiance refus-ing to listen to conscience and the Word of God, why do you never turn to him?' Do you know that? Is there anything more terrible and more awful? And then that sense of fear. You feel you have no right to turn to God at all, that you are such a cad for only turning to him when it suits you and using him to please yourself and your own convenience. But you are utterly helpless and you know that you are in his hands. You realise his power now and feel your own guilt. You have to admit that you deserve nothing but punishment for conduct so small and despicable. Have you not known it and felt it? If not, you do not believe in God at all, for no man can anywhere view the presence of the living God without feeling that sense of fear and shame. Have you not felt it already when you have gone to him in the various ills and accidents of life? But think what it will be like to face him like that at the end! No, we cannot fool God. We cannot pick and choose from his way of salvation. We either accept it all as it is or none at all. If you think that you can work your way to heaven by fooling and deceiving God you will awaken one day to the realisation that the only person you have fooled is yourself.

Jeroboam never repented. Had he repented and gone himself to the prophet, and confessed his sin and folly and shame, the whole story might well have been different. We do not know. We can but surmise and guess. But we do not surmise and guess when we tell you that if you realise now the folly and the vanity, the utter madness of this attempt to deceive God, if you but realise it, and confess it before him, in shame and sorrow – casting yourself upon his mercy, and confessing all, asking him to forgive you, promising him that you will forsake that evil way and live only to please him – then he will not only receive you but abundantly pardon you and forgive you and shower his blessings upon you. How do I know that? How can I prove that? The answer is Jesus of Nazareth, the Son of God. He came on earth and lived and died and rose again in order to purchase our pardon and deliverance. He gave himself unto death in order that we might be forgiven and have a hope of heaven, yes, but not only for that, but also 'that he might redeem us from all iniquity, and purify unto himself a peculiar people, zealous of good works' (*Titus* 2:14).

I have tried to reason and to argue with you, but it is all summed up in the cross. Isaac Watts is perfectly right. The man who truly sees the cross and what it means must argue and reason as Watts does in that hymn – 'When I survey the wondrous cross'. We dislike the holy life and the commandments of God because we desire and like other things. But look at these other things in the light of the cross. Look at your pride in its light, look at your little possessions – how vain they all seem and how base we are for ever having regarded them at all and for having placed them before him and his holy will.

He died, he gave all, he gave himself – look again to where 'sorrow and love flow mingled down'. 'He died to make us good' and to reconcile us to God. Can there be any other response than that of the last verse:

> *Were the whole realm of nature mine,*
> *That were an offering far too small;*
> *Love so amazing, so divine,*
> *Demands my soul, my life, my all.*

Give these unto him!

10

The Disease Man Cannot Cure[1]

Now Naaman, captain of the host of the king of Syria, was a great man with his master, and honourable, because by him the LORD had given deliverance unto Syria; he was also a mighty man in valour, but he was a leper.

2 Kings 5:1

This is the first verse of a chapter which records for us the extraordinary story of this man Naaman, captain of the host of the king of Syria. I am calling your attention to it because it provides us with a very striking illustration of a principle which is taught everywhere in the Scripture and which is vital in connection with the whole of Christian salvation. The message of this Book is really but one – two Testaments, one Book, one message. And the purpose of the Bible is really to deal with just one thing and that one thing is man in his relationship to God. The Bible is the most practical book in the world. There are foolish people who say that they are so practical they have got no time to read the Bible or to listen to sermons out of the Bible, 'We want to get on with life', they say. Well the Bible will certainly enable us to get on with life. It is not a theoretical book at all, it is a book that comes to us exactly where we are to tell us the cause of our troubles, and to tell us about the only way in which we can be delivered from those troubles. It does that in the Old Testament as well as in the New. There is only one real difference between the two Testaments, and that is the form in which the message is presented. In the Old Testament you have types, prophecies looking forward, you have got the shadows suggesting the substance. In the New Testament you see the great thing itself in its fullness but the same principle is operating in the Old as in the New. The Apostle Paul is always telling us in his

[1] Westminster Chapel, 14 February 1960.

Epistles that there is only one way of salvation, and that is by faith alone. Abraham was saved by faith as much as was the Apostle Paul. Take that great eleventh chapter of the Epistle to the Hebrews, it tells us how all these men were saved by faith. There is only one way of knowing God, of being saved and delivered from this evil world and from the devil, and that is this way of faith. So you have got it everywhere in the Old Testament in these great characters such as Abel and Abraham, Isaac, Jacob, Moses, David and the prophets. The same salvation in the Old Testament as in the New. In a very interesting way you also find people stumbling at this message in exactly the same way in the Old as you find it in the New, and this man Naaman is a great illustration with respect to that fact. So as we consider this man we shall be looking in a pictorial, dramatic manner, customary in the Old Testament, at the self-same principles as are taught more clearly in the New Testament. I am doing this deliberately because we are all helped by an illustration. We have been concentrating for a number of Sunday evenings on the doctrine, on the teaching, on the principles. Some of us may now be helped if we see all this in a concrete instance and example. The kindness of God and his concern to help us are such that he does not only give the teaching, he gives these pictures, illustrations and stories. It is good, then, that we should look at this great question in the terms of the picture and portrait of this man Naaman, the Syrian.

The first thing which we gather from this passage is that *sin is something which spoils life*. Listen to it: 'Now Naaman, captain of the host of the king of Syria, was a great man with his master, and honourable, because by him the Lord had given deliverance unto Syria; he was also a mighty man in valour'. Such is the citation – a man who has been honoured by the king, and honoured because he was a remarkable man, a man of natural abilities and powers, possessed of great prowess and highly successful in conducting his campaigns. So he was 'a great man with his master'. As we read of him, he seems to be rising from step to step and to be well-nigh perfect. Then comes this little word 'but' – '*but* he was a leper'. In just that phrase you really have got everything that the Bible tells us about sin for it is conveyed perfectly by this picture of leprosy. Leprosy in the Old Testament, and in the New, ever stands as a kind of type of sin, an illustration of sin.

Now we are all aware of this, that there is something which is spoiling life. There are so many things that are good about life today, and yet it is probably true to say that not one of us would be in this building at this moment were it not for the fact that we know there is something that is spoiling life. We know that about life in general and we know it in our individual lives and experiences. How easy it would be for me to give you a list of the excellences of this twentieth century – all the advances in knowledge, particularly scientific knowledge, the phenomenal strides that have taken place in the realm of medicine and the healing of diseases, the advances that have taken place in housing, education and culture. Everybody is better off today and 'never had it so good'. But nobody says that everything is all right. This fatal 'but' seems to come in, it is always there and it has been there throughout this century. If you cast your minds back to the 'thirties, those of us who are old enough to do so, you recall the tendency then was to say everything would have been all right but for this man Hitler. It is always like that. Everything would be perfect 'but. . .' 'But' is always there. So at the present time the world is like this man Naaman of Syria. You can say this and that are true of it; the world has never been so wonderful; we have never had so many amenities; everybody is being lifted up – circumstances, conditions, everything is better. So is it perfect? No, it is not – 'but'. There is something wrong, something which, like this leprosy, seems to spoil it all – the insecurity about the future, is all this prosperity going to last, what is the world going to do, are we working up for another war, or are we not? Just when we think everything seems almost perfect this 'but' comes in and you cannot get rid of it.

There it is looking at it in general. Take it in particular and you will find exactly the same thing. The life of man, according to the Bible, ever since sin entered in, has never been whole, it has never been entire. Man as God made him at the beginning was entire, his life was whole. There was nothing lacking in the Garden of Eden, man was made perfect in correspondence with God, with a life to enjoy all things, there was nothing lacking at all – no disappointment, no unhappiness, nothing going wrong at all. God looked at it all and he saw that it was good. The characteristic of life then was this wholeness, this perfection, with no blemish, nothing at all to detract from it. And then that fatal thing called sin came in.

Sin has robbed life of its wholeness, its completeness and its perfection. So the life of every one of us can be described in this way, we are this, that and the other *'but . . .'* Life has been spoilt and ruined by sin.

However successful a man is in this world there is no such thing as perfect and complete success, there is no such thing as perfect and complete happiness, there is no such thing as perfect and complete and entire peace. Nothing to me is more instructive when you read biographies and autobiographies of the world's great men as to see the very point which is made here by this word 'but'. There you see a man, able and ambitious; he says to himself and to his family, 'If only I get there everything is going to be all right.' He does get there, but everything is not all right, there is always something detracting. I am not being pessimistic, I am being realistic, I am simply telling you what you find described in these biographies. You will see it in the novels, if the author is a true novelist and not merely out to be popular. In other words, it is what a philosopher once called 'the tragic sense of life', there is always a fly in the ointment, there is always something that is detracting from the perfection of the thing we think we have. You have arrived at that great position, yes, but you are aware that people are jealous of you and envious of you? that they are watching for you to make a mistake, waiting perhaps for you to fall altogether in order that they may get there? They would not be at all disappointed or unhappy if you were taken ill and had to retire. You know all that and it spoils everything. The poet has put it for us, 'Uneasy lies the head that wears the crown'. He lies uneasily because he knows that there is another man who would like to have that crown and who has got a dagger somewhere. He has got there, he has got the crown, he has reached the acme, yet there is this 'but' that comes in. There is always something wrong.

The Bible is full of this. In the Book of Esther there is Haman who was a great favourite with his king Ahasuerus. Haman was exalted, he had everything and he thought he was so great that nothing could spoil him, so he let it be known that whenever he passed along the streets everybody had to bow to him. Everybody did bow to him except one man, Mordecai, and because he would not do it, all was spoiled for Haman. He went back and complained to his wife; he was miserable and he was unhappy – this man who had been honoured by the king, put into the supreme position, who could issue an edict and have it carried out, virtually having the power of a king, with everybody bowing to him. Yes, but there was one man who would not do it, and it spoilt the whole thing. When his wife says, 'What is the matter with you?', he replies, 'There is this man Mordecai, he won't bow to me.' What a parable, what a picture of life!

Naaman was a great man with his master, and honourable, because by him the Lord had given deliverance to Syria: he was also a mighty man in valour, but he was a leper and it spoilt the whole thing. Sometimes it is other people who are the problem, sometimes it is a man himself, his own temperament, his own constitution. Read the record of people who excel in their professions, whatever it may be, then get to know the story behind the scenes, and you will find that they are victims of their own temperaments. You see great actors and you say, 'How marvellous'. If you knew what they were going through before they went on, or even while they are doing it, and what happens afterwards, you would scarcely credit it – some constitutional trouble, nerves, sense of strain, and so on. Their success seems to be endless and almost perfect, but if you really get to know the person you will find this leprosy, this running sore!

Or sometimes it may be some trouble in the family. How often of that realm do we hear it said, 'If only', 'If only'. There is always something – something which spoils the whole thing. This is the great problem of life, this is really the explanation of so many of the divorces. A man says, 'I have done this and the other, but I am unfortunate, I made a mistake, my wife does not seem to understand, she cannot keep going with me, if only'. This 'but', the fatal leprosy that always keeps on coming in and spoiling life. 'There is no peace, saith my God, to the wicked' (*Isa.* 57:21). It does not matter how wonderful he may be, how far he may go, sin like leprosy comes in and spoils the whole picture.

But sin is not merely something that detracts from happiness, it is something that positively makes us unhappy. Follow the life of sin, the way of the world, and you will know unhappiness and misery. You cannot help it, remorse is bound to come. You will cause pain to yourself and pain to others. Sin brings positive unhappiness. The trouble with this man Naaman was not only that his condition detracted from all he had got, it positively made him miserable. Wherever there is sin, there is pain and sorrow. 'The still sad music of humanity', the pathos of life, the tragic sense of life, what is it due to? Says the Bible, it is due to sin, life was never meant to be like this, but sin always leads to trouble.

Then look at it in this way, the ugliness and the offensive character of sin. Leprosy! a terrible, a revolting, a horrible thing. And that was the thing from which this man suffered. Sin is ugly, sin is foul – look at it as it really is. Do not merely read the newspaper, consider the things which are described, the dishonesty, the pretence, the sham, the cunning, the stealth – all the things to which sin stoops. Think of all the things upon which it tramples. Is there anything which is quite as ugly and as offensive and as foul as sin? We all talk about and bemoan our modern problems, but the question is, what are they due to? And this is the answer, it is this leprosy of sin.

Further, sin, like leprosy, is something which is no respecter of persons. Naaman was a great man with his master, a man of great valour, a man of great success, but he was a leper. It does not matter who we are, nor what we are, sin is the universal problem. Read the biographies of kings and queens, of captains and of prime ministers, read the record of men at their best in every walk of life, you will always find it. We are all subject to it and suffering from it. This brings us all to a common denominator. There is no success and failure when it comes to sin, we are all failures, we have all got this terrible leprosy of the soul.

There is the first point that I make – the Bible tells us that the thing that really is making life what it is, spoiling life and ruining it and making it ugly, is this terrible thing which it calls sin.

Then look at a second point which comes out here so clearly. *Man at his very best and at his highest cannot deal with this problem.* That is the essence of the story of Naaman. Everything is spoiled because he has got this leprosy. Obviously he had gone to his doctor and to all the doctors, and they had all done their best but Naaman goes on suffering and the disease gets worse and worse. Nothing can be done.

We are told very explicitly that even the kings are baffled. Here is his own master, the king of Syria, what would he not have done to be able to cure this favourite of his, Naaman; but he could not do it.

Then he hears of somebody who can heal in Israel and says, 'Very well, I will write a letter to my brother, the king of Israel, and I will send Naaman to him.' So Naaman departs and suddenly arrives at the king's doorstep with a letter from the king of Syria asking that he may cure him. Listen to the response: 'It came to pass, when the king of Israel had read the letter, that he rent his clothes, and said, Am I God, to kill and to make alive, that this man doth send unto me to recover a man of his leprosy? wherefore consider, I pray you, and see how he seeketh a quarrel against me.' He could not cure him any more than the king of Syria. They were both completely helpless; all their magicians, all their physicians, all their great men and they themselves, they can do nothing at all with respect to the problem. Do you see it? That is an epitome of the whole history of civilisation for you, that is the story of the human race throughout the centuries and throughout known history.

'What do you mean?' says someone. What I mean is this, that ever since the dawn of history man has been aware of this trouble in his life in particular and in general, and he has been trying to deal with it. That is the story of all the thinking and the research and all the delving into the mysteries – man trying to find a cure, trying to get rid of this thing. It is the story of civilisation but never has it been more true than it is at this present hour. I see the world today in the precise position that is depicted here. Here is Naaman, the leper – that is all of us, that is society, that is every one of us by nature – and the world is trying to get rid of the leprosy and is completely failing to do so. How has the world been trying to get rid of it? Go back to the most primitive societies that you can find anywhere in history and you will find that they had tribal laws. What is the point of a tribal law? Well that is just their bungling way of trying to deal with the problem, trying to get a certain amount of order into the chaos and the confusion. Tribal laws to cure the leprosy. Then move up the scale a bit and you come to kings, emperors, governments, whether elected popularly or not does not matter. The whole notion of government is still the same, it is an attempt to deal with this problem, to solve it, to get rid of it and to set man free from this fatal leprosy. Look at it in terms of acts of Parliament, they are all trying to bring order into life, trying to get rid somehow or other of this chaos, to give man relief and release and 'improve his lot'. Until about the end of this last war, we were told that the real cause, the most drastic cause of the ills of mankind was poverty, and if we could only get rid of poverty by means of new arrangements and enactments, 'if only' – then man could be delivered from sin. But we have got rid of the poverty and yet what is our major problem today? Sociologists now begin to tell us that the major problem today is that people have got too much money and therefore there is this increasing sin and vice and crime. The problem, they say, today is the problem of our 'plentiful' society. The exact opposite of what they taught before! Before they also used to say that the trouble was that men had to work so hard that they got tired out, they did not have time to think or read. 'If only' we could give them more leisure, more time to think and to read, then they would lift themselves up and would no longer be the victims of evil. But now we are being told that the great problem facing us is the problem of leisure, people have got too much time on their hands, and because they do not know what to do, they go and do things they should not do – the 'problem' of leisure! It is always this or that which is the cause of our troubles. What is the matter, why are people behaving as they are, why do we get these wars, why is there this unhappiness, why is there mounting crime and all the rest? These are the questions with which men have been trying to deal throughout the running centuries. The real business of philosophy is to try to understand man, to try to understand life, and we have had great philosophers in many centuries but the problem still remains. The philosophers cannot get at it, they themselves are suffering from leprosy. They tell us what to do but they cannot do it themselves. Even if we do what they say the problem remains. The world today is full of agencies designed and brought into being to solve this problem. We have never had so many, the world has never been so busy in trying to treat itself as it is at this moment. You are aware of the agencies – Marriage Guidance Councils, psychology introduced into the schools, into the home, into the prison, and so on. But the problem is not only there, it is becoming more and more evident and obvious.

All this is nothing but the old picture of Naaman, the leper, whom no-one could heal. The world that you and I are in at this very moment is desperately ill, the leprosy is here, it is staring at us in the face. Look at all our acts of Parliament during the last century. Man has never passed such good legislation as he has passed in the last hundred years and I am not here to criticise it. That is no part of the business of preaching. What I am here to say is that all this noble, beneficent legislation leaves the fundamental problem, the leprosy remains, man is still sick, still miserable and unhappy, still failing. Man does not understand, he is bewildered, he feels he is the victim of forces round and about him from which he cannot escape. This trouble is in his very constitution and all that is being done does not seem to touch the problem. The kings of Syria and Israel failed completely, the problem was evidently too deep for them, too subtle for them, the disease was too foul, and their medicaments were inadequate. There is the second point that is made here so plainly.

The third point is that *man is ignorant of the only way to deal with the problem.* Notice the way in which it is put. Here is this great man suffering from leprosy, everything has been tried, everything has failed and they are beginning to feel utterly hopeless, but now the remedy was to be had, it was there, there was a remedy available. But these great people knew nothing at all about it, they were completely ignorant of it. The solution is there in Elisha the prophet, and these great kings, looking for a solution, were unaware of its presence by them the whole time. There again is the picture of the world, is it not? We would not be in this building at this moment, and I would not be standing in this pulpit, if there were no solution. That is what I am doing here, that is what I am here for, I am here to announce a solution, an absolute solution, a certain cure. But the world does not pay any attention to this, it does not seem to be aware of it. Is there not some other physician somewhere? is there not some great astrologer somewhere? is there not another king? That is what the world is thinking.

The world is unaware of the fact that the whole time the answer is at hand. It is ignorant of it because it is concerned about what it calls 'great matters'. The world is not interested in anything small, Everything for the world must be on a big scale, it does not matter what it is. Everything must be in the grand manner because man is so great, he has got such a conceit of himself that nothing but some great solution is adequate, and he is always looking for that. You see these two kings, they are concerned about great affairs of State, they think in terms of great armies and great conquests. A servant girl happens to have been captured in a skirmish with Israel but a king knows nothing about a little servant girl. How could he? The very idea is ridiculous. What if a man went in to the king and said, 'Your Majesty, you know in that last fight we captured a little servant girl', can you imagine what would happen to him? He would be thrown out of court and dismissed from his job probably – what is a servant maid to a king? The solution is there, but kings are concerned with great matters, and the whole world is like that. The world spends its time in setting up Royal Commissions, acts of Parliament, the profundities of some great philosopher, some wonderful discovery of science. It is looking, scanning the heavens, something big, great, marvellous, outstanding, something absolutely new, something hitherto unheard of – that is what the world is always interested in, is it not? And it is because it is like that, that it is unaware of the solution which is at hand. Or to put it in another way, the world is unaware and ignorant of the only real solution because this solution is so essentially different from everything that it had ever imagined. That is the thing that comes out in this story.

There is a sense in which the whole of the biblical message, the whole of the Christian salvation and what it has got to tell us this evening, is all in this little servant girl. I like the way the Scripture puts it: 'The Syrians had gone out by companies' – so we are told immediately after what we learn about this great man Naaman – 'and had brought away captive out of the land of Israel a little maid; and she waited on Naaman's wife' (*2 Kings* 5:2). Nobody knew about her, she was too unimportant, someone who did not matter or count for anything. But here is the glory of this gospel. The message of this Book has its irony and its extraordinary paradox. The great are looking for great things, kings may provide a cure, send the leper to the king of Israel, ask him to heal him. But the solution and the answer is there in the little servant girl, the unknown maid who was attending on Naaman's wife. The answer to the problem is not in the palace, in the court room, not amongst the courtiers and the sycophants; it is in the kitchen, in the lowest and the humblest place in connection with the whole establishment. Had you ever realised that that is what we are told in the Bible from beginning to end? Here, you see, are these great dynasties, these great empires, Egypt and Babylon and Assyria and the Chaldeans, and this, that and the other great people. Here are the great kings and captains, the astrologers and the wise men. These are the things and people in which secular history is interested. But the real key to the history of the world is to be found in a very little country called Palestine, just a little bit of strip of land, small and insignificant by the side of these great spreading empires. This little country figures everywhere in this Book, it is always bringing in the solution, turning everything upside down and giving the answer for which the great and the mighty are looking. Such is God's way. He chose the smallest nation of all, but this little race in this little country are the people who have got the answer. They are the ones who believe in the one and only true and living God, while other nations believed in their animism, their polytheism, their many gods. Here was the testimony of which the others were ignorant; they laughed at it but they had to come to it.

In Scripture you find many wonderful stories which illustrate the same point exactly. It is always some unexpected, humble and lowly person who does not seem to count at all who has got the solution. Let me give you one example. Do you remember the story of Joseph? Here is a great man in Egypt, Pharaoh, endless wealth and power; there seemed to be no limit to his authority and to his success. He can command everything. But suddenly he is threatened with an awful and a devastating problem, a famine is coming and what can they do about it? He has had a dream and he does not understand it. He sends for his wise men and astrologers, they are dumbfounded, they are absolutely confounded, they do not know. All the might and the understanding of Egypt is put to bear upon the problem, commission after commission is set up, all the subtleties of science and of art and everything that can be produced address the problem. None of them has an answer. Where does the answer come from? It comes from a man who is a prisoner in a prison. Who is he? Oh, he is some fellow that was sold to slavers by some travelling merchants. He was never in the court, never known to the king Pharaoh, but from that prison Joseph is brought to give Pharaoh the true interpretation of his dream, and through this unknown man comes Egypt's deliverance from famine (*Gen.* 41).

The same truth is equally clear in the story of David and Goliath. Here is a colossus striding the earth and everybody is trembling and quaking in their shoes, who is the man who can defeat Goliath? Not a great captain in the army, but a little shepherd boy called David. He cannot even walk in the armour that is given him, or handle a sword, but he can use a sling and one stone, and it is enough. That is the message of the Bible. The world is not aware of the answer, but the answer is there the whole time. Man is looking for great things, God does it in this way.

You see it at its very acme in the Lord Jesus Christ, the Son of God. 'Where do you see it there?' says someone. Let me tell you. The whole world was looking for a Messiah, in a sense they were scanning the heavens, but there was one place where they never thought of looking. He was born in Bethlehem, one of the least of the most despised of the cities of Judah. The Saviour of the world was not born in Jerusalem, he was born in Bethlehem. We read in the second chapter of Luke's Gospel of the census of the people and of how they went up to be taxed. They were all talking about the taxation and the politics, and of how this and that ought to be put right. They did not know it but the Saviour of the world was about to come into their very midst. They would not go out of the hotel to make room for a woman about to have a child – 'No, no, we are not going to shift out', so she had to go and sleep in a stable. And it was there that the Son of God was born. A little helpless babe lying in a manger, with the cattle amongst the straw, is the answer. Kings knew nothing about him, the great people knew nothing, the great thinkers knew nothing, the philosophers were unaware of it, they were still seeking for something strange and new and wonderful, but it was there he came. Always the same principle, the little servant maid, the unknown, the unexpected – there is the answer! And where did this Person spend his time after he came to manhood? We find him up in Galilee and read that men were all stumbled and offended at this. They said this man claims that he is a unique teacher, if he is why does he spend his time up there in Galilee, preaching to a rabble of poor, common people. If he is the Son of God, why does he not go up to Jerusalem, why doesn't he set himself up as a king, why doesn't he gather a great army and deliver us from the power of Rome, why doesn't he? 'This fellow', 'this carpenter' – always up there in Galilee with his rabble of ordinary people. He cannot be a philosopher or a great man – impossible. And finally they saw him nailed to a tree and expire in apparent utter weakness upon it. They saw his body taken down and buried in a grave, and they said, 'Is this your Saviour? is that your salvation? No, no,' they say, 'You don't get salvation out of kitchens and out of stables; we want something big and something great.'

The world, you see, has never been aware of the solution to its problem, the only satisfaction of its need. And this was not only true when the Son of God himself was upon earth, it has been true of the church ever since. Look at the church as it was at the beginning, a handful of ordinary men, workmen, fishermen, he leaves his kingdom to them and the world is not aware of it. But the world soon began to pay attention to them because they proceeded to turn it upside down, and in those centuries when the great Roman Empire was reeling under the attacks of the Goths and the Vandals and the Barbarians, and everything was being lost, it was the Christian church that preserved what was preserved of civilisation and of truth. The thing from the kitchen again, not the people in the Imperial Palace, but the people in the catacombs, the solution which the emperors did not know and could not see. And so it has continued throughout the running centuries. The solution has been there, and sometimes when men have been desperate they have had to turn to it as Naaman had to turn to the little servant girl. I am thinking of Martin Luther, just one man, an ordinary monk, not a cardinal, and in an unknown place in a corner of Germany, but there was God with the man, and the answer came forth. It is the great story of revivals and the position is still the same this evening. There is only one answer to the problems of society and it is the answer that the Christian church possesses. But ninety per cent of the people in this country are not interested in the Christian church. We are told that only ten per cent affect any sort of interest, and only half of those prosecute it at all actively. Of course not, they are interested in great things! What has Bertrand Russell got to say? what has this great thinker got to say? what acts of Parliament can we pass? what new commissions can we set up? how can we bring our scientific knowledge to bear and find the solution? You will never find it! There is only one solution to the problem of sin, it is this Christian message of salvation and the despised, derided, forgotten Christian church alone has the answer. We are in the kitchen of life, the newspapers know nothing about us, the world has never heard of us. What does that matter, we are God's servant maid, we are the unknown, the despised minority, the little remnant that remains. But we have got an answer to the problem, we have got a cure for the disease, it is our testimony alone that stands between the world and destruction.

That testimony is the same as was given by the little servant maid to her mistress. We do not say that we can cure the world, but we do know that the power of God can. That is all this girl knew, she could not cure leprosy, but she did know that there was a cure. She had come from a land where the power of God had been manifested and she said, 'If my master could only get under this power, then his leprosy would be healed.' And that is what I am doing in this pulpit, we are just bearing witness to this, that when the world has come to realise that with man it is impossible, we go on to say 'But not with God: for with God all things are possible' (*Mark* 10:27). There is an almighty power, there is a miraculous power.

> *There is power, power, wonder-working power,*
> *In the precious blood of the Lamb.*

There is a dynamic in this Christian message this evening that is able to eradicate sin, to cleanse men and purify them and restore their skin to its original condition. 'I am not ashamed of the gospel of Christ', says Paul. Why? 'It is the power of God unto salvation to every one that believeth; to the Jew first, and also to the Greek' (*Rom.* 1:16). I am here to tell you that whatever your problem, whatever the running sore of your soul, whatever the thing that gets you down and damns and ruins your life, there is one cure, it is an absolute cure, it is the cure of God. There is a power, and the little girl was able to testify to the One through whom the power was exercised. She said it like this: 'Would God my lord were with the prophet that is in Samaria'. There is power in Samaria, and it is exercised through a prophet, she pointed to a person. And thank God that is my privilege in this pulpit at this moment. I am not here merely to preach a vague, indefinite power, I am here to point to a Person, the One in whom all the fullness of the Godhead dwells bodily, the One in whom God has treasured up all the riches and the resources of his grace and wisdom and power, Christ Jesus. 'We preach Christ crucified, the power of God and the wisdom of God.' And what I tell you this evening is that you have but one thing to do in the depth of your disease and in the agony of your need; go to Jesus of Nazareth, the Son of God and you will be cured. He can remove your guilt because he has already taken it away, he can give you new life, new power, he will heal you, he will restore you, he will make you anew, he will lead you on. Go to him, that is all you have to do, he is the *all*-sufficient Saviour, he is 'the power of God unto salvation to everyone that believeth'.

What the world could not do he does. Your one need is to go to him. He knows all about you, he can heal you, heal your soul, heal your spirit, rid you of the thing that spoils life for you, and give you life indeed, life more abundant. The world by wisdom knew not God, but it has pleased God through the foolishness of preaching, to save them that believe. It is still the same tonight, 'Not many wise men after the flesh, not many mighty, not many noble are called', they are all scoffing at Christianity, dismissing it all. Yes, but they are ill, they are lepers. 'God has chosen the foolish things of the world to confound the wise' (*1 Cor.* 1:27) – a servant maid knows what kings do not know, 'God has chosen the weak things of the world to confound the things which are mighty', yes, 'things that are despised, things that are not', people like ourselves, so that our testimony should be a continuation of the witness of the little maid who had the answer of which the great and the kings were ignorant.

My dear friends, in the midst of all your reading and all your thinking, wait for a moment, listen to this old, old story, listen to this despised message of Jesus and his love, of Jesus and his blood, of Jesus of Nazareth, Son of God dying that you might be healed, rising again to give you life, and to present you to God. Go to him and you will be healed.

11

The Gospel and the Natural Man[1]

And it was so, when Elisha, the man of God had heard that the king of Israel had rent his clothes, that he sent to the king, saying, Wherefore hast thou rent thy clothes? let him now come to me and he shall know that there is a prophet in Israel . . . Then he went down, and dipped himself seven times in Jordan, according to the saying of the man of God: and his flesh came again like unto the flesh of a little child, and he was clean.

2 Kings 5:8-16

We looked at this story last Sunday night in general; it is a great representation of the Christian gospel, the Christian message. 'What', says somebody, 'in the Old Testament?' Certainly. It is the same God in the Old Testament as in the New. This Book is one. We call them Old Testament and New Testament, but it is only one book. Some people say this is a library of books – that is a terrible fallacy. This is not a library, this is one book, sixty-six sections in it, but only one book, as there is only one theme, only one message. That message is about what God has done about man in sin. That is the only message in the Bible from beginning to end. It is a Book about life – a portrayal of man in his misery as the result of sin, of his attempts to deliver himself and of his utter failure. With that theme we have the revelation of what God has done for man in his hopeless distress and of how God has made a way of redemption through his only begotten Son. Such is the message of the whole Bible. In the Old Testament there are the prophecies of redemption and foreshadowings of it in illustrations and pictures. Everything is pointing forward to it. In the Gospels you have got the very thing itself taking place, then in the remainder of the New Testament there are further elaborations of it, explanations of it, looking back

[1] Westminster Chapel, 21 February 1960.

upon it. The subject is the same, for God deals with man in exactly the same way at all times. So that here in this Second Book of Kings we are given a perfect portrayal of man in his need and in his sin and of how God deals with such a person.

Last Sunday we dealt with it in general. We saw how sin is that which ruins and spoils life. Every unhappiness in the human heart at this minute is due to sin. If sin had not entered into this world nobody would be unhappy; there was no unhappiness in life until sin came in. Sin ruins everything. Nobody is perfectly happy, there is always something missing. 'If only', we say. Yes, but we always do say 'if only'. Sin is the cause of all that. Naaman was a great man and great in valour, *but* he was a leper and it spoiled everything.

Then we saw how the great of the world could not do anything about this. The kings were completely helpless, as were all their great men. The world can do nothing about sin. Is that too strong a statement? No, the history of civilisation proves that. The story of civilisation is the story of man's attempt to deliver himself. But he cannot do it. Leprosy is too fell a disease, sin is too profound a problem for the ability and ingenuity of man.

Then the third point was that the world is also blind and quite ignorant of the cure, even though the cure is there. This little serving maid knew where Naaman should go: 'Would God my master could go to the prophet that is in Samaria! for he would recover him of his leprosy.' She knew but nobody else did. The cure was there, but Naaman and his wife and the kings of Syria and Israel knew nothing about it. The world is always looking in every direction except the one direction which has the cure. It knows nothing about this, dismisses it as insignificant and unworthy, and laughs at it.

My last point was this: that the business of the Christian church, as was that of the serving maid in the house of Naaman the Syrian, is to point to the cure, and to the only cure – 'prophet in Israel'. Yes, and Isaac Watts looking at the Lord Jesus Christ says, 'Great Prophet of my God!' He is! Prophet, Priest and King. He is the cure. He can cure sin. He can deal with it by his blood. He provides a 'double cure', which cleanses from both sin's guilt and power.

That is the point where we take up the story again. Perhaps you think there is no more to be said. Here is a man desperately ill with leprosy, he is told of a cure, he receives from his master a letter of introduction, obtains great presents, and goes to Israel where he hands his letter to the king. The king reads it and cannot do anything about it, but the prophet, hearing of it, says, 'Send him to me'. Here is the very prophet that the little girl was speaking about, the prophet Elisha. 'Well', you say, 'now everything is all right, she said he had only got to go to the prophet and he would be healed. Now Naaman has come to the door of the prophet surely the problem is solved and the story is ended.'

Unfortunately the story has not ended. Naaman came to the prophet who could heal him but he very nearly went home with his leprosy. Why? Ah, because of certain other things that were still wrong in him. This man was suffering not only from leprosy but certain other things as well and these very nearly robbed him of the cure. The world is still like that. Here in this Book is a message that would solve every single problem of the human race tonight. I do not hesitate to say that. If everybody in the world tonight were to live the Sermon on the Mount there would be no problems left. There would be no need to pile up these armaments and make these bombs, and there would be no need for the people who spend their time protesting against them. There would be no war. There would be no dishonesty, no immorality, no separations, no divorces – if only the whole world kept the Ten Commandments and the Sermon on the Mount! Or put it like this, if the whole world tonight believed on the Lord Jesus Christ and became linked to his power, there would be no problems left, none. Here is the answer, here is everything the soul needs, and yet though it is here, as Elisha was in that house, the world remains in its leprosy, its sin, and in its unhappiness. What is the cause? We shall be shown exactly what it is. The remainder of the story puts before us the difficulties still to be overcome before Naaman could be healed, and as it does so it brings out some of the most fundamental principles with regard to this gospel message.

Look at Naaman stumbling just at the very moment when he was to be healed. He nearly missed the blessing. Why? Because there are certain things about this gospel which the natural man hates, as Naaman hated them, and it was because he hated these things that he walked away in high dudgeon and almost went home. But for the plea that was put to him by his own servants he would have gone home in a rage and temper and still a leper. The trouble, I say, is this; there are things about the gospel of Jesus Christ which the natural man hates and that is why he does not turn to it, that is why he is not cured by it, that is why he is not rejoicing as he should be and as he could be this evening, in spite of everything that is happening round and about him.

Let us look at it and especially in the light of the commentary on it which I read to you earlier in 1 Corinthians 2. There you have got it in a doctrinal form, here in 2 Kings 5 you have it in a pictorial form. A picture like this is helpful, so let us look at what Paul is saying in 1 Corinthians 2 in terms of what Naaman did in actual practice in this world so long ago. The first thing which we find is this: that *the natural man hates the gospel because it hurts and humbles his pride.* That is the first thing. You remember how the story puts it? Naaman arrives with his gifts and money and clothes and all the rest of it, and came with his horses and with his chariot to the door of the house of Elisha. There he is – the horses, the chariot, the gifts, the retinue, all standing at the door of the humble prophet. Then we read: 'Elisha sent a messenger unto him, saying, Go and wash in Jordan seven times and thy flesh shall come again to thee, and thou shalt be clean.' He had gone there in order to be cured, had he not? Well that is the way to be cured, says Elisha. 'But Naaman was wroth, and went away, and said, Behold, I thought, he will surely come out to me, and stand, and call on the name of the Lord his God, and strike his hand over the place, and recover the leper. Are not Abana and Pharpar, rivers of Damascus, better than all the waters of Israel? May I not wash in them, and be clean? So he turned and went away in a rage.' Most of what we find in 1 Corinthians 2 is in those words.

Naaman's pride was hurt, he was humbled, he felt he was humiliated. For he was a great man, a great captain, next to the king in his own country. After all he had come with a letter of introduction, he had been to the king of Israel, and he now comes to the humble prophet – surely, he thought, he was going to have some special treatment or, at the least, he would have the usual courtesies extended to him. A man in his position cannot be treated in this way with just a verbal message sent down; why did the prophet not come out and bow to him and express his pleasure at seeing such a great man visiting him? Why did he not 'put his hand upon the place, and heal the leper'? Nothing of the sort, Elisha does not even see him! Naaman was insulted, humiliated, this was something he could not put up with, leprosy or not. Instead of having some very special treatment because he was a great man, he found to his chagrin and annoyance that he was treated like everybody else, as if he was just an ordinary man like every other ordinary man. He disliked it, he hated it, he lost his temper, he was furious, the thing was insulting, it was utterly impossible – and away he goes in his rage.

Naaman is not the last to have done that, you know. There are many in this congregation who are in the precise position at this very minute. 'What do you mean?' says someone. I mean this. People are offended at the first statement of the gospel, which is that there are no divisions nor distinctions recognised in the house of God. Whatever you may be outside this building, when you come in here you are the same as everybody else. Incidentally, that is why I am a Free Church man. There is no human head to the church of God. There is but one king in the church, it is King Jesus. There are no divisions and distinctions here. But we do not like that, we live on these things, we are so accustomed to them, and when we are confronted by this which is a blank contradiction of all we have believed and gloried in, we are taken aback, we are upset, we are annoyed. There are no divisions and distinctions in terms of birth or background or race or social status in the church of God, they are completely irrelevant. At the same time there are no divisions and distinctions or special categories as regards intellect in the house of God. You may be the greatest genius in the world, it does not matter, when you come in here you are like everybody else, you are in the same position as the biggest fool in an intellectual sense. You may be a man of great learning and knowledge, it does not make the slightest difference when you come in through that door, it avails you nothing. You come in, in exactly the same way as if you knew nothing, precisely in the position of the uttermost ignoramus. In the same way there are no distinctions in terms of one's moral behaviour and conduct in the past. You may be a paragon of all the virtues, it will not help you here, you will be annoyed if you listen to this gospel, because it will tell you that all your righteousnesses are as filthy rags and that you are in exactly the same position as the most profligate sinner who has come in off the streets. No difference! That is the message of the Christian gospel. There are no special cases here and that is what is so infuriating about it, that is why people dislike it and get annoyed. No special cases. None at all.

I will tell you another thing – it makes no difference at all from the standpoint of the gospel what century you belong to. This is a point which hits the modern man so hard. 'Why', he says, 'do you mean to say that we in the twentieth century are in exactly the same position as the people of the first century?' Absolutely – there is no difference at all. 'But my dear sir', says somebody, 'look at what they did not know, look at what we know, look at all our advances and developments in knowledge.' My reply is, It does not make the slightest difference, you are in the same position as Naaman even, who lived centuries before Christ. There is no difference at all.

Shall I try to put this before I pass on in terms of an incident that once happened in my experience and which I think will help you to remember it. It was my privilege, I think about 1941, to be asked to take part in a university mission at Oxford. As one of three speakers, I had to preach in St Mary's Church in Oxford on a Sunday night, and it was announced that there would be a meeting for questions in the Old Rectory immediately following the service. At this question meeting, which was crowded with undergraduates, I was attracted by an intelligent-looking young man sitting in the front, and when questions were invited he was the first man to speak. He told us that he was a man prominent in the Union Debating Society and he certainly spoke with all the polish of a practised debater. First he paid some compliments to the preacher – that is part of the game – and he went on to say how very much he had been attracted by parts of what he had heard. 'But you know', he said, 'there is one thing which seemed to me to be vitiating the whole sermon. I admit the logic and the arguments and the arrangement but I really could see no reason at all why that sermon, the same sermon, should not have been preached in exactly the same way to a congregation of agricultural labourers in Oxfordshire.' That was his question, and the chairman called upon me to respond. There was only one thing to say. I freely confessed that until that moment I had always taken the view that even undergraduates in the University of Oxford were only ordinary common human clay like everybody else, and that from the standpoint of the gospel there is no difference between your brilliant undergraduate and your so-called agricultural labourer. That is what the gospel itself says: 'There is none righteous, no, not one . . . For all have sinned, and come short of the glory of God' (*Rom.* 3:10, 23); 'the whole world' lies guilty before God. Yes, I would preach the same sermon to agricultural labourers because when you are face to face with these things there is no difference between one and another.

Take this point of intellect, what is the value of a man's intellect when you are dealing with God. God is infinite, God is eternal, God is everlasting, God is absolute in all his qualities. I know that a mind is a good thing and an intellect is a valuable thing in examinations in this world and in human knowledge, science, art and all the rest. In those realms ability counts. But, my dear friend, you are facing God, the absolute and the eternal, and what is the value of the biggest intellect the world has ever known? It is as helpless as that of the greatest ignoramus. For a man to pit his intellect against God is just to show that in a sense there is something wrong with his intellect, he cannot think straightly. If he thought straightly he would say, 'Who am I to span the mind of God, if I could I would be as big as God.' That is what man tries to do, and when he is told that his great intellect is of no value here he takes offence as Naaman did, and it is the same with everything else.

Sin is not an intellectual problem, it is a moral problem. And the problem of every one of us in this world is a moral problem not an intellectual problem. I do not care how great your intellect is, I do not care how high your birth is, you are just a miserable sinner like every one of us, you are a creature of jealousy and of envy and of passion and of lust and of desire, you are unclean, you have got leprosy in your soul! I do not care who you are nor what you are. What is the use of talking about your great qualities to me, while you are a leper. That is your problem – you don't know God, you commit evil, you are unworthy, you are unclean! That is how the gospel starts. Elisha did not come down to receive Naaman and give him special treatment and attention. Of course he didn't! Naaman was only a leper like any other leper, why should he have special treatment? What he needed was to have his leprosy cured and the prophet told him how that was to be done. Everything else was to be left aside, nothing else matters for a man in sin facing God! Your intellect and all the other distinctions make not the slightest difference.

Let me hurry to the second point: *the gospel annoys us and we hate it by nature because it shows that all our thoughts and ideas as to salvation are all wrong.* All that we have thought is wrong, completely wrong. Did you notice that here in the case of Naaman? Listen to him, he really betrays himself: 'Naaman was wroth and went away, and said' – now we hear Naaman giving his view about how a man is to be saved – 'Behold, I thought he would surely come out to me, and stand, and call on the name of the Lord his God, and strike his hand over the place, and recover the leper. Are not Abana and Pharpar' – if it is going to be a matter of washing in a river – 'are they not better than all the waters of Israel?' – this miserable country and its Jordan – 'may I not wash in them and be clean? So he turned and went away in a rage.' That was Naaman's idea as to how it should happen. His king was guilty of the same error; he sent a great present with Naaman. 'He departed, and took with him ten talents of silver, six thousand pieces of gold, ten changes of raiment, and a letter of introduction'. The same point comes out at the end, even after he is healed Naaman still has the wrong idea. 'He returned to the man of God . . . and he said, Behold, now I know that there is no God in all the earth, but in Israel: now therefore I pray thee take a blessing of thy servant'. Elisha replied, 'As the Lord liveth, before whom I stand, I will receive none'. Naaman urged him to take a present but he refused. Naaman could not understand it because all his ideas about salvation were entirely wrong and that is still the problem with the natural man. Elisha did something entirely different from what Naaman expected.

I do not want to stay with this but this is where the sheer folly of sin comes in. There is nothing more foolish or unintelligent in the world than sin and unbelief. Look at this man Naaman. Here he is, a leper, he cannot cure himself; the physicians, wise men and astrologers cannot cure him; his king cannot cure him; the king of Israel cannot cure him; nobody can cure him, the whole world cannot cure him – and yet, look at the fool (what else can you call him?), though he is helpless and hopeless as a leper and everybody can do nothing for him, he is fool enough to criticise what Elisha does and to argue and to put up his objections and his protestations. What can you say of the man but that he is a lunatic and a fool!

To start with, it is obvious he knew nothing. If he had known something about the cure of leprosy, he would never have gone to the door of Elisha at all. It was because he knew nothing, and nobody else knew anything, that he is standing at the door of Elisha – and yet there is the fool arguing with what Elisha says, criticising it, 'Is this right, is that right? if it is to be washing why cannot I go back to Abana and Pharpar, why this Jordan? why does he not come down and put his hand . . .' He speaks as though he knows all about it and yet he knows nothing. Is the thing not obvious to you, my friend? Can you cure sin? Can you rid yourself of it, the running sore of your soul? Are you perfectly happy and content? Have you through your philosophy, whatever it is, found the way? Of course you have not, otherwise you would not be in this service at this moment. Then I say, do not be a fool like Naaman; if you are a failure, and a terrible failure at that, who are you to criticise the gospel way? Why put up your ideas and theories, why say, 'No, I don't approve of that'? You see that was why the Jews, when Christ came into this world, rejected him though he was their own Messiah. They said, 'Is he not the man who spends his time up in Galilee speaking to a handful of poor people? The Messiah is one who will gather up an army and conquer Rome and set himself up as king in Jerusalem, elevate the nation above all others and conquer the world, that is the Messiah.' Their idea of a Messiah! Because this was not Christ's idea of a Messiah, because he would not conform to it, they hated him and the Pharisees and scribes and Sadducees and doctors of the law plotted against him and killed him. Ah, the tragedy and the madness of it all! And people still, who are miserable sinners, go on doing the same thing. They say, 'I cannot see why living a good life alone is not enough, I don't see that if a man lives a good life it is not sufficient, I don't see this and that' – and away they go in a rage. 'Abana and Pharpar better than Jordan'. Though they are miserable failures, though they are sinners, they have the effrontery, the folly to criticise the way of salvation which has been sent into the world by God. Is it not madness? But that is why they are annoyed with it, as Naaman was so annoyed. All his ideas were demolished immediately by Elisha's words. Nothing happened according to his plan and pattern, according to his notions, and yet he sticks to them and he battles and he argues and he objects, and still he remains a leper. Of course! The first thing we all have to learn is that all we have ever thought about Christianity is all wrong. We thought that being born in a Christian country made us Christians; we talked about 'pagan nations'. 'This is a Christian nation, why I was brought up in a Christian home, I have always believed in God, always been a Christian, always gone to a place of worship, always done good, never done a . . . of course I am a Christian!' The first thing that the Holy Spirit does when he convicts us is to show how tragically wrong all that is. That is not Christianity! That is the biggest obstacle to Christianity and it has to be got rid of. Elisha saw that that should be done, he knew his man, he knew his thoughts, he demolished them all and Naaman was furious. The gospel still does that. God does it.

The next point is this: *the gospel is annoying to the natural man and makes him hate it because it proposes a way to him that seems to him to be utterly contemptible and ridiculous.* It not only smashes what we thought and what we imagined it was going to do, all that is demolished, but then when it does show us its own way it is still more infuriating. You know I am sounding harsh about this man Naaman, I am really very sorry for him because I understand him so well. I have been in Naaman's position, like everybody else you see, but I do want to try to show you how ridiculous this position is. Here he is. He has come with his letter of introduction – chariot, horses, retinue, followers, servants, money, change of clothing, all these things, and then all that happens is that this prophet sends down a messenger, he does not even come to see him, merely a messenger saying to him 'go and wash in Jordan seven times'. That is the last straw. It is bad enough that he doesn't come down and do this and that, but *Jordan* when he already knows about Abana and Pharpar! The thing is insulting, the thing is utterly ridiculous! Yes, what the gospel says to every one of us is most galling to the natural man; it seems to him to be completely insulting and humiliating because it does not come and tell us that we have only to live a good life and that we have only to look at the Lord Jesus Christ and see his perfect example and then go out and follow him, practising the imitation of Christ. We are all ready to go out and imitate Christ, using our powers, making great self-sacrifices, doing marvellous things. 'This is Christianity', we say, 'this is fine – the imitation of Christ!' No, says the gospel, it is nothing like that at all. God does not invite us to imitate Christ, to try and put his teaching into practice, and promise to reward us by getting rid of our sin. No, no! that is not it at all! The message is not to look at 'Jesus' (as they call him), as the great moral exemplar, the great teacher; it is, look at a gibbet, at a man with a crown of thorns upon his brow and an agonised expression on his face, crying out 'My God, my God, why hast thou forsaken me?' – a man dying in apparent weakness, his body taken down and buried in a grave with a stone rolled over it. That is what you are called to look at – Jesus Christ and him crucified! The gospel says that is the way of salvation; that is the way to get rid of your sin and your problem; that is the way to be made whole and to be made happy – go to Calvary. Look at Christ dying upon the cross, realise what was happening – what it means, that there he was bearing your sins in his own body, that your sins were being punished in him, that God has laid your iniquity on him and has dealt with it there. This is all; you have nothing else to do but to acknowledge your sin, to repent, to confess it all, and then simply to believe that Christ, the Son of God has died for you and for your sins – and if you do it you will be immediately saved.

'What', says the man, 'just that? the thing is monstrous! Don't I have to go out of the service and decide to be better and to go in for a course of instruction on how to take up Christianity seriously, read books, try and do good works and then . . . ?' No, all you do is to look at the cross and see the Son of God dying, and say: 'I believe that message, I believe what you are telling me to believe, that he is the Son of God and that he has died for me and for my sins and I am immediately forgiven, I am immediately made a child of God, I am made a Christian, the Spirit puts life into me'. Just that, nothing more. No programme, no long-continued treatment, nothing at all, just that. 'Why', says somebody, 'that is all right for some ignoramuses in the East End of London or women and children, but don't you know I have spent my life reading philosophy, I have spent my time studying sociology, I am doing good works, I am battling with great notions and delving into the mysteries? You are insulting me, this is childish, this is ridiculously simple, this is immoral, even asking me to say that one died for me and that another could bear my sins; surely a man has to save himself by a good life.'

Isn't that what you have been saying about this gospel? You say, 'If that is the gospel what is the point of my education and my knowledge, what is the value of all my morality and all I have been trying to do for years? You seem to say it is of no value, I have simply got to believe, something a little child can do.' The answer is, Yes, a little child can do it. Because what is at work here is the power of God and it postulates nothing at all in us except our need, our poverty, our penury, our helplessness, our utter hopelessness. You come just as you are:

> *Just as I am, without one plea,*
> *But that Thy blood was shed for me,*
> *And that Thou bidst me come to Thee,*

as helpless as a child, the simplest thing in the world. That is what the gospel says. That is the message that was sent by Elisha to Naaman so long ago. Just come and dip yourself seven times in the river of Jordan and you will be healed, you will get rid of your leprosy. Naaman was furious, and the natural man still objects to it. Did you notice how Paul put it? 'The natural man receiveth not the 'things of the Spirit of God' (*1 Cor.* 2:14). Why? because 'they are foolishness unto him', and as he has already told those Corinthians in the first chapter: 'We preach Christ crucified, unto the Jews a stumblingblock, and unto the Greeks foolishness' (*1 Cor.* 1:23). 'What', said the Greeks, 'our great philosophers asked to believe that a carpenter in Nazareth dying upon a cross is the Saviour of the world, and that we have got nothing to do but believe in him and to surrender to him? Utter folly! Where is our understanding, where is our philosophy?' That is why they refused it. The princes of this world did not know him, 'for had they known it they would not have crucified the Lord of glory'. The gospel method seems insulting and childish. We want to do some great thing, as this man wanted to do.

The gospel insists that this is the only way, there is no other. 'Ah but', you say, 'what about Buddhism or Mohammedanism or Hinduism or Confucianism?' There is only one answer to that – they are not the way. There is only one way. Everything else had been tried by Naaman but it had led to nothing; everything had failed, and everything else is failing tonight. This is God's way, this is God's only begotten Son, Jesus of Nazareth, he is the Saviour of the world. 'There is none other name under heaven given among men, whereby we must be saved' (*Acts* 4:12). 'Other foundation can no man lay than that is laid, which is Jesus Christ' (*1 Cor.* 3:11). 'I determined not to know anything among you, save Jesus Christ, and him crucified' (*1 Cor.* 2:2). You will never find another way. Go after your philosophy, go after your other religions, you will never find peace and rest. Here alone is the cure. There is no alternative to this. If Naaman had turned away from that door in his rage and his anger, and had gone back to Syria he would have gone back as a leper, and leprosy would have spread all over his body until it killed him.

You may reject this gospel, but if you do you will remain a moral leper, you will remain a sinner, and when you die – because sin it is that brought in death and still leads to death – you will be condemned in the presence of God. You will remain a moral and a sinful leper through all eternity, without hope, without remission, with nothing to cheer you. God has sent his only Son, his only begotten Son into this world for us men and our salvation and the only way in which even he could do it was to die for us. That is why he died, there was no alternative, it was the only way:

> *There was no other good enough*
> *To pay the price of sin;*
> *He only could unlock the gate*
> *Of heaven and let us in.*

My dear friend, may I take up the position of the servants of Naaman who, seeing him turning away from Elisha and going home in a rage, went to him and said, 'My father, if the prophet had bid thee do some great thing, wouldest thou not have done it? How much rather then, when he saith to thee, Wash, and be clean?' May I plead with you in the same way? Is it not folly to refuse this gospel because it is simple, because it can save a man in the heart of Africa who has never had any education at all, or a man who was once a cannibal? Is it rational to refuse it because it can save him as well as you? Is it sense to criticise and to assert your ideas when you know already that you are a failure, that you cannot heal yourself, and that your sin is getting you down? The one question is this: Does this gospel cure? Well go and try it and you will find it does. You will get the same experience as became that of Naaman. He listened to the argument, saw how reasonable it was and 'he went down, and dipped himself seven times in Jordan, according to the saying of the man of God'. It cost him, it was not easy. Of course it wasn't. We have all been through this. But 'his flesh came again like unto the flesh of a little child, and he was clean.' Believe in utter simplicity on the Lord Jesus Christ and you will be saved. Confess your sins to God at this moment in this service, confess your inability, confess your arrogance and your folly. Say to him: 'I don't understand, but I have heard that message, I will believe, I do believe it. I repent, I acknowledge, "I believe; help thou my unbelief", I believe that Jesus is the Son of God and that he died for me. O Lord, have mercy upon me, enlighten me by thy Spirit and give me understanding.' Say that to him and I assure you that he will forgive you, that your sins will be blotted out like a thick cloud, that you will be given a new life, a new nature, you will become a child of God, the Spirit of God will enter you.

Paul, in writing to those Corinthians in the third chapter of that Epistle says: 'If any man among you seemeth to be wise in this world, let him become a fool that he may be made wise'. 'Become a fool' means admit that your intellect is of no value at all and that everything you have got is of no value – you must admit it. Or let me put it in the words of Horatius Bonar:

> *I heard the voice of Jesus say,*
>   *'Behold, I freely give*
>   [Without your doing anything]
> *The living water; thirsty one*
>   *Stoop down, and drink and live.'*

The water is in a fountain and you cannot drink it without stooping down. You have got to come down – your intellect, your morality, your religion, everything has got to come down. 'Stoop down' – get down on your face, let your lips just touch that water and you will begin to drink, and life will spring up within you:

> *'Stoop down, and drink and live.'*

> *I came to Jesus, and I drank*
>   *Of that life-giving stream*
> *My thirst was quenched, my soul revived,*
>   *And now I live in Him.*

Naaman's leprosy was healed, his skin became whole, he was clean. You can be cleansed from the guilt of your sins. You can be cleansed from the power and the pollution of your sins, a process will start in you that will end in your perfection in glory in the presence of God. Stoop down, submit to his way, obey him! Stoop down, and drink and have life which is life indeed, life eternal.

12

Assessing the Old and the Modern

But he forsook the counsel which the old men gave him, and took counsel with the young men that were brought up with him, that stood before him.

2 Chronicles 10:8

The historical fact which is narrated in these words is one of the most important in the whole history of the Jewish people. It marks a momentous turning-point not only in their own history as a people but also in the history of the whole world. For it was as the result of the action taken by Rehoboam and of which we are reminded in my text that the kingdom over which David and Solomon had reigned became divided into two kingdoms, the northern and the southern or, to use the alternative names, the ten tribes and the two tribes, or again, Israel and Judah. Here then is the key to the understanding not only of the books of Kings and Chronicles but also to the books of the prophets. Here we find the explanation of many of the woes and troubles and crises that followed and to which references are made by the prophets in their books.

From the mere standpoint of history alone, therefore, this event is worthy of our consideration and there is a great lesson and warning to be found in it for all nations and countries. However, this must not be my primary focus because the New Testament does not really concern itself with nations, as such, for its chief concern everywhere is with the individual. It does not propose to save nations or countries as a whole but those who believe *out* of every nation, kindred and tongue. The Bible is in a general way concerned about nations losing their power and their greatness and with the loss of human life consequent upon men's refusal to adopt the way of settling their disputes peaceably and amicably but its real concern is about the loss of the soul. We make no further apology, therefore, for using this historical incident in a personal, rather than in a general and national, sense. But even with respect to the personal use of it there is a danger confronting us, and that is the danger of treating it merely as a piece of human wisdom and philosophising upon life. *There* is perhaps one of the greatest dangers that always confronts us when we are considering the Old Testament. It is a book that is so full of wisdom about life that we tend to regard it merely as a book of wisdom. Its moralising and its pronouncements upon conduct and action and behaviour are so perfect and so incomparable that there is a danger of our seeing that only and stopping at that without proceeding any further. The Old Testament is the most perfect piece of what is called wisdom literature that can ever be found but it is not merely that. Over and above that it is the revelation of God and his ways and his purpose. It is not only out to inculcate morality but also to reveal spiritual truths and eternal values. In other words, it is not out merely to tell us how to live and how to make the best of life, over and above that, its purpose is to reveal God and to bring us to the right and vital relationship to him. As we regard this particular incident, therefore, from the personal aspect rather than from the general, we must not stop merely at noting certain general truths which might also equally well be found in secular literature. I refer to such lessons as the importance of the choice of the right friends, the importance of listening to our elders and of respecting their judgment and their wisdom, the folly of losing everything because of our inordinate desire, and the obvious homily that might be delivered from the basis of the incident on the old adage, 'pride comes before a fall'. All these things are of value and of great importance but after all the Bible is not concerned about preparing us for life only, its real object is to prepare us for eternity.

Here, then, I maintain, is one of these great Old Testament stories which is also a parable that teaches us ultimate truths concerning our souls and their relationship to God. Let us look at the story.

It is perfectly simple and direct. Rehoboam as a young man comes to the throne of his father Solomon and begins to face life. Naturally he has certain ideas and desires. What he desires above all else is power and to be able to rule over the whole of the kingdom. He desires the allegiance of all the people, he is anxious to be supreme over all. There is a case in which the desire is perfectly legitimate for one who was a king. However, the important and interesting thing for us to note is that at the very beginning, he is confronted by two possible and alternative methods of attaining unto that end. There is first of all the way preferred by these people led by Jeroboam and commended by the old men to whom he put his case. And then there is the way and method proposed by the young men. What I would have you observe very closely is that the two methods, the two suggestions, the two ideas propose precisely and exactly the same end. The difference is not in respect to the end but to the means. 'Do what we tell you' say the old men in effect, 'and these people will serve you and give you allegiance and do whatever you desire of them'. And the young men say exactly the same thing. The difference is to be observed in the two ways in which it is proposed that the common and agreed end can be brought to pass.

Please observe the order in which the two respective bits of advice were given. It is not accidental and unimportant that Rehoboam listened to the statement of the old men before that of the young men. It is only after rejecting the advice of the old men that he accepts that of the others. But this is what he does and you remember the sequel. When Jeroboam and his people came on the third day to hear his decision he treated them roughly and speaks to them rudely and threatens them with more and worse tyranny than that which his father had imposed upon them. And the result was the division of the kingdom, wars, and ultimately the captivity of Babylon. There is the story in its essence.

Need I trouble to point out the striking and exact parallel which it offers to the case and the life of each and every one of us? We all enter upon life exactly as Rehoboam did. And as we do so we have certain ideas and desires, certain thoughts and certain things which we propose to ourselves and which we intend to carry out. We all have a goal and an objective exactly as he had. It is not precisely the same thing in each case but it is there and it is always definitive. In some sense or other we all want to live a full life. We cry out for life. As Rehoboam wanted to rule, so we all desire to make the best of life and to get the maximum out of life. This is expressed in very different ways according to the different persons that speak but the underlying idea is constant. Some express it in terms of happiness and joy. Others phrase it rather as a question of obtaining knowledge and truth and understanding. Others again would speak of it more directly in terms of life and living. Others, still more definitely, would put it as seeking for a knowledge of God and a desire to please him. So in one form or other we all tend to set out in life cherishing certain hopes and nursing certain fond ambitions.

Someone may think and say that in these statements I am granting too much and that many people today, if not the majority, set out in life without any ideas at all. I am not concerned this evening to argue concerning that, as I believe we have something still more important to do. But I claim that all set out with the idea of living a full life and if we prove (as we can prove) that even these fail in their object where they approach along one given way, the utter failure and hopelessness of those who do not even make the attempt will be still more obvious and apparent.

We set out, then, as Rehoboam set out. And at the very outset we also are confronted by two ways and two possibilities. On the one hand is the Bible way and on the other is the way preferred and advocated by contemporary opinion and modern thought. I would have you observe that the parallel is still perfect. The difference is still as to method. The Bible and the world, in a sense, offer us precisely the same thing. No man deliberately goes wrong or desires to make a failure of his life. And the world and its way always presents itself as our best friend, concerned to aid us in the fulfilment of our desires and objectives. The Bible comes to us and tells us what is best for us and how we can obtain life which is life indeed. And the world and its thought do precisely the same thing. The difference is in the method. Both propose to give us life, truth, happiness and joy and all that we can desire.

It also remains true to say that it is the old proposal that comes first. Every person brought up in this country, with very few exceptions, if any at all, become acquainted first with the case of the Bible and religion. As Rehoboam consulted the old men first, so we all are taught about God and about his Son Jesus Christ and about the way of salvation. It is only after we have rejected that, that we turn to the world and its thought. And alas, men may still do that! How constantly is the story of Rehoboam being repeated! Why is that? Why is it that men reject the very things they say they desire most of all when the Bible offers it to them? Why is it that this particular way is still rejected and men seem to prefer any and every other way? As we consider together the case of this man Rehoboam I think the reason will become abundantly plain and clear. Our method divides itself into two main questions:

1.   *The first is, Why did Rehoboam reject the advice of the old men and choose that of the young men?* Actually, of course, the answer can be put in one word and that is *prejudice*. He accepted the advice of the young men because it tallied with his own ideas and confirmed his own thoughts. At first glance he appears as if he is an open-minded and wise young man. He states the case to the old men as if with the aid of their judicial minds he is prepared to consider and to weigh the facts on both sides and the evidence in favour of both views. And he even seems to be so wise that he consults the old men first. Yet the very narrative itself makes such a view of the man utterly untenable. The words 'he forsook the counsel the old men gave him' (*1 Chron.* 10:8) suggest that, and the rough way in which he speaks to Jeroboam and the people more than confirms it. Rehoboam regards the advice of the old men with contempt and he hastily and gladly accepts the other because it gives perfect expression to what he himself had felt and had thought. He does not really consider the situation and completely apply his mind to it. He is governed by his feelings, his desire, his ambition – in a word by his prejudice. When I shall mention the evidence on the other side I think that will become abundantly plain and clear. But even before I do so, is it not obvious? The very brusqueness of his manner, his hastiness and his arrogance reveal not a careful thinker and honest seeker but a man governed by prejudice and pre-conceived ideas and intentions. He did not really consider the advice of the old men. He just disliked it and dismissed it. As for the proposal of the young men he liked it and acted upon it.

Shall we examine ourselves honestly in the light of this? Those who are outside the church and religion truly would have us believe that they are there as the result of honest thought and consideration of the two sides. They would have us believe that they have con-sidered the case of religion and of Christianity honestly and dispassionately, and that it is only after seeing its fallacy and its error that they have given it up and have espoused the other view and belief. On the surface they appear to be as wise and judicially minded as Rehoboam seems to be before we examine him closely.

But is that really true? If you are not a Christian, my friend, let me address to you the following questions – Why are you not a Christian? Can you give me any good reason for your position and your attitude? Do you really *know* the case for Christianity? Have you really considered it and tried it? Have you any real argument against it? Is your case based upon anything besides and beyond certain loose, general statements about church members being hypocrites or what you say you have seen and know about certain people who claim to be Christians? I ask these questions not only because of my knowledge of other people and what they say and which I hear them saying so frequently, but also because of my knowledge of myself and the deceitfulness of the human heart. Men talk glibly about 'science' having proved this or that, and modern knowledge having demonstrated something else, but if questioned closely they reveal that they really have no knowledge of facts but are just repeating general phrases. Can you honestly say that you are not prejudiced against religion? If you can, let me remind you that it should mean that you never speak contemptuously of it or of any of its followers, that you are ready to listen to its case fairly and patiently, that you are as equally prepared to acknowledge its triumphs and its successes as you are ready to laugh and scorn its apparent failures. Can you say that? Alas, is it not far too evidently the case that men dismiss and condemn and forsake religion without ever really listening to it and merely on the basis of their prejudice?

But that does not really answer the question, for it raises another question. Why is there such a prejudice? How do we explain the existence of this prejudice? Let us return to Rehoboam. He accepted the advice of the young men only because it agreed with his prejudice. Again the answer can be given in one word – *pride*. Am I unfair to him? Look at the facts, study his personality, especially in the light of the words 'And the king answered them roughly' (*2 Chron.* 10:13). Why is he so annoyed and so rude? Why does he dismiss the old men's advice with such contempt? The answer is that he felt that it was insulting. But why should he feel that? For the proposition which is made by Jeroboam and his followers and which is commended by the old men seems to be the very essence of justice and fairness. And it was. Why is Rehoboam annoyed then? There can be only one answer. It is pride. Pride is always ready to see insults and to take umbrage and it is not difficult to see how Rehoboam saw an insult in the proposal. His mind, I suggest, worked along the following two lines:

First he saw that to accept this proposal would involve a confession and an admission that the position as it was at the moment, and as he had inherited it from his father, was wrong. They asked that he should 'ease somewhat the grievous servitude' and 'the heavy yoke' that his father had placed upon them. To do so meant to Rehoboam an admission that these people were right, which in turn would mean that his father had been wrong and that he also would be wrong if he did not do so. And that was something he was not prepared to do. Had the request of these people been something purely positive which did not imply any acknowledgement of something that was wrong, if their request could not by any stretch of a proud imagination be interpreted as suggesting anything wrong in Rehoboam, then probably he would have granted it. But such was not the case. This request could not be granted without confessing and admitting that these people were right and he, therefore, wrong.

The other way in which this proposal touched and hurt his pride was that it cut across everything that he held dear with respect to the office and function of a king. He desired the allegiance and the service of this people, but in his way and not in their way. No, he would not stoop to have it at their terms and at their price though they were perfectly fair. Who was he to compromise with people like that! That way might appeal to a weakling or to a spineless nonentity but certainly not to anyone who had even a vestige of virility and manliness. The idea of a king listening to a proposal from the people, the idea of having their allegiance on terms, the idea of gaining his desired object not as the result of something he had done but rather as the result of conforming to what someone else had suggested; above all, the idea of gaining what he desired at the expense of admitting and confirming that there was something wrong in himself and his system – it was unthinkable, insulting! No one could possibly commend and advocate such a way except these miserable old weaklings who were probably entering the state of second childhood if they were not actually already in it. No, he would rather not have the people at all than have them on such terms. But he would have them! He would fight for them. He would win them for himself without any loss of honour or of dignity.

It is clear that the pride of Rehoboam was touched in both these ways and along these lines and because of that he rejected the first advice and accepted the second. Prejudice is always ultimately to be traced to pride and the prejudice against religion today is to be explained in precisely that way. What is it that men object to in religion? Why do they refuse the gospel which offers to give them life, joy, happiness and knowledge of the truth? Why is it treated with such contempt, why is it ridiculed, why is it regarded as something laughable and a fit subject for mirth and ribaldry that one should still believe and accept the gospel and its offer of life and of salvation? The facts which have emerged in our analysis of Rehoboam still provide the answer.

What men find intolerable and insulting in the gospel is that it demands repentance and admission of wrong and of sin at the very outset. The gospel touches our pride by telling us that we are not all right as we are and by demanding and insisting upon our acknowledgement of that. There is nothing that the natural man so hates and detests as the biblical view of sin. We are all prepared to admit that we might be better but we are not prepared to grant that we are bad – 'born in sin and shapen in iniquity' (*Psa.* 51:5). We are all prepared to advance and to go forward but we hate a gospel which says 'Ye must be born again' (*John* 3:7) because we are so hopeless and so lost. We do not dislike a gospel that talks of love and of forgiveness but we dislike a gospel of grace because that tells us that we are utterly undeserving of that love and mercy. We are prepared to listen to a teaching that proposes to start from the basis of what we already have but when we are told by the gospel that what we have is useless, and that we need to be created anew, we become as annoyed as the Pharisees were by the teaching of Jesus Christ himself. The trouble about the gospel is that it regards us all as condemned helpless sinners, that it says, 'There is none righteous, no, not one . . . all have sinned, and come short of the glory of God' (*Rom.* 3:10, 23). The Pharisees rejected and ultimately crucified Christ because he convinced them of sin; men reject him and his gospel today for precisely the same reason and accept the opposite teaching because it praises them and flatters them.

But, further, the gospel not only tells us that we are wrong as we are but also announces that by it alone and only can we ever be put right. It demands our acceptance of that. But why does that annoy and offend? For the simple reason that it tells us something which we cannot do in and of ourselves. And there comes the rub. We have such faith in ourselves and in our powers. We desire to save ourselves and believe that we can do it. We put our trust in what we can do, in the world and its knowledge, in science and its achievements. We claim that we can find God, that we can create a new world and a new society and a new order. We ourselves can find happiness and joy and truth. To be told that we cannot and that we must become as little children if we desire to enter the kingdom of heaven is insulting; to believe that we can only see God and enter heaven by trusting ourselves helplessly to another, even though he be the Son of God, appears to be utter weakness and entirely unworthy of us. And to believe that he actually died our death, paid our penalty and bore our punishment – why, we feel the idea might be all right for the brainless and sentimentalists, all right for illiterate barbarians, but certainly insulting and almost immoral to the enlightened men and women of twentieth-century Britain. It is unthinkable, unworthy of our thought – it must just be dismissed with contempt and abhorrence and detestation.

We are prepared to listen to a teaching that will tell us how to save ourselves and help us to do so; we feel insulted by a gospel that tells us that we cannot save ourselves, but that God in Christ offers to do so. It is ultimately because man believes in himself and in his own powers that he rejects the gospel. It is his pride that creates the prejudices that lead to his rejection out of hand of what offers him his own greatest and everlasting good.

There we see why Rehoboam rejected the advice of the old men and chose that of the young men. As you admit it to be true of him, cannot you see that it is also true of you if you are not a Christian? Oh! face it honestly and without prejudice. See it, hate it and forsake it!

2.   But let me encourage you to do so by putting the other side to you, let me appeal to you to do so by showing you why Rehoboam ought to have done the exact opposite to what he did. *Let us consider why he should have listened to the advice of the old men.* The reasons are quite clear, if we but apply our minds to the

situation instead of judging blindly in terms of prejudice and passion.

Surely the age of Rehoboam's first advisers, with their knowledge and experience, should have been enough to influence him, in and of itself. I would not be understood as saying that age is always right, for history shows fairly clearly that most reforms and revivals have taken place through the instrumentality of young men. Slavishly to listen to that which is said merely because it is old is madness. Nothing can be so deadening and soul-destroying in its influence as traditionalism. But at the same time there is nothing which is quite as blind and so utterly foolish and unintelligent as to ignore the past entirely and to jettison everything that has been handed on by tradition simply because it comes on to us from the past. That a thing has been believed for centuries does not prove that it is true, but it certainly ought to cause us to think seriously and ponder long before we lightly throw it overboard. To Rehoboam the age of these men and their wisdom and knowledge and experience and understanding was nothing. Indeed it told against them. They belonged to a past age, they were behind the times, their age alone proved that they were wrong and that they must be wrong.

I need not point out that that is precisely the cause of most of the modern attitude towards religion. The idea is that it belongs to the dark past and that by now the world has outgrown it. The argument more or less is that religion must be wrong simply because it has been in the world for so long. We regard ourselves as being so entirely different from and so infinitely superior to all who have gone before us that for us to believe anything which they believed must of necessity be wrong. So we reject it. Now this is something which we can show to be wrong as a principle and not only in the matter of religion. A man who refuses advice based upon knowledge and experience simply because it is old is just a fool and will certainly fail in any business or profession or whatever else he does. Of course if he can prove that all past knowledge and experience is irrelevant for his particular case or problem, because it was never concerned with them, we grant that he may be right. Or again, if he can prove that the old are untrustworthy he is fully justified in not accepting and acting upon what they say. We are not very interested, for example, in what past centuries may have had to say about flying or telecommunications or various other subjects clearly connected with scientific knowledge and its advance. Neither are we interested in the opinions of people who are known to be incompetent.

But is such the case with respect to the whole question of religion? Have the problems of life and living, the questions of happiness and joy, morality and purity, truth and knowledge of God changed? Men through the ages have been concerned about precisely the same things as you, your problems were theirs, your desires were also theirs. To reject out of hand, therefore, evidence from the past on these matters simply because it is from the past is sheer fool-hardiness and ignorance and utterly unscientific. And what of its witness? Whose are the voices that speak to us from the past and whisper to us from the records of antiquity? Look at them! Abel, Abraham, Jacob, Moses, David, the prophets, the apostles, Augustine, Luther, and in the centre Jesus of Nazareth, the Son of God! Does all this mean nothing to you? Can you ignore such testimony? Can you lightly reject an offer that has faced mankind steadily and unchangeably throughout the centuries, the acceptance of which has made the noblest souls the world has ever seen and which is commended by One who towers above all mankind and upon whom all history converges? Is all this nothing and is it to be forsaken for the opinions of certain modern writers and teachers whose views and theories change about from day to day and whose lives are as changeable as their views? The man who thinks that he can live happily, regarding everything that is most glorious and uplifting in the whole story of the past as being based upon utter error and fallacy, surely needs to reconsider his whole position and that seriously. And that is precisely the position of all who reject the gospel of Jesus Christ. The Christian tradition alone, the mere continuance of the church should save a man from such an act of utter folly as was committed by Rehoboam and is committed by all who act in a like manner still.

But Rehoboam should have hearkened unto the old men also because of the essential rightness and justice of what they commended. If ever there was a fine and a reasonable proposal it was this. It was essentially right and fair and just and true. Whether recommended by old or by young, in and of itself it should have commended itself to the king. The truth is greater than its advocator and their business is but to point and to lead men to the truth. What is amazing is that Rehoboam should have felt the need of consulting anyone at all. The case was perfectly clear, the wrongs and injustices under which these people suffered should have been renounced. There was no excuse for them. The demand of the people was absolutely right and just and nothing so condemns Rehoboam as his failure to see this and his determination to do the exact opposite.

Precisely the same is true of the gospel and its way of salvation. Look at it and consider it again, not in terms of what you like and what you feel, but in terms of truth and history and justice. Is the gospel unjust when it condemns our sin? Is there anything wrong in exposing evil and removing masks and pretence and make belief? Is it a crime to state the truth about life and to expose its ills? Is it unfair, is it unjust? Does the gospel really wrong you when it tells you the truth about yourself, when it exposes all the hidden things of your heart and all the inmost recesses of your soul? Do you really claim that your life is what it ought to be? Are you perfectly content with it? Would you be ready and prepared for all your thoughts, desires and misgivings to be printed in a book or to be flashed upon a screen? Are you not aware of the existence within yourself of the foul and the ugly and the cruel? Must you not confess that you are not really what you appear to be and what you try to impress people as being? Is not the Bible stating the literal truth when it says that the human heart is desperately wicked and deceitful? Was not Charles Wesley describing you as well as himself when he said 'Foul and full of sin I am'? Is there not something radically wrong even in your best and highest? Is not the case of the Bible perfectly fair and just when it says these things? Why object to it then and why resent it and become annoyed? Why not rather thank God for an honest book which tells you the truth about yourself instead of something which tries to please you and to flatter you by telling you something which you yourself in your own heart of hearts know to be wrong?

And is there anything wrong or unjust or unfair in the demand that comes to us to humble and abase ourselves and repent in sackcloth and ashes before a Being who is a Holy Absolute Eternal God. To be asked to do so before man would be unjust but the Bible asks you to face God! Is it insulting to tell you that you can never by your own efforts arrive at and attain unto such a Being who dwells in eternal light? Is it degrading and dishonouring and insulting to you to tell you that you must accept his way of salvation simply because he asks you, whether you can understand it and grasp it with your mind or not? And where is the insult in being told that all your efforts and striving will never make you fit to stand in his presence and that you must be clothed with the righteousness of his Son, his spotless Lamb, who was made an offering for your sin? And is the kind of life that he maps out for you one that suggests weakness and flabbiness and lack of virility and manliness? Look again at the Sermon on the Mount and read once more the lives of the saints. What have you really to say against the gospel and its way? It is the very truth of God himself – the one and only revelation of him.

Yes, Rehoboam should have listened to the old men because they were old and especially because of the essential rightness and justice of what they commended. But also, and as a further inducement and encouragement, he should have accepted it because it promised to give him, and really guaranteed to give him, the very thing he most desired. 'If thou be kind to this people, and please them, and speak good words to them, they will be thy servants for ever' (*2 Chron.* 10:7). That was the very thing he desired. He refused this way and felt that he had a better way of his own. But you remember the result. His rejection of the right and true way led to utter and complete failure. Oh! the tragedy. And how often is it taught and pictured in the Bible. Indeed it is its whole message from beginning to end. If man could save himself why should the Son of God ever have come? But man cannot save himself. Try as he will, he fails. He cannot find happiness and peace and joy. He cannot find truth. He cannot arrive at a knowledge of God by his own effort and striving. Look at the modern world – in spite of all its learning and knowledge and wealth and power. No, it never has been done and it never can be done. There is but one way of life which is life indeed, there is but one way to happiness and joy, there is but one way to proceed in life, there is but one way to know God as your Father, there is but one way to triumphant dying and to heaven, it is through the One who said, 'I am the way, the truth and the life' (*John* 14:6) – Jesus of Nazareth, the Son of

God. In him you get not merely what you desire, but how much more:

Thou O Christ! art all I want:
More than all in Thee I find:

Go back again and ask the saints. They will all tell you that at one time they trusted to themselves and their own powers, but they never found peace or rest or joy or the knowledge of God. The moderns write a lot about these things and try to understand the infinities. But have they found them? Have you found them? Recognise tonight that there is but one way. Acknowledge and confess your sins, humble yourself before God, accept his way of salvation in Jesus Christ and cast yourself upon him and you will know peace and joy, power and freedom in your life and a certain assurance that all is well between you and God. Do so now.

13

The One Question[1]

Then Job answered and said,
I know it is so of a truth: but how should man be just with God?
Job 9:1–2

I think it is generally agreed that one of the greatest arts in life, in most realms, is the art of asking questions. Nothing is more vital in any study of any subject whatsoever as the capacity of being able to concentrate and to fix attention upon that which is most important. The ultimate distinction I take it between the good student and the bad student is that the good student can sift between that which is more or less relevant and that which is vital. The art of study, the art of understanding in every realm, is to know how to avoid missing the wood because of the trees – it is, I say, to pick out the significant, the important, the striking and the vital. You think for instance of the whole art of the advocate handling his case, his real art consists in being able to fasten attention upon the most relevant facts and factors; his whole purpose is to call the attention of the jury and the judge to the salient features. The successful advocate is the man who, by a kind of instinct, is able to read his brief and immediately pick out that which is vital and important. Or take the art of the physician. Is it not exactly and precisely the same with him. He discovers multitudes of facts, he may be face to face with great hosts of details, but the essential part of his business is to sift these and to realise which are the significant ones and to follow them, ignoring the others. And is not this true of any subject of which you may choose to think. The good lecturer is the man who emphasises the vital principles. The worst lecturer I have ever had to sit and listen to was a very well-known man who had failed at that point. He was a poor lecturer, though an authority

[1] Westminster Chapel, 21 September 1947.

on his subject, because he gave the same amount of emphasis to comparatively unimportant details as he did to the great central principles. The secret of lecturing is to extract those big central principles which are most vital and to present them in an orderly and in a well-arranged manner. At whatever aspect of life we may look, the first necessity has to do with the art of asking questions. In other words, when you approach the position, if it is a case in law, if it is a patient in the consulting room, if a subject on which you have to lecture and make plain to others, you start by asking what is important here, what is unimportant, what is relevant, and so on; the whole art, I say, is ultimately the art of asking questions.

Now that is exactly the position with regard to the whole question of life and living. One of the most difficult things in this world is to know what questions to ask. There are many questions being asked – men are full of questions and questionings – the real art of life is to know which questions to put, what questions to ask, what material on which to concentrate. This is something which is perhaps unusually difficult at the present time. Life as we are living it at this hour is utterly bewildering. There is no need to prove that contention. The world in a sense has never been more confusing than it is today. Questions are being asked on all sides; we are all reading articles in the newspapers, in books and in journals. The whole world in its present state of turmoil is raising an almost endless number of questions, and nothing is more difficult at this present time as to discriminate and differentiate between the important and the unimportant.

What is it that really matters in life tonight? what is it that really counts? what should come first? – that is the question. What is it that I should start with as I view myself in life tonight, and as I see the world around and about me with all these problems and difficulties and trials? I say the most difficult thing of all is to be able to go right through all these masses of questions and say, *this* is the first thing, this is the thing on which I must concentrate. Never perhaps has it been more difficult to face the true and the ultimate questions than it is at this present moment. The whole business of the preaching of the gospel as I understand it, the whole business of the message of this Book which we call the Bible, is to direct our attention to the first and the most fundamental question. There are those who would have us believe that the business of the church today is to make its pronouncements upon the questions that are being asked by other people. You are familiar with them – questions on economics, questions on the social conditions, questions about war and peace and a thousand and one other things. There are those who would have us believe that the business of the church is to express her point of view upon this great host of questions. Now I want to try to demonstrate that that is a travesty of the whole business of the church and the message of the church. As I see it the first fundamental business of the Bible and of the church is to raise a particular question and to ask the most relevant question. It is to direct the attention of men and women to the things that are tending to be forgotten and submerged in this welter and vortex into which mankind by its sin has turned its world and its life.

We can state this in a slightly different form by putting it like this. The whole tendency of man at the present time is to concentrate his attention upon what we may well describe as the symptoms of his trouble rather than upon the trouble itself. If you read the books and the journals, if you listen to the discussions on the wireless, you will find the great scientists and others are discussing the whole problem of life. They are all raising questions. From the biblical standpoint the difficulty and the trouble with them all is that they are concerned not with the disease itself but with certain manifestations of the disease and certain symptoms. They stop at the symptoms and fail to consider the disease itself. Or to use other language, the danger at the moment is to be over-interested in facts and to forget and ignore the cause. Now the whole contention of the Bible itself and of the gospel is this – that its message is the only agency in the world that can really both speak to us about the disease and explain the cause. It is here and here alone that we are led right back to first principles and made to confront and face those fundamental issues upon which all the remaining problems and difficulties of life ultimately depend and from which they originally issue.

There is nothing, therefore, that is more important or so important as to know exactly and precisely which is the first question to ask. The answer is given in these words that we are considering together this evening, 'how should man be just with God?' Now I need not take time in pointing out to you that this is a question which was asked at the very dawn of history. We are so much the slaves of our own time and generation, we are all so persuaded that there has never been a world like the world of the twentieth century, we are all so accustomed to being told that man has never been as man is today, that we are a separate and unique people, that it comes to us in rather a surprising and startling way to realise that the most important question today is the question that was propounded all these centuries ago by this man called Job at the very dawn of history. What does the question mean? The question can be put in this form: how can a man really present himself to God? how can a man speak to God? how can a man go on to live with God? how can a man find God? how can a man arrive at God? how can a man have fellowship and communion with God? That is the question – what can a man do about himself in his relationship to God?

I put it to you that in the midst of all the questions and problems of this modern life, this is the first and the most vital and the most important question. I therefore say to the modern man with all the things of which he is so well aware that he should brush them all aside for the time being and say, I cannot consider any other question until I have first of all dealt with this and settled it and answered it finally, once and for ever. But of course I cannot make that statement without remembering at once the many objections that men put forward once one makes this assertion. There are those who, when they are told something like this, immediately reply, 'You cannot assert that that is the most important question; surely this is too small a question for you to demand for it that it should come in the first place. Are you not aware of the whole world situation, cannot you see the nations arming for war, issuing their threats one to another, are you not aware of all the trouble and suspicion of the modern world, are you going to tell us that the first question is man in his individual relationship to God? Is your question not too small and too insignificant for you to describe it as the first and the most important?'

Then there are those who would say that it is too selfish a question. 'Fancy in a troubled world like this where there is so much unhappiness, so much suffering and uncertainty, when the whole destinies of man are hanging in the balance, fancy directing our attention to this question of your own personal salvation, your own destiny beyond death and the grave and in eternity. Why', they say, 'that old gospel of yours is so self-centred, it is so unutterably selfish, surely this is no time for man to be thinking about himself – that is the cause of so much trouble in life. Should not you Christian ministers be dealing with the great questions of the moment, the political question, the international question, the economic question, should we not as citizens be concerned about these things and not merely about man and his own soul and salvation? It is unutterably selfish!' This is another very common objection.

Then there are those who dislike and dismiss it because they believe that the most urgent problem at the moment is not man in his relationship to God but man in his relationship to man. 'Look at it', they say, 'in the labour realm, in the realm of industry and commerce, look at it between nation and nation, between husband and wife and family, look at it in relationship to the law; surely the most urgent problem is not man in his relationship to God but man in his relationship to man. You are surely not going to tell us we must be looking at ourselves and examining ourselves and saying, "How can I save my own soul?" when there is this problem of man and mankind?' Now a great deal is being written on this subject. One of the favourite words tonight is the word 'community' or 'society' – we are told we must consider man in society, man in the communal setting, and that this and not religion needs first attention.

And then there are those who ask us seriously whether we are right in asking man to consider his own little soul and his relationship to God when we are in a world surrounded by such immense issues as atomic power. 'We are thinking', they claim, 'in terms of the stars and this mighty universe, we are thinking in terms of space and infinity and you narrow it all down to this question of man and his soul. How amusing to say that that is the first and the most fundamental and the most vital question!'

What do we say in reply to these people? Let me simply give you some of the answers that are given by the Bible itself to those who object to concentrating first on the question, 'how should man be just with God?' Here is one good and sufficient answer to this objection: *this is the only question that must inevitably be faced at some time or another.* I accept that there are these many problems and troubles in the world tonight and it is no part of the preacher of the gospel to say that they are unimportant. These questions have their importance, but I am here to say that there is only one question which every man and woman must inevitably face and it is this question propounded by Job. I may never have to face the reality of atomic power; it is in the world but it may never become an acute problem to me. It is among the dangers which may or may not come – dangers which do not of necessity affect every individual person, but here is a problem that all must face sooner or later. Man is set in this world, he has not chosen to be here, he finds himself here; and we pass through this world, we have no control over it in an ultimate sense, our times are in the hands of God and whether we like it or not, and whether we believe it or not, the fact of the matter is that we shall go out of this world, we go on to another world and there stands first and foremost this old question of Job – 'GOD' and my relationship to him. You may remember some of the Psalmists who have written finely and dramatically on this theme. Some of them describe man as trying to avoid God and to get away from him but they always come back to this, that God is inescapable. You recall the words of 'The Hound of Heaven' – 'I fled Him down the nights and down the days' – man tries to avoid this problem but the message of the Book is that though you travel up to the heights and down to the depths, to the East and to the West, to the North and to the South, you will come back one day and there will be God and yourself and you will realise that Job put the first question when he said 'How shall a man be just with God?' I ask you, my friend, am I not right, therefore, in putting this first and in the most prominent place?

If this question is absolutely certain and if I cannot avoid it, I must face it and face it first. But then there is a second principle which must be added and which is still more inevitable. Not only must I of necessity face this question some day, *I never know when I may have to face it* and that makes it surely still more urgent.

Let me give you this in the form of an illustration. I have referred to this whole question of the atomic power and of the possibilities and the dangers if you like of future world conflicts and conflagrations which may result. Yes, but there may be many of us here tonight who will never have to face that problem at all. You may say there may be a terrible war in ten or fifteen years, you may say then these atomic bombs may be used, but you may not be here in ten or fifteen years' time. I say that all these questions are contingent

– they are not certain, but here is a question that is certain. I never know when I may have to face it. Surely every man who has any wisdom must start with this question. If I knew for certain that I was going to live for another twenty or thirty years, I might be entitled to relegate this to a later date, but I never know and no one else knows. In the midst of life we are in death – we are here today and gone tomorrow. 'What is your life?' Scripture asks us. Job is using the same language in this very chapter. The uncertainty of life! Now surely because life is so uncertain, and because I may have to face this question at any moment, I must put it in the first place and in the first position. It is the most vital question because of the uncertainty of this matter.

But let me give you a final reason for considering it. 'How should man be just with God?' is the first and most vital and most urgent question *because of what depends upon it*. Here is the greatest and the ultimate thing. Consider how much depends upon the right answer to that question. Consider how much depends even in this present world here and now upon the right answer to that question. It is not for me to forecast the future, but we do know certain things are bound to happen, illness, old age, perhaps disappointment, perhaps industrial depression causing semi-starvation, perhaps war, some of these things may happen to us and therefore one of the questions a man asks himself in life must be this – 'How can I prepare myself for these possibilities and for these eventualities?', and here I say is the answer which is found in the Bible and confirmed by the experience of the saints everywhere. It is the man who has answered Job's question who is best able to face the vicissitudes of life. Look at a man like the Apostle Paul, for instance, surrounded by troubles and trials and tribulations and yet you remember how he speaks – 'this light affliction which is but for a moment worketh for us a far more exceeding weight of glory' – or listen to him again as he speaks in the midst of trouble – 'I am persuaded that neither death, nor life, nor angels, nor principalities, nor powers, nor any other creature, shall be able to separate us from the love of God which is in Christ Jesus our Lord.' Here is a man who is put in a world in which there is so much against him but, whatever happens to him, his serenity, his peace, his joy remains. Why? because he knows the answer to Job's question. Now if some or any of these things are the things that are going to happen to us, how am I to face them? Surely the very world around and about us is proclaiming loudly that the only way to answer that question is first to answer this question of Job. How does a man of today who does not believe in the gospel, how does he stand up to illness, how does he stand up to sorrow and bereavement, how does he stand up to financial loss, or anything that upsets his life? Read your newspapers and the accounts of men and women. Life without God does not work, it is not a success even here and now. While we are in this life and in this world the real way to live is to answer the question of Job. But when you consider what depends upon this question in eternity, why then I think you see still more clearly how much depends upon the question. If this Book which we call the Bible is right, and if its message is true, this is the fact, man's whole and eternal destiny is determined and decided by his answer to the question propounded by Job. How shall a man be just with God? I have to face him, I shall be judged by him and the whole of my everlasting destiny will depend upon my capacity or my incapacity to present myself before God in such a way and manner that God will say of me, 'Well done thou good and faithful servant, enter thou into the joy of thy Lord'. Or if I fail I am confronted by the other statement, 'Depart from me'. Can there be any question that is more urgent than this? Is there any single question that should come before this? Life depends upon it. Death, eternity, everlasting existence depends upon it. I plead, therefore, in the name of God and upon the authority of this Word and message, dismiss every other question, forget every other problem and face this question – how shall a man be just with God? Are you ready to meet God, have you an answer to this question, have you something to say to him when in a moment, in a flash, you may be placed in his holy presence? This is the first and the most fundamental question.

Let me say a word on the false answers which have frequently been given to the question and the false answers that are still being given. Some say, 'Well, I agree with you, that is the great question. "How should a man be just with God?" – Let him live a good life, let him do his best, let him do as much good as he can, let him pray, let him try to be benevolent, and let him do a good turn to someone else.' Others add, 'That is not enough, we must go further. Let a man become religious, let him be attached to a religious society, and belong to a church.' Such a person, they feel sure, is better than the vast majority of people, he is making an effort and trying to do something about his position before God.

Are not these the answers that are being given? Raise Job's question in conversation with any man you like at the present time and I think you will find these are the answers that are given. Put the question: 'When you come to die and go on into eternity and face God, what will you be relying on, what are you going to say to God as he looks at you and asks you what have you made of your life, what have you done with that soul, how are you going to justify yourself before God?' We know the answers you will be given – 'I have not done anybody any harm, I have always tried to be as good as I can, I have indeed tried to help others, I have had my standard which I have tried to live up to and I feel I am better than many other people.'

All these answers are false answers and that is in a sense the great message of this Book. Have you noticed how Job speaks, he tells us that all these answers are utterly wrong and false. Listen to what he says in the twentieth verse, 'If I justify myself, my own mouth shall condemn me'. Does not our own conscience condemn us? When I put up my theoretical and intellectual arguments a voice within me condemns me. Every man alive and breathing has this inward monitor and knows his own heart is condemning him and telling him he is not true. No man can finally satisfy himself, still less can he satisfy God. When a man is perfectly honest with himself, he knows nothing about him is good enough. It is one thing to argue and try to gain your point in debate rather cleverly, but when a man is left to himself, and when a man looks at himself and examines himself, he knows he is unworthy and inadequate. My own mouth shall condemn me if I try to claim in the presence of God that I am perfect.

But there is something infinitely more important, and here is the final difficulty. 'For he is not a man, as I am, that I should answer him, and we should come together in judgment' (*Job* 9:32). And that is where the whole tragic failure of our position becomes revealed. It is not a question of being a little bit better than somebody else. The standard of God is not a standard of just doing a certain amount of good, being religious, being benevolent – the standard of God is an eternal standard. The problem confronting man is how to dwell with God, how to speak with God – that is

Job's problem. Where is he? 'Oh that I knew where I might find him! that I might come even to his seat!' (*Job* 23:3) – I cannot get at him, he is so far removed from me. He is so great in majesty and dominion and power and I am so weak. And in addition to the might and power and majesty of God, I must face the holiness of God. 'God is light, and in him is no darkness at all' (*1 John* 1:5). There can be no harmony between light and darkness; no compromise between the true and the false – there is no medium between those opposites. But God is thus described in the Word – 'It is a fearful thing to fall into the hands of the living God' (*Heb.* 10:31). Let us approach him with reverence and godly fear, 'For our God is a consuming fire' (*Heb.* 12:29).

I think increasingly that the whole trouble not only in the world but in the church at the present time is that our whole idea of God is so tragically inadequate. We forget the character of God, the holiness of God, the nature of God. If only we realised the nature of God we would put our hands upon our mouths and we would be afraid to speak – the holiness of the character of God! 'If I wash myself with snow water', says Job, 'and make my hands never so clean' (*Job* 9:30), it is not good enough; if I spend the rest of my life trying to purge and purify myself, that cannot get rid of the sin. God sees into the very mind and the thought and the imagination. He knows the desires that are never given expression. He tells us a look is as bad as an act. God sees into the very depths. It is not mere actions, it is our nature, it is our sinful condition.

And thus all these answers that men put forward from time to time in an attempt to answer the question of Job are utterly false and utterly inadequate. There is only one answer to this question, it is the answer that I am privileged to give you tonight in the name of Jesus Christ. 'How shall a man be just with God?' What hope have I of standing before that searching light? Think of an X-ray multiplied by infinity and that is the eye of God. How can a man stand before that – what hope have I to stand in his presence? There is only one answer to this question, it is the answer of this Book. Here Job cried out for a 'daysman that might lay his hand upon us both' (*Job* 9:33). Oh that there was somebody who would take the matter up, that would bridge the gulf! Oh that I had a robe to put on which would enable me to stand before God and he would see nothing but the robe and not the vileness and the foulness within. Thank God there is, and this is the very central message of this glorious gospel. God has sent his only begotten Son into this world, Jesus of Nazareth. He came because man could never justify himself in the presence of God. He has done something to justify man – he has taken upon himself your guilt and mine, your failure and mine. He has come into this problem, he has entered into the vortex with us, he has identified himself with it, he has taken our sin upon himself and God has dealt with our sin in him. 'For he hath made him to be sin for us, who knew no sin; that we might be made the righteousness of God in him' (*2 Cor.* 5:21). Before I can face God I must have a nature like God's nature. Before I can stand in the presence of God I must get rid of this foulness, this guilt of sin and all that is true of sin, and there is only one way – Christ clothes me with his own righteousness, he even promises to take hold of me by the hand and to present me faultless before the presence of the glory of God with exceeding joy. 'How shall a man be just with God?' 'The just shall live by faith' (*Rom.* 1:17). The righteousness of God in Christ is given to every believer (*Rom.* 5:15–17). This is God's way and it is of necessity the only way.

May I leave you therefore with the question. 'How shall a man be just with God?' How are you going to be just with God? Let me put it more urgently. If you had to stand before him tonight what would you say to him? Do you still believe you could point to your record and say, 'Not so bad, isn't that good enough?' Do you still feel you can trust to your own efforts and righteousness? There is only one plea, make certain that you can make it – do so by turning to the Son of God and saying:

> *Just as I am without one plea*
> *But that Thy blood was shed for me.*

The only thing that will avail in the presence of God is that you can look at him and say 'Jesus my Saviour, my Lord and my God'.

14
The Wrong Questions

Therefore they say unto God, Depart from us; for we desire not the knowledge of thy ways. What is the Almighty, that we should serve him? and what profit should we have, if we pray unto him?

Job 21:14–15

There can be no doubt that the main explanation of the ignorance and neglect of the Bible which characterises the present time is the fact that people in general no longer believe in its divine inspiration in a unique sense. While men still regarded it as 'the Word of God', written by men who had been 'moved by the Holy Ghost', they obviously believed that they should credit its teaching. But as the idea gained currency that the ancient view of the Bible is false and that it was only the result of human composition – the account of the religious ideas and pilgrimages of a particular people – men began to say that though it was remarkably interesting it was no longer vital, and eventually they ceased to read it. By regarding it as the expression of a phase in the history of the development of mankind which has long since passed, it was felt that these documents only remained interesting for those concerned with religious matters, history and the science of anthropology. The Bible could no longer be of general interest for the present age which has advanced so much and which therefore needs correspondingly advanced ideas. In other words, men argued that when you have dispensed (as they thought!) with the theory of the plenary inspiration of the Scriptures, then their antiquity alone does away with their value in any real sense.

Now that is a conclusion with which I find myself in utter and complete disagreement. Were I not to believe that this is the very Word of God I should still say that it is the most important book on earth and the one above all others which all men should read. And my reason for that would be its very age and antiquity. Drunk with the theory of progress and development, men today assume that an old book is a useless book. But were they to read these old books carefully they would have to come to the same conclusions as the author of one of the books in the old Book, namely, that 'there is nothing new under the sun' (*Eccl.* 1:9). And amongst the endless number of things which they had always thought to be brand new, but which they would discover to be very old, there are two of very special importance of which we are reminded in my text.

The first is that irreligion and godlessness are not new. Now I would have you remember that it is generally agreed and admitted that the book of Job is probably the oldest book in the Bible. The Bible itself is the oldest book extant and in its collection the oldest is the book of Job. And here in this book (as we are shown in our text where Job states and refutes the argument of the ungodly) we are reminded of the existence at that time of the ungodly and the irreligious. That one fact alone is more than enough to answer and to demolish the assumption on which the average person of today rejects the gospel of Jesus Christ and the godly and religious way of living. I say 'assumption' deliberately because there is nothing which is quite so clear as the fact that the vast majority do not think about that question at all. They just dismiss it, and they dismiss it because they take for granted that it is wrong simply because it is old. Their view is that people in the past were ignorant and that their religion was the result of that ignorance. Religion belongs to that primitive stage. We are advanced. You are all perfectly familiar with the talk which ends by saying 'No-one believes that sort of thing now'. The assumption is that in the past everyone believed it and that had they lived in those times they would have believed it also, but living as they do in enlightened times, with all the discoveries of science and the advance of knowledge, they have seen through it and they have given it up. They think it is purely a question of time, merely a matter of the passing of the centuries and the advance of mankind. How fortunate we are that we happen to live in the twentieth century and not in the past! And how sorry we feel for those who have gone before. Is that not the assumption?

But irreligion is almost as old as religion. People said in the time of Job exactly what they say today. To say that you do not believe in God and religion and to turn away from him, far from being new, modern, up-to-date and the special hallmark of the enlightenment of the twentieth century, is simply to show that you conform absolutely to something that has always been true of mankind. Every age, this old book tells us, likes to think of itself as being superior to all that has gone before it and likes to express that superiority by turning against God and fondly imagining that it is the very first to do so!

We are also shown here that irreligion is not only not new but that it always *expresses* itself in precisely the same way and always makes the same claims. In other words, in that main assumption about the historical element in this question of religion there are two other assumptions which are constant. The first is that intellect and thought are always on the side of irreligion or that religion lives and thrives solely on ignorance. '*Therefore* they say unto God', says Job. What they say is claimed to be the conclusion of a logical process, the result of an intelligent examination and investigation. 'Therefore', in view of what they have considered, they came to that conclusion! These people of Job's time claimed that as the result of their thought they had seen through religion. The claim is still made in precisely the same terms. Men still say that they were brought up to believe in religion and that as long as they just accepted it uncritically they did believe in it, but that the moment they began to think things out for themselves, to read and to face the facts, they saw that it was all wrong and that there was nothing in it. And thus they produce their proofs which, strangely enough, as I am going to show you, are generally expressed in the form of questions! Intellect and religion are regarded by the majority today as being hopeless incompatibles. Many of Job's contemporaries took precisely the same view.

The other subsidiary assumption is that when a man turns away from God and religion he emancipates himself and truly enters into his own for the first time. Those who are still religious are regarded as being held in the thraldom and tyranny of an ignorance and superstition which prevents the true development and unfolding of one's real nature. To be a man worthy of the name one must shake off such shackles and cry out 'What is the Almighty that we should serve him?' Mankind has felt from the beginning that Satan was right when he suggested that God desired to keep us down and to rob us of our rights.

For these two reasons, then, men turn away from God today as they have done throughout the ages and they do so by asking the sort of questions of which these in my text are quite typical. We have seen already that the general assumption on which this attitude is based is one which is utterly false. What of the two subsidiary assumptions? We can only answer the questions when we have considered and analysed the statement which these people make. They tell us that having thought and reasoned they have decided to turn away from God and to reject him, and that in so doing they are emancipating themselves. They pass their verdict upon God. 'Who is he?' they ask, 'that we should serve him? and what profit should we have, if we pray unto him?' They think that their case is unanswerable. What have we to say to it? What is our reply to their questions? We shall divide it into two sections.

1. *First of all we shall consider the background of the questions, the assumptions on which they are based, and then we shall give a direct reply to them.* And as we consider the background we are forced to the conclusion that these statements about God do not in any way add to our knowledge of him but they tell us a great deal about the persons who made them. Let me prove that to you.

With regard to the claim of intellect and understanding, let me first assert quite bluntly that there is nothing which is quite so obvious about irreligion as its superficial thinking, its utter and complete failure to think clearly and straightly. This is a large subject which might be considered along many different lines. Obviously we have no time to do so in the space of one sermon and all I am proposing to do is to consider this as it is demonstrated in the particular context of this twenty-first chapter of Job. For here we have a very typical and thoroughly representative example of the type of argument that is used. It is an argument about God which is based solely on what men observe round about them. The people of Job's day put it thus. They observed that certain people were godly and that others were not. They observed further that whereas the godly often suffered a great deal, the ungodly seemed to flourish and to prosper and to have a thoroughly 'good time' in life. On the basis of their observations they drew the following conclusions:

That if there is a God he must be helpless, *or*

That if he is not helpless he is at any rate unjust.

On the basis of these two deductions they came to the final conclusion that God can be ignored altogether. People who ignore him 'get on' and do well. What, therefore, is the point of worshipping him and obeying him. 'What will it profit us if we pray unto him?' Here were the arguments of the irreligious of Job's day. Have they not a peculiarly modern note about them? What are the current arguments brought by people today against religion? Why is it that the masses have turned away from it and live the life they do? On what grounds is God denied and ignored and dismissed by so many? The arguments are still the same. Here are some of them. 'If there is a God and if he is a God of love why did he allow the Great War?' 'If there is a God why do the ungodly succeed and flourish and the godly so frequently suffer?' 'If there is a God why are there incidents such as floods and disasters, and why does he allow good people so often to die when they are young and the evil to live to old age?' And, still the same conclusion is drawn that it does not matter whether one believes in God or not, that it does not seem to affect life in any way, and that therefore the whole religious view of life is probably utterly and entirely wrong. Why worry to be religious any further? Why strain to live the good life and obey God when those who do not do so seem to be perfectly happy and contented and eminently successful?

These are some of the reasons which account for the present irreligion. By means of such statements men and women think that they dispose of God and religion. And they claim that they have proved their case. When they ask the question, 'If there is a God why this and that?', it is just another way of saying that there is no God. The argument seems complete, there is no need to discuss it; and people give expression to this point of view as though the matter was finally settled.

Now there is nothing about all this which is quite as pathetic as the fact that it displays, above all else, superficial thinking. Men cannot see that their whole argument is based upon a false assumption, namely that God and his ways must of necessity be intelligible to them and conform to their ideas. In other words, they start by stating what God ought to do. And then they conclude that because he does not do what they think he should, there is no God, or else that he is without power and that, in any case, it does not matter whether he is obeyed or not because he cannot affect our lives either way. It never occurs to them that God in his infinite wisdom may allow various things which we are not able to fathom. They ignore words of one of the Old Testament prophets which remind us that God 'hides himself'!

'Why does he do that?' they ask. I cannot tell you and for the time being I am not concerned to attempt to do so, because what I desire to prove is the utter fallacy of arguing from the mere silence and non-interference of God either to his impotence or to his non-existence. What would you say of the intelligence of a man who argues that there is no sun simply because he cannot see it because of the clouds? Or the intelligence of a person who mistakes patience for impotence and wisdom for weakness? But such is the mentality of all who so lightly turn away from God today. They suppose God must do certain things and behave in a certain way. And just because he does not they draw their sweeping conclusions. But who said that God should behave like that? Why should not God in his infinite wisdom permit things which we cannot understand? Surely the wisest assumption when you come to consider a person whom you call God is that his ways are past finding out? If I could understand God I should be greater than God, and if he is only to do what I can understand, and what I think he ought to do, he will no longer be God but my servant.

People who turn from God and give up religion simply because they do not understand God's ways are just confessing the smallness of their own minds and their intellectual bankruptcy. They look at one incident in their lives or in the world and from that draw sweeping conclusions. They have never considered all the facts – the fact of the world itself, creation, history, etc. Are chance and luck a sufficient explanation? No one of any real intelligence believes so today. The more life is studied, analysed and pondered, the more it leads to wonder and to God. The only true conclusion to draw from the fact that we cannot understand the ways of God is not that there is no God, but that our understandings are impaired and insufficient. The man who thinks that his mind and thinking are big enough to inspect God is just confirming that he does not know how to think truly. So much for the claim that to be irreligious is to be intellectual.

But what of the other claim – that to give up religion emancipates man and brings him to his own? Precisely the same conclusion must be drawn here also. It utterly fails. Listen to the claim as it is put here: 'What profit shall we have, if we pray unto him?' That is the question they ask. What a flood of light that question throws upon the questioners. How they reveal not only their own mentality but also their own nature and their view of man and his well-being. The word 'profit' is in and of itself interesting. It is the great word of today. There is a sense in which it is quite legitimate, as I shall show. What matters is the connotation that one gives to it or the terms in which we measure and assess profit. It is not difficult to see what Job's contemporaries meant by profit. Their idea was perfectly plain and clear. Profit to them was something that was to be measured only in terms of material goods and benefits. They had a sufficiency of everything – goods, friends, money, children, health, happiness – everything! 'What more could we desire?' they say. 'What could conceivably be better?' 'What could God add unto us?' That was their idea of life and that is also, therefore, their idea of man. They were perfectly satisfied and content. They desired nothing more and nothing greater. Indeed they could conceive of nothing bigger and greater. They claimed that in turning away from God they were liberating themselves and becoming men worthy of the name. To ask men to worship God and to serve him was evidently, in their minds, the same as telling men what they should lose and give up. They were the liberators of mankind, the defenders of the rights of man, the upholders of the true dignity and greatness of man! Their idea of man and his world was something conceived solely in materialistic terms.

Is this merely true of the men of Job's time? Look around, listen to the truth of the ungodly and inspect their lives. To what do they give themselves when they turn from God and religion? What is the nature of the emancipated life to which they offer to lead us? What are the things which they covet and which satisfy them? They are still the same. First and foremost is material wealth and comfort. This is true not only of those who have it but also of those who would like to have it and who are jealous of those who do. Money and wealth has never meant more to the average person than it does today. The ideal life for most people is a life in which they would not only have sufficient money not to have to worry about it but also so much that they would have no need to work. The whole idea of the dignity of work and labour has gone. To have to work is almost regarded as an indignity and a disgrace. The idle rich are not only admired but also envied. The ideal life is a life of leisured wealth in which one can do exactly as one pleases. And what is it that pleases? Sports and entertainment: football, cinema, drink, gambling and betting; or in a quieter way, a nice house, motor car and to be surrounded by one's family and friends. But I need not elaborate. The facts are familiar to all. What men like is revealed in the newspapers which cater for men and their tastes. And it is because these things satisfy men that they ask, 'What shall it profit us though we did pray unto God?' That is the freedom which they desire. Freedom to live a life which appeals only to the lowest part of man's nature. Men give up God and his service in order to have physical comfort and ease, pleasure and excitement, worldly success and applause – preferring to drink and gamble, to play games on Sunday, to be immoral and licentious.

Such is their emancipation, such is their liberty, and is the experience to which we can attain if we but shake off the chains and fetters of God and religion and really become men worthy of the name! Nothing about the spirit and the soul! Not a word about the higher part of man and his most noble faculties! Not a word about striving and effort and self-denial! Nothing to call forth that in man which differentiates him most from the animal! This is what we are asked to regard as an advance upon the other view which places first and foremost the soul and the spirit, and their eternal needs. Come, face these facts honestly. Stop repeating your superficial prejudices and answer direct questions. What is your view of life? What is your ambition in life? What is your highest object? What is your ideal? Is it measured merely in terms of money, pleasure and ease? Has it reference merely to that which is animal and material, or does it include the soul and the spirit? Is your view of the ideal life one which includes and necessitates the calling forth of effort and the exercising of all the powers of the mind, heart and spirit? There is nothing about the modern view of life which makes it more inconsistent with man's true nature and being as the fact that it always offers ease and comfort and represents these as so easily attainable. The modern view never challenges us. It passes over and excuses our weaknesses and the worst in us; it describes sin in terms of self-experience and nature; it caters only for the physical, panders to our pride, ministers to our creature comforts, tells us that we are wonderful, 'master of our fate and captain of our soul', and makes no demands upon our honour, self-restraint and temperance; it leaves alone our intellect and our souls! No longer need we deny ourselves and discipline and control ourselves. No longer need we wrestle and fight and pray. No longer need we examine ourselves and condemn ourselves. No longer do all the powers and faculties we possess need to be roused to fight the good fight and attempt to scale the heights and achieve a higher and a better type of life. We need only recline and relax into a life of indolence and ease!

These are the things that are offered us today in the name of intellect and emancipation. Could anything be more false and fatuous, could anything be more unintelligent and debasing? But these are the assumptions from which the questions 'What is the Almighty, that we should serve him? and what profit should we have, if we pray unto him?' always arise. It is because they enjoy this kind of life which is so degraded that men still cry unto God, 'Depart from us; for we desire not the knowledge of thy ways.'

2. *Having shown the utter hollowness of the assumption on which these questions are based, let us now proceed to answer the questions themselves.* Have you asked them? Do you still ask them? Are you doubtful as to whether you should believe in God or not? Do you serve him and pray unto him? Are you tempted to turn away from him simply because everything does not happen just as you would like it to happen? Do you feel that God is unfair to you and are you, to any extent, envious of the wicked and the ungodly, who seem to be prospering so much and whose lot always seems to fall in pleasant places? If so, listen to these answers to their questions. They are the answers which are given partly by Job himself and by the Old Testament everywhere, but especially by the New Testament and above all by Jesus of Nazareth, the Son of God. Listen to them.

'What is the Almighty that we should serve him?' The question itself partly indicates the answer. He is the Almighty. Apart from any other consideration God is to be served, obeyed and loved and worshipped because he is God. He is the Almighty, the Great, the Eternal and the Absolute. He is the Maker and Creator of all things, the Lord of all being. It is he who created the world out of nothing.

It is he who has designed all being. It is he who brought you into the world and placed you in it. He is from the beginning and will be for ever. His greatness alone demands our worship and our service. But think also of his power and his might. He upholds all things and all things are in his hands. He is outside the world and greater than it. He has lived without it and is still doing so. He is the creator of time and is greater than time.

'What is he that I should serve him?' He is not only my maker but also my judge. Men in their arrogance ask their questions as if they sat as judges at a trial where God is to come and appear before them. The folly of it all! As you are asking your questions you are moving nearer and nearer to the end which will soon answer your questions for you in a terrible manner. 'What is the Almighty that we should serve him?' You will soon know! You will stand before him. But you will not stand, you will be incapable of standing. One glimpse will be enough! One flash of that eternal light, the consuming fire! Because in his infinite love and patience, mercy and compassion, he does not now strike all the ungodly down at once, they assume that he is powerless. They mock him because of his kindness and ask their blasphemous arrogant questions because of his long-suffering. 'I do not understand this and that', you say. 'I want to know how God allows this and permits that.' You say you cannot, you will not serve him and worship him until you do understand. One day, you *will* understand and see clearly that God is to be worshipped because he is God.

'Though he slay me', says Job, 'yet will I trust in him' (*Job* 13:15). Job did not understand God nor his ways but he continued to worship because he knew he was God and that there was a perfectly good reason though he could not see it. And he who was greater than Job, the very Son of God himself, said, 'If it be possible let this cup pass from me, nevertheless not my will, but thine, be done' (*Luke* 22:42). 'What is the Almighty that you should serve him?' He is God. He is your maker. He will be your judge. He is the eternal. A king does not give reasons and explanations for his requests and demands – he just makes known his will. A dutiful child does not withhold obedience until he has satisfied himself that his parent's request is right and good. He obeys because it is that parent's request. God is to be obeyed because he is God, whatever the circumstances or conditions may be.

'What profit shall we have, if we pray unto him?' From the standpoint of what we have clearly seen to be the worldly man's idea of profit, the answer is 'nothing'. With this standard of values, communion with God not only gives nothing but is an actual hindrance and waste of time. Yet Jesus of Nazareth spent much of his time in prayer and even went without sleep and rest in order to obtain that communion. Why? Where is the profit? What is its value? The answers to these questions are endless. Let me note some. What can confer greater dignity upon man than to talk to God? There are people in this world paying large sums of money and giving time and many other things in order merely to see certain people who are accounted great. They will pay still more in order to be allowed to speak to them. An audience with the king, or to be presented at court, is considered of much greater value than mere money and wealth. But what is all this in comparison with talking to the King of kings and the Lord of lords. Even though I get no material benefit, even though I may have nothing tangible to show for it, I have spoken to him! He has granted me an audience! What is the world and all its wealth in comparison with that. Job had lost his children, his wealth, everything. But his greatest desire was not to get this back; his cry was, 'Oh that I knew where I might find him!' (*Job* 23:3). But the profit does not end merely with the audience. God does bless those who serve him and who seek him. Not as the world counts blessing, but in an infinitely more glorious way. He blesses the soul. He gives peace and rest to the troubled breast.

> *He smiles, and my comforts abound;*
> *His grace like the dew shall descend,*
> *And walls of salvation surround*
> *The soul He delights to defend.*

The profit? Ah, perhaps it takes trials and troubles in order to measure it and to assess it. While things are going well, the ungodly may *seem* to have all the profit. But what is the position when trials come, when illness visits us, when old age creeps on, when the jaws of death gape widely before us? It is then that our Lord's question, which is the exact reverse of the ungodly, may be heard: 'What shall it profit a man though he gain the whole world and lose his own soul?' (*Mark* 8:36). It is then that the profit of knowing God and praying regularly to him and serving him is seen. But even before that, for all who have been delivered from their old nature the profit is evident. Living life with God and in obedience to him one finds one's whole nature affected and benefited. Sin is condemned and conquered, a new view of life is obtained which gives us something to strive after that is greater than ourselves, our noblest faculties are all called into play and exercised – 'old things are passed away; all things are become new' (*2 Cor.* 5:17).

This is the profit in life with God. It is the way that has produced all the saints and all the greatest benefactors of mankind. It has enriched life in every department. In trouble and in death, the fear of the grave is removed, the sting of death is drawn; instead of going on to the judgment in fear and trembling, and with terror and torment, we know that we are going to the Father to spend eternity with him and all the blessed angels in heaven. 'What shall it profit us?' It all depends whether you think only of a few years here on earth or whether you think of eternity! It all depends upon whether you think only of the flesh and its desires or the end and its inevitability. It all depends whether you think in terms of man only or introduce God also.

Just as with the ungodly of Job's age, many are saying today, 'Depart from us; for we desire not the knowledge of thy ways.' And they turn away from God, fondly imagining that their turning may somehow affect the situation. But it does not. God remains! Death remains! The judgment remains! Surely these people have been asking the wrong question. There is only one vital question to ask, not 'what shall it profit us if we pray unto him', but Job's question, 'Oh! that I knew where I might find him.' Do you know God? Are you ready to meet him? Have you served him and obeyed him? Are you ready for the judgment? Can you not see that the situation is desperate? You are in God's hands, you have sinned against him, forgotten him, ignored him, criticised him and asked your blasphemous questions concerning him. You see now the utter folly of that. You will see it still more clearly after death. What can you do? What can be done? Blessed be the name of God there is an answer greater than anything Job knew. God is Almighty and the Judge, but he is also Love and such wondrous love that he sent his only begotten Son, Jesus of Nazareth, into this world to bear our sins, die our death and reconcile us to himself. Though mankind had turned away from him, God in his love did not turn away from us. He sent his Son after us to save us, and yielding ourselves to him the profit we desire is pardon from our sin; peace with God; power to live life worthy of the name; the removal of the fear of death; sonship of God and heirship of eternal bliss. That is offered to all now. It is the only offer and the last offer. The consequences of your choice you will experience to all eternity. Surely none can hesitate.

15
Four Pictures of Life

Oh that men would praise the LORD for his goodness, and for his wonderful works to the children of men . . .

Psalm 107

I always point out whenever I happen to preach from the book of Psalms that a psalm is a song and should therefore be always taken in its entirety. Certainly there are individual verses in the psalms which merit prolonged and separate attention but a psalm is generally composed so as to give expression to some one big prevailing thought or mood. Now if this is true of almost all the psalms, it is particularly true of Psalm 107. For this psalm, though it consists of forty-three verses, has only one great message to give. It has only one theme though it varies the expression of it some four times. And the psalmist is particularly concerned to show that the four variations are simply variations on the one theme. That, in a sense, is his whole object and purpose – to show that there is one theme and that all men should be giving expression to it in their own different and separate ways. 'Oh that men would praise the Lord for his goodness, and for his wonderful works to the children of men!' (verses 8, 15, 21, 31).

Now by repeating these words, the psalmist (as if anticipating much of what is being said in these present days) reminds us of one of the most remarkable facts concerning the Christian church and, at the same time, refutes one of the commonest charges which is brought against her. You are all so familiar with that charge, perhaps from having uttered it yourself so frequently, that I need not take up much time in describing it. It would have us believe that religion and the need for spiritual experience, far from being the great common denominator for the whole of mankind, are nothing but the manifestation of odd racial or temperamental characteristics, particularly of those instincts which are most primal and unintellectual. Out of the kindness of their hearts these observers are prepared to grant that some people ought more or less to be religiously inclined – indeed they expect them to be so inclined. What they hotly deny and deeply resent is the Christian claim that all men need God and spiritual life, and that without him they are dead. They are prepared to allow others to worship if they will and if they think it helps them, but what they cannot tolerate is that religious people should invite them to join, indeed should plead with them to do so and finally threaten them with awful consequences if they persistently refuse!

Regarding the Christian religion as a safety valve for certain individuals, for whom it is a more or less harmless weakness, they naturally are somewhat annoyed and infuriated when it is suggested that they should deliberately cultivate the same taste. As one of these people once said to me, 'You Christians are so thoroughly impudent and interfering. I do not try to force you to drink or smoke or take up golf or accept the Conservative theory of politics or take up my particular intellectual hobbies and amusements, so, why should you try to interfere in mine? What right have you to claim that your particular view is universally true? Why not allow each man to go on in his own way, recognising that we are different and that our tastes and ideas must correspondingly differ?'

In other words, they regard the Christian religion and view of life as being mainly a matter of opinion or personal preferences and therefore they generally expect to find such beliefs and opinions held by people of the same type or similar temperamental make-up. As you have the artistic or musical or scientific or political or poetical temperament in different people, so, you must expect to find the religious temperament in a certain type. It is one of the possible types and they think it is as foolish to say that all people should be religious as it is to say that all should be artistic or musical. Every man, they argue, must work out or find his own salvation according to his own particular need and it is monstrous, they add, to suggest that there is such a thing as a common salvation for all in spite of temperament and all these natural differences.

That is the theory, stated at its baldest and in its most common general expression. There are variations of it which are very much more subtle and are not infrequently heard from the lips of many church members these days. The commonest, perhaps, is that which states that a man can be a Christian without knowing it and without professing actual faith in Jesus Christ our Lord. 'No', they say, 'the man doesn't belong to a church, he doesn't believe the various things that are taught about Jesus Christ by the church. He's not that sort, not that type. But he's all right, his good life and his good works prove that.' There you have the same idea. Here is a man or woman that would not profess faith openly and actively, not the type that would enjoy joining in praise with fellow-believers, but 'all right' in spite of that, if not indeed very much better than those who do profess to believe and attend their chapel! Alas, how often do we hear that these days even from the lips of church members. Probably without realising what they are doing, they are granting the whole case which is put forward by the attackers of the Christian faith.

Now the author of this psalm refutes all that by reminding us of one of the most striking and notable facts about the Christian church and the Christian faith, namely, their universality and all-inclusiveness. He reminds us, I say, of a fact not a theory. Look at the church today or any time you like during her long history and you cannot fail to note that one of the most amazing things about her is the way in which, precisely as her Founder and Lord was able, she has been able to attract to herself men and women of all types, shades and possible combinations and permutations of psychological and temperamental make-up. There has been literally no limit to this power which she possesses. There has been and there is no type of person who is not represented in the Christian church – volatile and phlegmatic; emotional and logical; sentimental and intellectual; aesthetic and mundane; ethereal or practical; artistic or scientific, credulous or sceptical, mercurial or dull – all, all have been and are today found within the fold of the Christian church. How thoroughly dishonest it is to talk glibly about the religious temperament and make-up and ignore facts which have stood the test of nearly two thousand years!

Yes, the psalmist here reminds us of that fact. Let us observe how he does so. He is calling the church together. He is calling a meeting or, as it were, assembling the massed choirs of the Christians of all ages and places. He recognises none of these artificial distinctions of which we have been talking. He ignores all the talk which says that religion is related to racial or ethnic characteristics. 'Let the redeemed of the Lord say so, whom he hath redeemed from the hand of the enemy; and gathered them out of the lands, from the *east,* and from the *west,* from the *north,* and from the *south'* (verses 2, 3). Such is his cry, such is his invitation. East! west! north! and south! They come from everywhere; there is no point on the compass in which they will not be found. But not only do they thus come from different places from the four quarters of the globe, their experiences differ also and they themselves differ in temperament and in their approach to life. Still, he invites them all to sing the same song, 'O give thanks unto the Lord, for he is good: for his mercy endureth for ever', with that oft-repeated chorus, 'Oh that men would praise the Lord for his goodness, and for his wonderful works to the children of men!' They come from different places, they speak different languages, they have different stories to tell in a sense and yet he invites them all to sing the same song, this song of thanksgiving and praise to the Lord. But he does not stop at that. He proceeds to show us why it is that he calls all these different people with their different experiences to unite in their common hymn of praise. He analyses the reasons which underlie this remarkable unity. What are these reasons?

1. In the first place, he makes it quite clear that *all these different people have, in spite of all superficial appearances, had precisely the same experience.* That all, as it were, had been suffering from the *same* disease. In so doing this man displays himself to be a true psychologist and a thoroughly shrewd physician of the soul. He takes each symptom as he finds it but he is not content merely to note the symptom. He examines it completely and traces it down to its origin and root cause. A symptom, he seems to say, is not something in itself. A symptom is always a manifestation of a disease and the wise man does not lightly treat or palliate the symptom but makes use of it in order to arrive at and discover the disease or root cause of the trouble.

Now, in this psalm, as I have already reminded you, we are told of at least four different reasons why people should praise God. Four experiences are here described but, according to the psalmist, these differing experiences do not show four different diseases but simply four different symptoms or manifestations of that one great disease called sin. Though the experiences of these people, when looked at hastily and superficially seem to be so different, fundamentally, they are all identical. Now that is really the great case for the Christian religion. It looks deeply at life, it analyses it and dissects it and teaches that there is this great common factor to the whole of mankind – sin. The Christian religion, therefore, is not the hobby of just a few special people. It has something to say to all men. It is of vital importance to everyone. It is a superficial view of life that divides and separates mankind into various groups and compartments; the profoundest view of life, not only Christian but also pagan, recognises the essential unity or solidarity of the entire human race. 'One touch of nature makes the whole world kin.' It is the devil who would have us believe that we are all fundamentally different, it is of the very essence of the Christian religion that face to face with God we are all one and the same. But let us see this truth as illustrated by the psalmist in his four cases.

The first picture which we are given in verses 4–9 is that of travellers wandering hopelessly in a wilderness. They have lost their way and are going hither and thither looking for 'a city' in which to dwell. But they cannot find it. And they have become 'hungry and thirsty' and 'their soul fainted in them'. The psalmist may well have had the picture of the children of Israel in the wilderness for forty years in his mind. He may have been referring specifically to that or to the return of the Israelites from Babylon. However that may be, it provides us with a perfect picture of the spiritual pilgrimage of many a man, it is a perfect description of the way along which a certain type of person eventually arrives at Christ. These people are generally intellectual in type. They are concerned about life and think and read and meditate. They have not done so for long before they realise that they know very little about life and its ultimate meaning, purpose, and destination. They feel they are in a wilderness and that it is their duty to get out of it as soon as they can. So, they set out upon their journey almost invariably full of confidence and hope. They begin to read more deeply, to attend classes perhaps on philosophy or psychology or other subjects which claim to deal with the problems of life. They pursue such studies eagerly and with intellectual zest and enthusiasm. But they have not proceeded very far before they begin to realise that the psalmist was quite right when he described life as a wandering in the wilderness 'in a solitary way'. They have come to a strange sense of loneliness and isolation. They observe their fellow men and women, placed in the same world and having the same problems, yet thinking little about it – most of them without the ability, the time, or the inclination and aptitude for such studies and pursuits. What would become of them? The people they meet like themselves in the wilderness are but few and exceptional people. Yes, it is a 'solitary way'. But on they go, still hoping and persuading themselves that they are pioneers and that after they have discovered the new country, the promised land, they will then be able to return and lead their duller and less intelligent fellows with them. That is how it has always happened with explorers and pioneers. So on they go, in spite of the loneliness and the solitariness. Intent upon their grand intellectual and spiritual quest: reading, thinking, studying, attending lectures and so on, they are out to discover all about life and death; the past and the future, indeed the whole object and purpose of life. They are looking for the 'city of habitation' in which their souls and minds might find rest and sustenance. Again and again they meet with people in this wilderness who assure them that if they only follow them they will lead them to the city. They follow, but after much travelling and toiling, no city is to be seen. Then they meet another and follow him or they discover some sort of a track which appeared to lead somewhere. But still with the same result – still no sign of the city wherein they could dwell. They cross river after river, are deluded by mirage after mirage, but still they have no rest. Their soul begins to feel faint within them, they are tired and hungry and thirsty. They begin to feel it is all useless and pointless and that they might go on like this forever and still be none the wiser. 'If only we had never set out at all', they say to themselves. 'If only we had never begun to think at all. Happy is he who lives like a vegetable and never attempts to solve the riddle of life.'

Yes, there they are – tired and exhausted, feeling as far away from the city of refuge as at the beginning, yet still longing for that rest and peace which alone could be found there. But I must not go on, fascinating as the theme is as a portrayal of this approach to Christ. My point is that all the combined wisdom of all the sages and all the philosophers has been totally and completely unable to answer these ultimate questions and to satisfy the deepest longings of the human heart. They lead us on and on, ever on, always promising great things, but at the end we find no city and have to be content with vague theories, ideas and suppositions. All who have ever been in that wilderness have done one of two things. They have either given up in despair and cynicism or else they have done what is described here, namely, 'they cried unto the Lord in their trouble'. In other words they have either given up in despair or have become Christians. What is certain is that they have never found the way out of the wilderness unaided and on their own.

But look at the second type, the second picture in verses 10–16. Here we find prisoners 'such as sit in darkness and in the shadow of death, being bound in affliction and iron'. Let us give the full force of the description and note how securely they are imprisoned. They are not only bound in iron, but the cells in which they are so bound are safely guarded at the windows by 'bars of iron' and outside all are 'gates of brass'. What a picture! How true it is of a certain type of sinner – indeed of all men and women in different ways! What could more clearly illustrate the tyranny and enslaving power of evil thoughts, vicious habits and bad company, than powers that correspond to the iron bands on the body, the iron bars at the window and the brass gates outside all. Is anyone so foolish as to deny the truth of this picture? Is it an easy thing to break with bad company? Can you without much effort break yourself of a long continued evil habit and practice? Above all, do you find it an easy thing to control your mind and rid it of all its impure thoughts, all its evil imaginings, all its unkind and bitter judgments and envyings? Tell me, are you free? Free from the control of friends and associates, free from the influence of others which you know is wrong, free from the grip of every evil habit and practice, free from all these sins of the mind which reduce us to despair and shame? Are you free? Have you ever tried to free yourself? Can you achieve moral and spiritual freedom? Can you break all the bars of iron and the fetters and the gates of brass? Has anyone ever done so unaided? Has it ever been achieved except in Christ Jesus our Lord and in the new life and power which he alone can give?

Ah, this picture seems at first sight to be very different from that first one. Who would imagine that the traveller in the wilderness is in the identical state of this poor fellow. The former can walk and move about, indeed is characterised by movement and apparent freedom; the latter is bound down by iron chains, is helpless and immovable in a well-guarded prison cell. Yet they are both the same. Both are failures, both are in a state of despair. The one mainly intellectual perhaps, the other mainly moral. But both *failures* and equally helpless.

The third picture is again different from both the others. This picture given in verses 17–22 represents a person lying ill on his bed who becomes so desperately ill that he 'abhorreth all manner of meat' and actually 'draws near unto the gates of death'. Here is no intellectual, intent upon his great quest, nor the person whose main characteristic is his moral slavery and his bondage to certain obvious sins. Here there is no suggestion of the lonely wilderness nor the closely guarded prison. This is a more homely picture of a much quieter nature. Here we have somebody who is pining away and apparently dying through sheer misery. They have built their hopes for happiness in this world upon some particular person or some particular thing and it has failed them, with the death of someone who was very dear, perhaps, or the failure of some great ambition in life. Or perhaps it has been some sad disillusionment, some treachery on the part of a trusted friend and the dashing to the ground of their greatest hope in life. A terrible disappointment has taken place. The main thing on which they had built all their hopes has failed them and they are left permanently miserable and without hope. They try to console themselves and others do their best to assist them. But nothing avails. They will not be comforted. They pine away and lose interest in life and in everything. The sheer misery of it all overwhelms them – they pine, they languish away.

Now we must not be too hard on this type of person. They really cannot help it. It is foolish, indeed cruel, to command them to forget and to go forward, to pull themselves together and be brave for that is just what they cannot do. They have not the energy to do so, they have not the energy to think at all. They cannot rouse themselves, the mainspring of their lives having gone. They are helpless and are as much the victims of their grief and sorrow and misery as the people described in the former group. Who would ever think of comparing such a person as this with the confirmed drunkard? Yet they are fundamentally the same. One is the slave of drink, the other the slave of grief and misery. Each is as helpless as the other. Though the one may be respectable and a member of a church, and the other riotous and immoral, it is clear that the essence of the trouble in both cases is the fatal helplessness with which Christ alone can deal.

The last picture, given in verses 23–31, is again quite different. Here we have a storm at sea, with a ship being tossed about helplessly and its poor occupants are in a state of desperation. The gale is blowing, the waves 'mount up to the heaven, they go down again to the depths' and as for the men aboard, 'their soul is melted because of trouble. They reel to and fro, and stagger like a drunken man, and are at their wits' end.' This picture need not be elaborated. We have all seen it far too often! We have all seen men and women tossed about by their sinful lusts and passions exactly like the ship here described. Poor things! They have entirely lost control of their lives, the very steering and tackle of the ship have been washed overboard and they are helpless. But still, you will observe, the main result is precisely the same as that described in the three previous cases. Though differing from each other so markedly at a superficial first sight, fundamentally they are all the same. They are all helpless, they have all failed – face to face with life, death and eternity, face to face with God and all he expects from man there is no real difference.

As it is with these four types, so it is with every other type that you can think of or can mention. Yes, says the psalmist in effect, you may well wonder at these different people whom I have called together to sing this one hymn of praise. You may well ask how they can all join together in view of their differences. I will tell you. Listen to me! They have realised the same common need, they have become conscious of their same fundamental helplessness face to face with life and death. Though apparently so different, it can be said of each one of them that 'then they cried unto the Lord in their trouble' (verses 6, 13, 19 and 28). Face yourselves, my friends, and stop thoughtlessly repeating these superficial clichés of the world. Be wise and learned. Face life, face death, face God and eternity. Keep on doing so until you feel your utter helplessness. Do you know how to live, are you master of your life? Do you know how to die? Realise your condition and plight and 'cry unto the Lord in your trouble'. Whatever temperament you may possess, whatever particular and peculiar manifestation and symptoms there may be in your case, however different from other people you may think yourself to be, remember you are common clay like the rest of us and that you are suffering from the same dread disease called sin.

2.   I fear I have given far too much time to the disease. But it is only those who realise that they are ill who consult the physician. Realisation of our need, however, will never make us sing. 'Crying unto the Lord in trouble' is not exactly an anthem or hymn of praise. It is, in a sense, what assembles the choir together, but it can never make them sing. *What, then, explains the singing and the music and the happiness and the thanksgiving?* Two reasons are given:

The first is *the graciousness of the Lord*. You remember we left all these poor people crying unto the Lord in their desperate troubles. They had tried everything else and everyone else. They had gone the complete round of all the professed remedies. They had often heard of the Christian religion and of Jesus Christ our Lord, of the love and mercy of God, but they had ignored and forgotten all this and had kept trusting to their own devices and those of other people. But, all else having failed them, they now turn to the Lord. In their utter desperation and perplexity they turn to him whom they have so persistently ignored and whom they should have consulted at the very beginning. They realise their folly now and see how they have insulted him. They are conscious now that they are entirely in his hands and that he can do as he wills with them. Indeed they could not blame him were he to refuse them and to crush them. They see that their sinfulness and independence and foolish pride deserve nothing else and nothing better! They, the pygmy creatures of time, defying the Eternal and Almighty God; they whose life is as a vapour or as a passing cloud turning their backs upon the Creator and Artificer of all things; they who were made by his hands and moulded by him out of the clay and the dust defying their Maker, the clay attempting to resist the Potter! Ah, what can they hope for except to be crushed, what do they merit but damnation and hell?

These are their feelings as they turn to the first cause, the uncaused cause, the Eternal God who exists from eternity to eternity, and turn to him as the last resort! These are their thoughts, these are their fears – God can exist without them, there is no need for him to listen to them or pay any attention to them, indeed, everything that they can think of is apparently against his doing so. But in their desperation they risk it. They cry to God, they place themselves entirely in his hands and at his mercy, they plead for pardon and forgiveness and for strength. And wonder of wonders, he listens, he hearkens, he stoops and bends his ear! And instead of casting them to hell, instead of damning them to all eternity, instead of laughing them to scorn, instead of gloating in delight at having them in his power – he delivers them out of their distresses! Oh, wonder of wonders! Oh, matchless grace! Oh, eternal love. In spite of everything. In spite of our sin and rebellion, in spite of our arrogance and pride, in spite of all the insults and abuses we have hurled at him, in spite of our treating him as the last resort of desperate sinners – in spite of all! Oh, wondrous grace and love that commends itself to us 'in that while we were yet sinners, Christ died for us' (*Rom.* 5:8). More than that, says Paul in the same chapter, 'when we were enemies, we were reconciled to God by the death of his Son'.

Do you see it? 'He led them forth' from the wilderness, says our psalmist in the seventh verse, 'by the right way, that they might go to a city of habitation.' Yes, he led them forth, but what is most remarkable and amazing and what should make us sing to all eternity is that he prepared the 'right way' of his own free love, without asking us, made it for us in spite of our rebellion and wandering, prepared it while we were still sinners and enemies. Yes, he saved us in spite of everything, in spite of ourselves and all our sins. Who cannot but sing who has realised that? What theme is more likely to stir the depths of our souls, what song is more appropriate? Indeed we are told that that is the song of heaven and eternity is to be spent singing the praises of 'The Lamb that was slain and that sitteth upon the throne'. 'Worthy is the Lamb that was slain to receive power, and riches, and wisdom, and strength, and honour, and glory, and blessing ... Blessing, and honour, and glory, and power, be unto him that sitteth upon the throne and unto the Lamb for ever and ever' (*Rev.* 5:12–13). Are you still surprised that they all sing and that they all sing the same song? There is but one song, they have all experienced and received that same free grace of God in Jesus Christ our Lord. They owe it all to him! They were helpless, they had failed. He did it all!

But consider the second main reason for their praise – *the wondrous and marvellous change which God produced in their condition.* Whatever their condition before they all were delivered and made happy. They came from different circumstances and with different needs but all the needs were satisfied. Think about the suddenness, unexpectedness, completeness of the change produced on the men who were previously lost, imprisoned, desolate and out of control. From their trouble and distress he delivered them all. 'He led them forth by the right way that they might go to a city of habitation.' 'For he satisfieth the longing soul, and filleth the hungry soul with goodness.' 'He brought them out of darkness and the shadow of death, and brake their bands in sunder.' 'He hath broken the gates of brass, and cut the bars of iron in sunder.' Oh, wondrous Redeemer and Liberator! 'He sent his word, and healed them, and delivered them from their destructions.' Finally, 'He maketh the storm a calm, so that the waves thereof are still. Then are they glad because they be quiet; so he bringeth them unto their desired haven.'

Now for the full chorus after the separate solos by soprano, alto, tenor and bass!

Oh that men would praise the Lord for his goodness, and for his wonderful works to the children of men.

Intellectual rest and peace; a spiritual city to dwell in; old habits broken and old sins conquered; happiness, joy and a new song in the heart, even rejoicing in tribulations and affirming that 'all things work together for good to them that love God' (*Rom.* 8:28); stability and a fixed purpose in life with a sure knowledge that we are being piloted safely into that desired eternal haven of God beyond death and the grave. This, then, is the glorious salvation given to all who 'being wise, and observing these things' (verse 43), cry out unto the Lord and trust themselves to our blessed Saviour and Redeemer Jesus Christ. Whatever your circumstances and conditions, turn to him at once. 'He *is* able. He *is* willing'. The way is already prepared. 'Doubt no more.' Having done so you will at once join the choir and mingle your voice with those who sing the song of Moses and of the Lamb.

16

Why Men Reject God

Forasmuch as this people refuseth the waters of Shiloah that go softly, and rejoice in Rezin and Remaliah's son; Now therefore, behold, the Lord bringeth up upon them the waters of the river, strong and many, even the king of Assyria, and all his glory: and he shall come up over all his channels, and go over all his banks.

Isaiah 8:6–7

It is no mere accident that in the arrangement of the books of the Old Testament Scriptures, the prophecies and the writings of the prophets should be placed at the end. For they undoubtedly are a true climax to all that goes before them and represent the topmost level of God's revelation of himself under the Old Testament dispensation. Their supreme position of exceptional importance can be shown along many lines and in many respects. They are very important, for instance, from the mere standpoint of history in that we find in them an account of the last stages of the history of the Jews as a people and of God's Spirit dealing with them under the Old Testament dispensation. That, I say, is something which is of prime interest in and of itself.

In the various other books of the Old Testament we read of the calling of Abraham, the bringing into being of a new and special race of people and we follow their history in these first and early days. How wonderful and glorious are the possibilities, how bright the prospects. We see God's mighty actions on their behalf and the special miracles and works which he performed in order to make of them a great people. Never were people given such a wonderful opportunity. No history is so romantic and so thrilling as the early history of the Jews as we follow it out from step to step and from stage to stage. We think of the conquest of Canaan, the greatness of David and his kingdom and also the greatness and splendour of the kingdom of Solomon. But as we go on we become aware of a gradual decline and fall, of a steady lowering of the standard, the division of the kingdom into two, increasing problems, troubles and difficulties. And then in these books of prophecies, as well as in portions of the history of Kings and Chronicles, we come to the last days and see Israel and Judah in adversity and in the lowest depths of national disaster and shame. What a contrast it all presents to those early days. It is the end of a period, the outworking of a certain principle and a certain process and here we see it described in all its ugliness and in all its nakedness. In the books of the prophets we read an account of the tragedy of Israel.

But in addition to that account we also have exhortation and predictions and prophecies as to the future and as to what is going to happen to Israel. The prophets do not merely exhort and preach but also threaten and predict. They present the people with the only two alternatives and make the consequences that will follow the acceptance of either perfectly clear and definite. And therein, of course, lies their great value as a support to faith and as a guarantee of divine revelation and inspiration. The prophet, as God's mouthpiece, warned the nation that if they did not submit certain things would happen. Now at that time, such warnings seemed utterly impossible and quite unthinkable and as they heard them the kings and the people treated them with derision and sarcasm and scorn. They continued in this sinful way confident, arrogant and unashamed and the warnings of the prophets, as Isaiah and others of them tell us, were regarded by them as but idle gibberish. Nevertheless the predictions were fulfilled, the prophecies were literally verified and that in a most extraordinary manner. And that in turn leads us to note what is, after all, the most important thing of all about these writings, namely, that they provide us with an explanation of the history. They show clearly why Israel declined and fell. They give us the explanation of why it is the prophets threatened Israel with such terrible consequences and of why these things actually came to pass. The mere consideration of the past history of a race or a nation is valuable and those who have eyes to see will always learn valuable lessons and greatly profit by so doing. But it does not always follow that such a study will lead us to the exact cause of the trouble. But in these writings the cause is laid down and that it is actually the cause is further proved and substantiated by the way in which the predictions as to the future were so literally and so completely verified. The prophet in addressing the people, and exposing their sins and ills, did not command their respect and might not command ours. We might disagree with his view and his diagnosis. But when he proceeds to threaten and to outline the future, the position changes and we begin to feel that he has a higher authority. Even so, we may try to dismiss him as a mere dreamer and visionary. But when the events which he foretold all come to pass we are silenced and have to admit that he knew. The prophets teach us, then, that history is not accidental, that things do not happen in an utterly uncontrolled and haphazard manner. They reveal that there are definite principles behind all these appearances, that the seen and recorded events are but the outworking of certain definite and eternal laws.

The fall and the failure of the children of Israel cannot be explained in terms of secular history and ideas of men. It is not merely the case that the nation eventually became weak and lost her position of pre-eminence and power as many another nation has done since then. It is not merely something happening in the nature of things or according to some rule of life and of history. The whole process can be easily and definitely traced. At any moment, if the people had but hearkened to the voice of God through his prophets the process of decay might have been arrested. Indeed when they were on the very verge of disaster and almost entirely engulfed, the prophet tells them that it is still not too late. He also warns them as to the consequences of refusal. His teaching is that God controls history and that the one thing that matters is that the nation should be right with him. Everything is explained in terms of that central position. Failure to grasp that, he says everywhere, is the cause of all their trouble, refusal to accept his offer is ultimately the greatest sin of all and there can be but one outcome to such action – destruction and desolation. That is the essence of the message of the prophet.

The early Christian church understood this because it took the view of the Bible which our Lord himself took and all the apostles and which every true Christian must of necessity take, that all these things are not mere history but are further, as St Paul says, 'written for our admonition' (*1 Cor.* 10:11). They represent a general principle, a principle which is still in operation and which we avoid or ignore only at our peril. What God offered to do for Israel under the old dispensation he now offers to all in Christ Jesus our Lord. And the conditions still remain the same.

Now here in this particular text which we are going to consider together tonight we have a typical and a perfect illustration and example of what I have been saying. At this particular point in their history the children of Israel were in great and grievous trouble. The prophet tells them the cause of this trouble and points the way out in the name of God. This they refuse, preferring to cling to their own ideas and devices and falling back upon human help and human alliances. Whereupon the prophet warns them and threatens them and assures them that there will be but one result – disaster, awful and complete. His words were literally verified on the actual field of history.

Let us then proceed to consider this case and learn the lessons God would have us learn. As we come to do so let me impress again upon your mind that here we have not a fairy tale or romantic novel but actual history. What God says, he also performs, what he threatens he also carries out. That people laugh at his Word today, treat it with disdain and regard it as something childish and ridiculous in comparison with what is called modern living and modern knowledge, should surely mislead no one who is really intelligent. For they did that in the days of Isaiah. But it made no difference to the outcome. And it makes no difference today and it will make no difference in the days that are to come. It is the Word of the living God, the eternal God, the God who sees the end from the beginning. Hearken unto it! Its principles are perfectly clear and it needs no ingenuity on our part to discern and to extract them.

1. *The first is that troubles and difficulties and all that renders life miserable and unhappy are entirely the result of sin.* We clearly must stand with this principle on grounds of mere logic and philosophy apart altogether from the teaching of the Bible. Finding ourselves, or anyone else, in trouble and in difficulty the exercise of wisdom is to try to discern the cause and the explanation of the situation. The man who is intent on trying to deal with the situation without reaching the cause is not a thinker at all. All true thinkers try to face a problem and try to discern the cause. It is at this point that the

Bible differs from all human ideas and conceptions. Men ever try to discern the cause of their ills in circumstances and surroundings and in various other factors and forces outside their own control. Failing to find anything definite they are prepared to fall back on what they call fate or chance. That they do this is not at all surprising. It is just an attempt to avoid personal responsibility and to fix the cause of our ills anywhere and everywhere except in ourselves. So we blame our environment, our lack of material prosperity or lack of education, the particular temperament with which we have been born, the chance meeting with a certain person, economic depression or prosperity, and many another factor, for our being what we are and for our misery and unhappiness.

That this is done is, I say, in no way surprising. It is perfectly natural. But very little real and earnest thought should demonstrate how utterly inadequate and insufficient it is as an explanation. A mere consideration of facts alone should be enough to refute the idea once and forever. And the facts are varied and prolific. Let me illustrate what I mean. I remember a discussion with a man who believed in the so-called social gospel. On being pressed he said, as all such are really prepared to say, that he blamed current conditions for the fact that many people are not Christians. In his opinion it was impossible for a person to be a Christian in a slum area and therefore the first and the most vitally important step in the evangelisation of the masses was the complete transformation of such surroundings. All that was necessary in reply to this was just to ask whether he thought that sin and misery and suffering were confined solely to the East End of London and were entirely missing in the West End! Put more directly I asked whether he really and honestly believed that it was more difficult to save the tenants in such districts than it was to save the landlords who owned the houses. He thereupon proceeded to denounce the landlords and to say that their case was infinitely worse. But the surroundings of the landlords are perfect! Where then is the argument for environment and surroundings? Precisely the same thing has been said about education and culture. Were it proved that sin and misery and unhappiness were confined only to the illiterate and uneducated then the case would be unanswerable. But the facts are almost the exact opposite. And so we could go through the entire list of causes and excuses and explanations. But our argument would not stop even at that. We would proceed to a more positive line and prove by innumerable glorious examples that some of the very greatest and noblest souls have come out of the very worst conditions and environment. We could show that all along it has been the case that happiness and true success in living have not been the monopoly of 'the wise and prudent', and that the real epics in life and history have been the stories of those noble people who in spite of 'cruel fate', yes, of persecutions and imprisonment and death, have never for a moment lost their calm balance and perfect serenity.

The attempt to explain the ills of life in terms of any or all of these external conditions will break down hopelessly in the face of facts whether negative or positive. We are not so foolish as to say that they do not count at all. What we deny is that they are the controlling factor and therefore of prime importance. We further reject such an explanation on the grounds that it is an insult to the true nature of man in any state or condition to suggest that he is entirely and utterly dependent upon his external condition. That is to make of him something lifeless and mechanical; it is certainly to destroy belief in the soul and the spirit. But what is most extra-ordinary about it is that modern men, who are so fond of boasting about free-will and their independence, and who so often reject the Christian religion because they feel that it binds and limits them, nevertheless, when they come to explain their lives, their troubles and their misery, invariably speak of themselves as mere machines who are entirely controlled by forces and factors outside their own control!

But all this is just preliminary to the clear and definite statements and teaching of the Bible. There we are told that man fell and went wrong in the most perfect and ideal conditions in Eden, in Paradise. And as we follow the history it is ever the same. Look at it at this point in the history of the children of Israel when Isaiah wrote. Why were they in such terrible and in such a desperate plight? Why that terrible change from the days of David and Solomon? Their environment and country had been perfect, their knowledge and their culture was superior to that of any other nation. Why, then, the present difficulties? The answer is perfectly plain. It is not that they were engaged in a fight against adverse circumstances, and attempting to rise amid great difficulties. The story of the children of Israel is not the story of the evolution of a great people against circumstances and powers, it is the story of the decline of a people who had been made great by God and who had been placed by him in a perfect position. What is the cause of the decline? One word answers the question. It is sin. They defied God, they refused to keep his laws. They refused to walk and to live in the way he indicated. It was just rebellion. While they served him and obeyed him they were happy and they prospered. Even the difficulties that came across their pathway were easily and gloriously surmounted. All their ills have but that one cause – refusal to walk in God's ways. That is a law, an absolute law. 'There is no peace, saith my God, to the wicked' (*Isa.* 57:21). Be not deceived by present apparent peace and plenty and happiness. For a while all seemed to go well with Israel after she had turned her back on God. But trouble came eventually as it always will come to all such. If not in life, then in death and beyond. But has that not come even now? Is all well with you? Are you really happy down in the depths? Are you not fighting a problem? What is the cause of the trouble? What is the real explanation? Do not try to blame circumstances and surroundings for there are others in precisely the same condition but who are happy. Do not blame knowledge or its lack for that argument, as we have seen, cancels itself out. Face up to my question. How do things stand between you and God? Do you acknowledge him? Is your life planned and lived according to his law and his ways? Had you realised that the only really important thing in this life and the world is to please God? Were you aware of the fact that your welfare depends solely and entirely upon him? Israel is in trouble because of her sin. Sin is the cause of all our ills and troubles.

2. But we cannot content ourselves with that statement or stop at that point. For were we to do so we should not see the real enormity of sin. This we now proceed to consider. The real nature of sin is to be seen when we observe that it not only brings us into trouble for our refusal of God's law and way of life but, further, *it refuses his gracious offer of deliverance* out of that very trouble. That is the precise nature of the charge which Isaiah, at this point, brings against Ahaz the king and his people. Though they were in trouble because they had deliberately disobeyed and flouted God and his laws, he does not turn his back upon them. In their trouble he

comes to them through his prophet and speaks to them. He assures them that it is still not too late, that if they but hearken unto him and turn to him, and rely upon him, all will still be well with them. He is prepared to forgive the past, to blot out all their guilt and all their enmity. Though they have dishonoured and offended him yet in his infinite love and grace he is prepared to look upon them again and to bless them. He sees them with a piteous eye, he regards them with compassion, he chooses to see not the sin which has caused the trouble but the pitiful state in which they are found because of the trouble. And he offers to deliver them, he even urges it upon them by raising up a succession of prophets and appealing to them in the most tender terms.

Furthermore, God shows them that his way out is the only way out. He warns them of the futility of trusting to any other expedient or advice. He reminds them of the powerful way in which he had delivered them in the past and of his place in all their history. In their utter extremity, caused by their refusal to live in his way, he comes to them with this offer of pardon, even deliverance and restoration. Is anything so wonderful? Could love do any more? Yet the terrible, the awful thing in the history of Israel is that it was all refused and rejected and that with sarcasm and arrogance. As God's way of life is refused, so his offer of salvation and deliverance is refused and spurned and Israel turns to men and to her own ideas and devices in an attempt to find release and escape from her problems and difficulties, 'This people refuse the waters of Shiloah that go softly . . .', which is just a pictorial way of describing God and his power, 'and rejoice in Rezin and Remaliah's son'. That men should forget God's love and sin against him is bad enough, and shows a nature which is sinful and perverted, but the real nature of sin is seen in this further act whereby they actually refuse and cast back into the very face of God himself the offer of his life and freedom and forgiveness. That his justice and his love are rejected is bad enough, that his love and grace are spurned and refused just defies description. Israel refused the salvation God offered them and trusted to themselves and to men. Men today refuse the offer of salvation and deliverance for the ills of life which is offered in the gospel of our Lord and Saviour Jesus Christ, and prefer to pin their faith on anything and everything else.

3.   What can explain such folly and such enormity? What explained it in the case of the children of Israel of old and what still explains it? Why is it that men persist in refusing a way of salvation that can do all they need and infinitely more? Why is it that mankind thus goes on spoiling itself and rejecting the Almighty as it does so? The reasons, alas, are but too evident and too obvious and show the subtlety of sin and the terrible perversion which it has introduced into human nature. Here are some of the reasons:

One is that the Israelites saw very clearly that *to accept God's offer of deliverance and of salvation would of necessity imply an acknowledgement and confession on their part of the real cause and nature of their troubles and their problems.* Away back in the early days of their history God had told them that if they disobeyed certain consequences would follow but that if, even out of them, they called to him and returned to him, he would deliver them. To accept God's offer of salvation and deliverance would simply acknowledge all that. But that was the very thing they were not prepared to do. They had turned from God and his truth and had espoused and taken up other gods and other religions which they believed to be much better, so much superior. Were they now to confess that all that was all wrong? Certainly they were in dire straits and terrible trouble, and they would welcome nothing more than deliverance and salvation, but they had not sunk so low as to lose their self-respect entirely and utterly! God's offer could not be accepted without their acknowledging that their departure from him was the cause of all their ills and that the trouble was entirely of their own making. Now that was something which they were not prepared to admit. Their troubles they felt, as we have seen, could be explained in other terms. Why were the other nations successful? And they did not worship God. No! it had nothing to do with God at all, it was purely a matter of chance and accident and what was needed to deliver them was a more subtle type of diplomacy and strategy. They could not see that they had been wrong, they felt that there was no case for humiliation and repentance and in any case this teaching seemed to them so childish and so primitive in comparison with what was to be found in other nations. No, they would not confess their sin to God, they would not say that all the trouble was directly traceable to themselves and to their own actions. They desired salvation and deliverance but not at the cost of acknowledging their sin and confessing their own iniquity before God. Mankind is still like that. That it is frantically in need of help is shown by all the many cults and movements that are to be seen and by all the devices of men in their attempt to find a way of peace and deliverance. Why then does it not accept the gospel, the gospel that has brought all that and more to countless thousands of souls? Pride is still the cause of the trouble. We want comfort, we desire salvation, but we prefer to go on suffering rather than to acknowledge the real trouble about ourselves. We like offers of salvation which tell us that we are more sinned against than sinning, which pity us and tell us that we have been having a very hard time which we in no way deserved, and which offers some kind of magic word which will change everything for us.

The one way of salvation which is hated and rejected is that which tells us that we have sinned, that we are where we are because we are what we are and which says that the very first and most essential step in our deliverance is not that everything around and about us needs to be changed but we ourselves. That is why the gospel of God is always the last way of escape to be tried. It insists upon our confessing our sinfulness and acknowledging our sin as the cause of all our troubles. We are ready to admit that we could be better and may even desire to be better but we hate to have to admit that we are bad and vile as we are! But such is the trouble and a recognition and acknowledgement of it is ever the first step to salvation.

Coupled with this and closely allied to it is another explanation which we must also consider. It is that these Israelites clearly *thought that they could succeed in extricating themselves from their troubles in their own way and by their own power without the aid of God*. Indeed it is perfectly clear that they regarded this way as being greatly superior and they thought of the words of the prophets, advising and advocating God's way, as but idle chatter. This follows inevitably upon the prime reason. Not realising that their troubles were due to their sin against God, they naturally could not see that there was but one way back which was obviously to accept God's offer. They 'rejoiced in Rezin and Remaliah's son'. They were proud of their actions and ideas and had no doubt whatsoever but that they would be highly successful. In spite of innumerable failures in the past they still trusted to their methods and ideas and they assured themselves and one another that all would be well. Mankind is still confident that it can cure its own ills both personal and national and international. There is nothing indeed about sin which is quite as remarkable as the sanguine optimism which it seems to develop in its dupes. They go on chasing happiness and peace and success in life, ever always confident that they are about to catch it. They break God's laws one after the other; they go back even on their own pet theories and solemn vows and cast consistency to the wind. They care not what it is as long as it appears a hope of deliverance, a hope of peace and happiness. They rejoice in all the modern moral muddle and compromises, feeling that they are superior to all that has gone before, and that they have discovered the way to solve the problems of life. Mankind, in spite of the passage of the centuries, with its usual failure and constantly blighted hopes, is still as self-confident and arrogant as it was in the days of Israel.

Then, again, the Israelites saw very clearly that *to accept God's offer of deliverance and salvation would mean of necessity that they would have to accept his terms* and proceed to live in his way and according to his ideas. And that was something which above all else they hated and to which they objected violently. It might well be that God's method of salvation would be to tell them to do nothing but just, as he had so often done in the past, to tell them to stand still and see his salvation! But that was useless because they desired to be wonderful and to do wonderful things themselves. And then if they accepted his salvation there would have to be an end of disobedience. They would have to give up all the false gods; they would have to finish with and say 'good-bye' to all the sins they had cherished for so many years. It would mean a complete alteration in their lives and a new life which seemed to them to be dull, unintelligent and uninteresting. No! such a price for deliverance was too great. They desired deliverance, they were intensely unhappy and indeed very alarmed at the situation, but even that, yes, anything seemed better to them than living 'the godly life' and subjecting themselves to the guiding hand of God.

Let me say this for them – they were at least logical and saw clearly the condition of salvation in the way that many people do not seem to do at the present time. There are so many who talk about the love of God and bank upon what they call God's way of salvation, who seem to think that that means more or less that they can continue to live as they please as long as they believe in God and in his Son Jesus Christ. These Jews knew better than that. God offers to deliver us in Christ not that we may continue in sin but rather that we may be delivered from it. 'Be not deceived' says St Paul to the church at Corinth, 'neither fornicators, nor idolaters, nor adulterers, nor effeminate, nor abusers of themselves with mankind . . . shall inherit the kingdom of God' (1 Cor. 6:9, 10). A Christian is not merely a man who believes that Christ died for him, he is one who shows that he believes that by living such a life as proves that he hates the sin that drove his Saviour to the cruel death of the cross to atone for his sin. Accepting God's offer of deliverance implies accepting God's terms and conditions with respect to the subsequent life to be lived.

But there can be no doubt but that the ultimate reason and explanation of the refusal of these people to accept God's way is that *they failed to appreciate and to realise the reality of the danger with which they were confronted.* That was ever the trouble with the children of Israel. They never really believed the warning. Look at them right through their history. They did not believe Noah. They thought he was quite mad. They did not believe Lot and caused him to remain in Sodom until it was almost too late. How frequently did they flout the authority of Moses and entirely ignore his commandments and warnings. There was always this trouble and it came out even in the life of Solomon with all his wisdom. And as the story continued it became more and more evident. They ridiculed Isaiah; they tried to kill Jeremiah; the words of many of God's servants all sounded utterly foolish and ridiculous to them. They felt that these men must be silenced else they would play on the imagination of the people and frighten the more illiterate. They scoffed at the warning of the destruction that was about to overtake them. They always felt they could explain away these warnings and that things would certainly never come to such a pass. Their own history was entirely against such a delusion, but still they continued to believe it. The situation is still like that today. Without the slightest shred of evidence with which to support themselves, men still confidently affirm that there is no such thing as judgment, no such condition as hell, and that whatever a man may be here that everything will be all right with him at the end. The teaching of history is set aside, the very word of Jesus Christ the Son of God is pushed aside. Men cannot believe, they say, that the threatenings of Scripture both New Testament and Old Testament can ever really be carried out. So they continue on their way and reject God's offer of salvation in Jesus Christ.

It is just here that the writings of these prophets as history is of utmost importance. Isaiah predicts here that because these people refused God's offer, and trusted to Rezin and Remaliah's son, that destruction swift and terrible shall overcome them in a certain definite manner. What happened? It was all literally and exactly fulfilled as all the predictions of the prophets were fulfilled and as our Lord's prediction of the destruction of Jerusalem was fulfilled. You say you do not believe in punishment and retribution. You pit your word against the Word of God! You are confident and sure and think Scripture to be childish and puerile – all right, you suppose, to frighten people in the past but not enlightened citizens of the twentieth century! My reply is just this: 'All flesh is as grass, and all the glory of man as the flower of grass. The grass withereth, and the flower thereof falleth away: But the word of the Lord endureth for ever' (*1 Pet.* 1:24–25).

4.   But I cannot leave you on such a note. I would appeal to you as I value your immortal soul and desire its salvation from disaster and doom. And I would do so, by just displaying to you as I close, *the glory and the wonder of God's way of salvation*. It is because he is blind that the sinner cannot see it. It is because he is so perverted that it appears to him to be so irksome and so distasteful. Oh! the tragedy of men refusing a salvation which is so glorious and so wonderful. Are you in trouble? Do you realise even vaguely your need? Are you unhappy and sore distressed? Are you finding the battle of life difficult and almost too much? Have you come here tonight because you are almost at your wits' end in some respect or other with a personal problem or sin or something more general? Are you afraid of death and the future life? Whatever your position hearken unto the gospel which is:

(i) *At hand*. There was no need for Israel to go outside Jerusalem and the confines of her own land – to Rezin and Remaliah's son – to make alliances and to find help. The God who had brought them to Jerusalem, who had kept them there, and who had always been with them there, was still offering his help there. That is always one of the most glorious things about the gospel – it comes to us exactly and precisely where we are. The trouble was in Jerusalem, the salvation offered was also in Jerusalem and is typified by the stream, the waters of Shiloah, mentioned in my text. My dear friend, you have no need to search or to look, or to travel far and wide. The gospel of Jesus Christ comes to you exactly where you are. Are you down in a gutter of sin? It comes there. Are you heart-broken and tried and frightened? It comes there also. You need not move. Where you are Christ Jesus the Son of God is standing by your side. He just asks you to look unto him. Place and time make no difference. Whenever and wherever you need him he is always there. Turn to Christ!

(ii) But it is also a way of salvation which is *simple and lowly*. The people refused 'the waters of Shiloah which go softly'. How quiet and unobtrusive is God's way in comparison with man's way. Men believe in armies and battalions, in organizations, in bustle and activity. And their way of life corresponds to that. God's deliverances are always simple in comparison as the Old Testament history shows everywhere and as we see supremely in the cross of Jesus Christ. He did not cry and shout aloud, 'a bruised reed shall he not break, and the smoking flax shall he not quench' (*Isa.* 42:3), and by dying on a cross he saves. No wonder the world in its wisdom felt it to be folly. It has always done so and still does. But such is the truth. The way of salvation, thank God, is simple, so simple that it is open to all. It is not high and difficult so that only the learned can understand it and avail themselves of it. It does not ask us to do the impossible but tells us that Christ has done it for us all and that all we have to do is to accept what he has done and then show our gratitude by yielding ourselves to him and living only to please him. It is at hand! Yes, and it is so simple that a little child can accept it. And so simple and direct in its teaching afterwards that all who are childlike can walk in these waters of Shiloah that flow softly. 'Learn of me', says Jesus Christ, 'for I am meek and lowly in heart: and ye shall find rest unto your souls. For my yoke is easy, and my burden is light' (*Matt.* 11:29–30).

(iii) And lastly, the salvation which God offers, like the stream, is *constant and never failing*. The empires on which the children of Israel so liked to depend were temporary and constantly changing.

But God remains the same. Circumstances and change make no difference to him and with him. Whatever the need, his strength is always sufficient. Drought might come and parch up everything. The waters of Shiloah still continued to flow softly. They never failed. Oh the folly of trusting to one's passing moods and ideas and the changing schemes of men which never really satisfy. Turn back tonight to the waters of Shiloah. They will satisfy you now. They will wash your guilt away. They will refresh you and revive you and fill you with new life and new power. They will never fail you. Such is the salvation God offers in Jesus Christ his Son who died for our sins and rose again for our justification and who waits to bless you now. It is the only way. And the alternative is damnation. Turn to the waters of Shiloah and be saved.

17

Sound an Alarm [1]

*And he discovered the covering of Judah, and thou didst look in that
day to the armour of the house of the forest.*

*Ye have seen also the breaches of the city of David, that they are
many: and ye gathered together the waters of the lower pool.*

*And ye have numbered the houses of Jerusalem, and the houses
have ye broken down to fortify the wall.*

*Ye made also a ditch between the two walls for the water of the
old pool: but ye have not looked unto the maker thereof, neither had
respect unto him that fashioned it long ago.*

*And in that day did the Lord GOD of hosts call to weeping, and to
mourning, and to baldness, and to girding with sackcloth:*

*And behold joy and gladness, slaying oxen, and killing sheep,
eating flesh, and drinking wine: let us eat and drink; for tomorrow
we shall die.*

*And it was revealed in mine ears by the LORD of hosts, Surely
this iniquity shall not be purged from you till ye die, saith the Lord
GOD of hosts.*

Isaiah 22:8–14

I think you will agree, having listened to a passage like that, that
there is nothing which is quite so remarkable as we read through
the Bible as the way in which, very frequently, we come across a
passage with a strange contemporary ring about it. We discover an
almost exact description of the situation in which we find ourselves,
not merely in general but even with regard to details and *minutiae*.
Now this is not a mere coincidence. It is not an accident. This is
really just an illustration of what the Bible says about itself, or, if
you prefer it, it is an illustration of the great message of the Bible.

The Bible claims to be the Word of God – the Word of God
about himself, the Word of God about man, the Word of God about

[1] Cardiff, 1 January 1957.

the world, the Word of God which tells us why the world is as it is, and the Word of God as to how the world can be put right. That is the whole case of the Bible. It claims that it has a unique teaching with respect to the problem of man. It tells us right at the very beginning that man's troubles in this world and in this life, whether you think of man as an individual or man as a collection of people, have come upon him because of something that happened at the very beginning, at the very dawn of history. The Bible says that man fell from God, that he sinned against God, and that as the result of so doing he is in a state of sin. It says that man, the whole world, has been in that condition ever since the Fall, and that that is the most important and the most significant thing about man that we can ever learn and understand.

In view of this, the Bible says that the whole story of man from that first beginning has always been the same. It does not matter what changes there may be, the real truth is that man is in a state of sin and alienation from God, and that is the cause of all his troubles and of all his problems. So whenever you read your Bible, it does not matter whether you read the Old Testament or the New Testament, whether it is an historical portion, prophetic portion or Psalm, it does not matter whether you are reading about one man, or whether you are reading about the children of Israel as a nation, you will find that the story, the message, is always exactly the same in principle. It is always this story of man in trouble because he is sinful. That is why the Bible is always contemporary, and always up to date, for it says that man is still what man has always been ever since that original sin, ever since that first fall in the Garden of Eden.

Thus it comes to pass that as you are reading through your Bible suddenly you come across a passage and you say: 'Well, that might have been written today, it is an exact description of what is happening at the present time!' Precisely, says the Bible, because all the changes that have taken place in the human race are entirely on the surface; they are mere changes in appearance, in clothing and in externals. Man *qua* man remains exactly what he has always been. So, as you read the account of an old king in the history of the children of Israel you are looking at a modern man; as you read of the children of Israel you are seeing the modern world.

Now the passage before us is a perfect illustration of what I have been saying. Must you not agree with me when I say that I defy you to produce a more accurate, detailed description of the state of mankind in the world today than that which we have in these very verses? You see, the Bible is right when it says: 'There is no new thing under the sun'. What we are told here of the state of the children of Israel, and especially of the city of Jerusalem at this particular juncture in their history, is an exact portrayal of the world at this very moment.

Very well, let us look at it and see what it has to tell us. Here, I say, is the Word of God to any individual in this congregation who is in trouble or distress, it is the Word of God to the whole world immersed and involved as it is in all these alarums and trials and troubles, of wars and rumours of wars, and the horrible possibility of yet worse things to come. Let us then listen to it, and pray God that he will give us his grace and his Spirit to take this message unto ourselves individually, and to ourselves as citizens of the world in which we live.

What is the picture? It is introduced by this remarkable phrase at the beginning of verse eight: 'And he discovered the covering of Judah, and thou didst look in that day to the armour of the house of the forest.' What does he mean by, 'And he discovered the covering of Judah'? You might translate it like this, 'He has taken away the covering of Judah'. He has taken away, in other words, the covering that was over the eyes of the people of Judah. They had a kind of veil before their eyes so that they could not see certain things; but now, says the prophet, the covering has been taken away, and they are suddenly beginning to see these things. How had the covering been taken away? The answer is already given in the early part of the chapter and the whole context and the contemporary history. This was the position. An Assyrian army had entered the land of the children of Israel and it had occupied certain parts of the land already. It was now advancing in the direction of the city of Jerusalem. Now it was that fact that had awakened these people, it was that fact that had taken the covering from their eyes, and had forced them to look at the situation and to recognise certain things. Before that they had been thoughtless and heedless, not paying any attention at all. Certain people amongst them had been trying to call them to their senses, a prophet such as Isaiah and other prophets, but they would not listen. They said: 'Everything is all right, do not bother us, do not trouble us, all is well.' The covering was over their eyes. But now, with the advance of the Assyrian army, suddenly the covering is taken away and they are made aware that something is wrong. And they begin to think and to consider and to face the facts.

How typical! What a perfect description of this present century! What an exact description it is of the late Victorian era and especially the Edwardian era – indeed, what a perfect description it is of what happened in the 1930s between the two world wars. 'Everything is all right. Why, things have never been so good', people said. I am never tired of repeating that, in a sense, the very essence of the gospel message today is to call attention to that fatal optimism! The Victorians seemed to be perfectly satisfied in general with their lives and felt that everything in the world was wonderful. Ah, yes, they said that it could be better, and that it would be still better in the twentieth century. Science was developing, knowledge was growing. Why, there was nothing left but to enjoy the golden era that was about to come. 'Everything is all right', they said; and if anybody ventured to suggest that everything was not all right he was dismissed as a pessimist. Man was inevitably going on towards perfection. Even after the First World War people still continued to say that everything was all right. Go back, those of you who are old enough to do so, and consider the mentality of the twenties and the thirties of this century. Even after the rise of Hitler people said: 'No, no, it cannot happen; you do not get two world wars within a quarter of a century. These things cannot happen.' The veil, the covering, was there, and they could not see. And it has been the same even after this last World War. This fatal complacency, this refusal to recognise what was happening in the world has persisted.

But here are people from whom at last the covering is taken away and they are forced to face it. Is not something like that happening to us, I wonder? Have not the events of the last months taken the covering away from the eyes of every person who is capable of thinking at all? Are we not being forced to ask certain serious vital ultimate questions? What is the matter?

The covering has been taken away. Then, what did they discover? We are told in verse nine: 'Ye have seen also the breaches of the city of David, that they are many . . .' The covering having been taken away, they were forced by the advance of the Assyrian army to begin to look at and to examine the wall, the defensive wall that surrounded the city of David. And for the first time they discovered that there were many breaches and many holes in the wall. They had never seen them before, but now they discovered that there were many.

Let us be clear about this. It was not the Assyrian army that had made the breaches. The Assyrian army had not yet reached the city of Jerusalem. Why then were there breaches in the wall? Here is the answer – simply because of the complacency and the indolence and the slackness of the children of Israel, the citizens of Jerusalem. They were enjoying themselves and having a good time. They did not inspect their walls. They did not examine them and make sure that everything was all right. Occasionally a mason or a foreman would come and say: 'Look here, it seems to me that you need to re-point the walls at certain places'. 'Don't be alarmists,' they replied, 'let us go on having a good time. Don't talk about the need of re-pointing.' And so they had neglected the wall and ignored all warnings; they had allowed things to go on. The result was that the mortar had crumbled and at last the bricks and the stones had collapsed and there was actually a hole, a breach in the wall. Sheer negligence, nothing else! This fatal complacency that said that everything was all right and that there was no need to worry or to be an alarmist!

Am I not still describing the modern situation? Is not this the fatal complacency that has been so evident in this country? Is not this the way in which this country, which was once a religious country, has become an irreligious country? Is it not entirely due to this slow subtle process that goes on almost unobserved? We will not listen, and when people call our attention to it they are dismissed. That is how it happens.

These points in the walls of Jerusalem did not suddenly fall in. No, no; it was a very slow, insidious process. But it had gone on almost imperceptibly from day to day. And at last there is a collapse and there is a hole. That is how it always works. That is how it happens in the life of a nation. The great Roman Empire did not suddenly collapse; it was a very slow process that undermined its health and its strength, its vigour and its life. And it has been the same with every great empire and every great nation. It was always the trouble with the children of Israel.

But it is exactly the same in the life of every individual. No man suddenly goes wrong and all to pieces; it is a very subtle, it is a very slow process. He starts by being just a little bit slack here and there. 'It is all right,' he says, 'nothing is happening.' He just forgets to say his prayers which he was taught to say by his parents. Nothing in it! Of course not! And he begins to play with drink. Ah, just another drink. Of course he is not going to be a drunkard. No, no; just a little bit of moral slackness. And so it comes in. It is imperceptible and you yourself do not know it. Someone else says: 'Look here, do you know where you are going? What is happening to you? You are not as faithful as you once were to your prayers, to your church, and to your Bible. Don't you think you are playing with fire?' 'Do not be an alarmist,' you say, 'do not be silly. I know what I am doing, I am well aware of where I am, and I am in control of myself.' That is how you speak, is it not? And you know nothing about it until there is an actual breach in the wall. You suddenly find that you have lost your chastity or your purity, you have suddenly lost your character. Something precious and vital has suddenly gone. That is how it happens. It is not the enemy coming in and smashing it down. No, no, it is sheer indulgence, complacency and negligence on our part. So these things happen, and suddenly we are confronted by the situation. Something happens and we are awakened. We have to wake up and rub our eyes and we discover the trouble – the advance of the Assyrian army.

Is not this happening today? Are we not all at last beginning to be aware that there is something wrong with man, something wrong with the world? The events of the last months must surely have awakened us!

Ah, yes, that is all right, that is very good. But the vital question arises just at that point. What are the children of Israel going to do about this? What did they do about it? The answer is that it was just here they went tragically wrong; and it was because of their failure at that very point that the prophet addresses this message to them. It was because of that tragic failure that eventually they were conquered and their city was razed to the ground and destroyed, and they were carried away captives into the land of Babylon. Here we have God's message to them designed to prevent that calamity. And it is God's message to us today to prevent the same calamity.

Let us look at it individually for a moment. Every one of us is like this city of Jerusalem. Every one of us is under the eye of God. Every one of us in this world is determining an eternal destiny. The most vital matter for us, therefore, is this. If we have discovered that things are not well with us, if we have any reason for being concerned about our lives, and for feeling that we have gone wrong or gone to pieces in certain respects, and want to be right, well then, the most important thing for us is to discover what we have to do. And the same applies to this nation, the same applies to all the nations, and to the whole world of man.

What do we observe? What did the citizens of Jerusalem do? We are told here, first and foremost, of the frantic and the futile attempts of the children of Israel to deal with their problem. Did you notice it? 'Ye have seen also the breaches of the city of David, that they are many . . .' And what did they do about it? 'Thou didst look in that day to the armour of the house of the forest.' 'Ye gathered together the waters of the lower pool . . . Ye have numbered the houses of Jerusalem, and the houses have ye broken down to fortify the wall. Ye made also a ditch between the two walls for the water of the old pool . . .' Now let us look at this. Here they are, the advance of the Assyrian army has at last taken off the veil, they are wide awake, and they say: 'We are in a desperate position. You see the breaches in the wall. What can we do about it?' And they began to get really busy and active. You notice that they first of all went to that 'armoury in the forest', the place where they kept their implements of war – their chariots, horses and various implements which were used in making war. They rushed to their 'Woolwich Arsenal' if you like, and to all their arsenals. They found out what they had there, and then added to them, and made great military preparations.

But they did not stop at that. They did something about their water supply: 'Ye gathered together the waters of the lower pool.' It seems they were even going to use that as a means of defence. And then they did a most heroic thing. They began to number every house in Jerusalem, and then they sent round the experts who said: 'We have not sufficient stones to build up the breaches' – no reserves you see! Not being aware of what was happening to the wall they had not provided bricks and stones and everything that was necessary. So they now become desperate and they say:

'What can we do?' So they numbered and inspected every house in Jerusalem, and then they decided that the only thing to do was to pull down some of those houses in order that they might have the bricks and the stones to repair the breaches in the wall. Some people were called upon to sacrifice their homes and their houses in order to defend the whole city. And so they pulled down certain houses and repaired the breaches. Then there was that pool between the two walls. Tremendous excitement and activity and bustle and busyness – trying to save the situation lest the enemy might come in.

Note the number of things they did. Note the variety of things they did. Note the heroic methods which they adopted. What a perfect description it is, once more, of this present century in which we live! Never has man been quite so busy in trying to repair the breaches in his life as during this present century. Never has there been so much busyness and bustle and organising and planning as during this present century! All designed, as was the case with the children of Israel, to stop the rot and to build up the breaches, and, somehow or another, to save civilisation against the threat that is coming ever nearer. That is the picture.

May I remind you of some of the heroics in which we have indulged precisely as the children of Israel did of old? Think of all the political measures. Think of them here in our own country – home politics. Think of the acts of Parliament we have passed in order to try to save the situation. Think of all that we have done in international politics – League of Nations, United Nations' Organisation, conferences, meetings – everything conceivable to bring people together and to solve our problems together. Has the world ever been as busy as it is at the present time? And as it has been during the whole of this present century? Pick up the biographies of statesmen who lived a hundred years ago and more. Oh! how leisurely their lives seem to us! Parliament used to have very long vacations, ministers were away for months. What a leisurely life it was! And look at the busyness of this present century, bustling to get this pool ready, pulling down these houses, getting that waterway into position, rushing to the armoury! Never has man been so busy, in a political sense, trying to save the world. Then think of it in terms of education – the social effort as well as the political. Look at all the money that is being spent on education in all the countries. Why, even in my lifetime I have seen it developing and increasing in an almost incredible manner. I remember the time when you first had Directors of Education in local authorities. They now have Assistant Directors and those who organise Further Education, and music and almost everything. The whole thing has become a mammoth organisation and we are spending millions of pounds upon it. All in an attempt to build up the breaches in the wall and somehow to save our civilisation. There are all sorts and kinds of Councils and Conferences, even Marriage Guidance Councils. They did not have things like that in the past; but now everything is being organised. We are aware, you see, of the social problem, and we say that it must be dealt with. We are working day and night in all directions, trying somehow to save the situation. It is but the bustle and the busyness of the children of Israel of old. And then all the talking and the writing about the application of the Christian ethic, and that that is all that is needed to put an end to war, and to make everything perfect. And then the economic remedies on top of that. 'It is finally an economic problem', say certain schools of thought, 'and if only you can put these right and make these adjustments everything will be put right.' We have done that in a large measure but still the problem remains. And then the military solution – the money we are spending on armaments. And so on endlessly.

We must not stay with these details. All I am concerned to show is this – that these children of Israel had done all these things and had indulged in those heroic methods in an attempt to save their city. But it completely failed. It was frantic but it was equally futile. And I tell you in the name of God that everything we have done as men in this present century has been equally frantic and equally futile as regards the real problem. Our world today is proving that. The nations have never been so highly organised in every department of life as today. Yet look at the facts, look at the breaches, look at the enemy that is advancing.

Why does all this fail? Listen to the answer. The first is that, even when the cover had been taken off their eyes, *they could still not see the real character of their problem.* They failed to see, first of all, the moral character of their problem. To them it was purely a military problem. They never saw that it had a moral aspect. As far as they could understand it was just a question of these breaches in the wall and making use of that armoury, supplementing it, and getting everything ready so that they could meet the enemy when he came. They never realised that it was essentially a moral problem. That is the message of verse thirteen. In spite of what God tells them in calling them to repentance, this is what happened: 'Behold joy and gladness, slaying oxen, and killing sheep, eating flesh, and drinking wine, for tomorrow we shall die.'

What does that mean? Let us divide it up in this way. The first thing that was so tragically wrong about these people was that even the situation to which they had become awakened did not make them serious. In spite of the desperate character of their plight they are still light-hearted, flippant, and still feeling confident and assured. 'Joy and gladness . . . let us eat and drink'! The Bible is a remarkable book, is it not? Is there anyone who can listen to things like this and still not believe that the Bible is the Word of God? This is just an exact description of what is happening today. We are awakened, we are disturbed. This business in Egypt, this business in Hungary, and the other possibilities. We are aware that something is wrong. It is on the front page of the newspaper. But side by side with it on the front page is the endless series of photographs of these women, these adulteresses, and their married relationships! As if it mattered to anybody or ever mattered to anybody at any time! When the world is perhaps on the verge of a third world war, we must hear all about these filthy details of these immoral livers on the front pages! We are still not serious, though we have passed through two World Wars. You cannot read your newspapers without getting all this trivial nonsense still! Side by side with the serious is the flippant and the carefree. The popular press of this country still shows a fundamental lack of seriousness.

But that is not the whole truth about this moral failure. The flippant and the carefree attitude is due to something else, and that is the love of ease and the love of pleasure. Though the enemy is advancing, though the breaches are in the wall, though they have not got reserves and are having to pull down houses and do things like that in order to save the situation, still this is the position – 'joy and gladness, slaying oxen, and killing sheep, eating flesh, and drinking wine. Let us eat and drink.' Nothing must be allowed to disturb our pleasure, not even a war! Even the last war was not allowed to disturb our pleasure. No, we must still have our drink.

There are many things we can go without, and did have to go without, but not without drink. Not without our pleasure, not without our sex, not without that kind of entertainment coming over the wireless. Nothing must disturb our pleasure. The things we like and the things we enjoy must always go on. That is the reason why we refuse to be serious. Did you realise that the industrial problems confronting this country today are ultimately moral problems? They are not economic problems essentially, they are moral problems. Whatever may be the final outcome of this business of the Suez Canal, according to some of the best economists the whole future of this country industrially and economically, is in jeopardy.

Why is the future in jeopardy? I say that it is for moral reasons. It is the love of ease and the love of pleasure. It is this new false, wrong attitude towards work. It applies on every side – the owners, the managers, the masters are as guilty as the workmen. Let us be quite clear about this. Sin is no respecter of persons and this moral rot is running right through the whole of society. There are too many owners in industry whose chief ambition is not to do a good day's work but to be called 'Gentry' and to enter the fringes of the Court circles. Their idea is to use their business in order that they may be gentlemen! They are interested in fox-hunting and racing and things like that. They are not interested in their work as such. It was they who began the long week-end habit and started the five-day week. There it is amongst them. But it is equally true amongst the working classes. They are simply repeating what they have seen the others do. They argue: 'If the owner can afford to work only five days a week, why should I work more than five days a week? If he must have his cigars, why should not I have my cigarettes? If he must have his wine and his expensive drinks, why should not I have my beer?' A perfectly logical argument. It is the same, all along the line, from top to bottom. Work is regarded as a nuisance, and the only value of business is that it provides money with which we can buy food and drink and have a good time and enjoy ourselves. So whatever may be the position of the country, 'I must still go fox-hunting', says one; 'I must watch that football match mid-week', says the other. And so together they neglect their work, and the whole country may be in jeopardy. It is a moral problem. The problem of this country industrially today is not fundamentally an economic one, it is not a social one, it is a moral problem. The attitude towards work is absolutely wrong. Work has become a nuisance – merely the means for providing money. This love of ease and of pleasure!

Then you notice the fatalism that always accompanies this. 'Let us eat and drink', they say, 'for tomorrow we shall die.' What is the use of anything? That is the modern man, is it not? He is an utter cynic. He is in a state of utter despair. He says: 'What is the use of anything? We all may be dead. If that bomb is used we are finished. Very well, in the meantime let us have a good time, let us eat and drink.' Absolute fatalism and despair.

But still more important and still more serious, the people of Jerusalem had not realised *the religious character of their problem*. Listen to the text. They had indulged in their heroic methods: 'But ye have not looked unto the maker thereof, neither had respect unto him that fashioned it long ago.' They ran to the armoury, they ran to the pools, they ran to the walls and pulled down houses. They ran everywhere, here and there, but there is one thing they never did, they never looked up, they never looked to God. They never realised that it was ultimately a religious problem.

In other words, the whole story of the tragedy of the children of Israel is just that they forgot God, and forgot that they were God's people. They forgot that it was God who had given the land and who had made them a nation. They forgot that it was God who had given them the city and every blessing and every victory that they had ever enjoyed. They forgot that. They did so because they had a wrong view of God and a wrong view of themselves.

Now that is as true today as it was of those children of Israel of old. Are the present calamities really causing people to think and to turn to God and to think of him? Are they even causing men and women to get a right and a true view of themselves as man? This is the ultimate and the only solution to the whole problem. Man is not an independent creature, an autonomous creature who can manage his own affairs. Man is a creature made by God, fashioned by God in his own image long ago, as this city of Jerusalem had been fashioned by him. Man has been made by God and for God, and he can only function truly as long as he is obedient to the laws of his own nature, the law of his being. The world is in trouble because man does not know the truth about himself. He does not know that he can never be successful and happy and truly prosperous unless he is being blessed by God. He may tackle his problems economically, politically, socially, educationally, and in a thousand and one ways, but until he realises that he is made for God and dependent upon God all will be in vain; because he is a creature of God, and he will never succeed without the blessing of God. It is this fatal failure to realise that the problem is a moral problem, and that it is a religious problem, that damns all our efforts.

Then the third thing they failed to realise was this – *the profound and the radical character of the problem.* The children of Israel always thought that though there was trouble it was but a little trouble. They were always listening to the prophets who said: 'Peace, peace,' when there was no peace. They said that there was something wrong, but that there was no need to be an alarmist, or to be frightened. There was only just a little wrong and it could soon be put right. They never realised the radical character, the profound character, of their trouble.

Listen to Isaiah putting it here in these wonderful terms: 'You have done all this', he says, 'but you have not looked unto the maker thereof, neither had respect unto him that fashioned it long ago.' What does he mean? Let me put it to you as a simple illustration. The problem of man as he is in the world today is a very profound, a very radical, a very deep, a very great problem. Look at it like this. Think of a man driving a motor-car. Often in his experience something or another has gone wrong. He has got out and he has lifted up the bonnet of his car; he sees a connection loose, he screws it tightly again and off goes the car. Again it stops. 'Oh,' he says, 'it is just a plug that needs a bit of cleaning'. And off he goes again. Then another stop. He fails to deal with it this time and turns into the nearest garage. In a few seconds the mechanic puts it right. But then a day comes when he has another stop, and he says: 'All right, I will see if I can put this right.' But he fails and he goes into the nearest garage. The man there does his best, but he cannot put it right this time. The local garage-man is no longer adequate. He says: 'You need something further.' So the man tries a larger garage. But there the expert comes to him and says: 'I am sorry to have to tell you that your car is hopelessly broken down. There is only one thing to do with it; it must be sent back to the makers, you need a new engine.'

That is the Bible's message to man: 'You must go back to the original fashioner. You yourself, the local mechanic, the large garage, are no longer adequate. Back to the Maker! Back to the works! There is something radically wrong, something profound. Something essentially new is needed.' That is what Isaiah is saying in effect: 'Your heroic methods and your tinkering with the walls, even though you pull down houses and make sacrifices is not going to deal with the situation. You must go back to your Maker.'

That being interpreted and stated in a modern form can be put like this. The real trouble with man in sin is not a problem that can be settled by Acts of Parliament, nor by education and culture, nor by economics and social methods and all your societies and organisations, good and essential as these things are negatively and in and of themselves. For man's trouble is in his nature. It is in his heart. Man is as wrong and as hopeless and as vile as this, that he cannot be improved, he cannot be put right by just a little adjustment here and there. He must go back to his Maker. He has got to go back to God. He needs to be made anew, he needs a new engine, a new nature, a new heart; he needs to be made a 'new man'. And nothing short of that will ever meet the situation.

But that is the very thing that the children of Israel never realised, and they went into captivity. Modern man does not realise it, or he would not still trust to his own expedients and his own devices. He does not realise the profound character of his problem.

Finally, and to cap it all, is *man's tragic blindness to the doom that awaits him if he continues as he is.* That is the message of verse fourteen: 'And it was revealed in mine ears by the Lord of hosts, Surely this iniquity shall not be purged from you till ye die, saith the Lord God of hosts.' God had spoken to these children of Israel and had called them to repentance: 'In that day did the Lord God of hosts call to weeping, and to mourning, and to girding with sackcloth.' What was their response? 'Behold joy and gladness . . . ' 'We could not care less . . . ' Who is God? Who is God to a modern man? Man is so brilliant that he can split atoms! What is God to a modern man with all his education? Sob-stuff! Tripe! Christ! Ha! suitable for an oath or a curse. To be spat upon! 'Your Christ and his blood', says the modern man, 'I have outgrown such rubbish!' 'Joy and gladness, slaying oxen and killing sheep, eating flesh and drinking wine: let us eat and drink'. That is the response. It is all because he does not realise that this is God's world, that God has made this world, that God is 'the Lord God of hosts', who has brought the whole cosmos into being out of nothing, who can smash an army by blowing upon it, who can raise kings and pull them down again. The Lord God of hosts! The modern man says religion is played out, that Christianity is old-fashioned. He could not care less. He is not interested. But he is talking about the God in whose hand his breath is, and whose are all his ways (*Dan.* 5:23).

We all have to meet this God. You cannot escape him, you cannot evade him. He has made you. You are in his world. He can take your breath out of you just when he pleases. And you will certainly stand before him in the judgment. These people scoffed at him and his Word; but his Word came true, was verified, and they were ruined and destroyed and carried away. Man is still facing God and the judgment to come.

What then can we do? It is all here, and it is very simple. We have but to listen to the Word of God, and this is the Word: 'In that day did the Lord God of hosts call to weeping, and to mourning, and to baldness, and to girding with sackcloth.' What does he mean? He means repentance, a true repentance. He does not just mean that when things are desperate you have a 'National day of prayer'! He does not mean that when things are very bad that the great of the land go to a service in Westminster Abbey, or elsewhere, and nobody can remember when some of them were seen in a place of worship before ! He does not mean just attending a civic or some other formal service annually. He does not mean that. He means that we must begin to realise that we are what we are, and that our world is as it is, because we have forgotten God, because we have desecrated and broken his holy laws, because we are proud and arrogant and mad, and drunk with our own self-importance. He means that we must realise that we are going to die and to stand before him, and having had a glimpse of his holiness and his law, and having seen the truth about ourselves, we become alarmed and terrified and begin to weep and to mourn and tear out our hair and shave our heads as an expression of our grief and sorrow and terror and alarm. (They did that literally in ancient times to express grief and sorrow. We must do what corresponds now.) He means that we must humble ourselves under the mighty, almighty hand of God and plead his pardon and his forgiveness; that we surrender our lives entirely unto him, that we go to him and acknowledge it all, and casting ourselves upon his mercy say: 'What wouldest thou have me to do?' And God will then say to us: 'Believe on the Name of my only-begotten Son. I have sent him into your world because it is as it is, and he alone can save it. I have sent him, he has done the work; he has died for you and for your sins. I forgive you in him and because of his blood shed for you. Give yourselves to him, receive his salvation, submit yourselves to him and let him make you anew.' That is God's Word to man today. Turn back to God. Recognise your need of his forgiveness. Recognise your need of a new life, a new start, a new nature, a new heart, a new beginning. Ask him for the gracious influences of the Holy Spirit. Submit yourself entirely to him and surrender your life to him. And then get up and walk in obedience to his laws. Let the world laugh at you! Say to them: 'This is God's way, it is the only hope, it is the only way of being saved from final disaster.' Repent and acknowledge and confess your sin to God. Obey him when he tells you to believe in his Son, who died for you and your sins. Follow him whatever the cost and you will find yourself saved, you will find yourself at peace with God, with a new life, a new nature, and a new outlook upon everything. Fear of death will go, fear of the judgment will go. Having gone back to the Maker, to the Fashioner and Designer, you will find yourself a new man.

This is essentially an individual message. Nations do not turn to Christ together, but individuals do; and as individuals do in large numbers, nations are influenced. Start with yourself therefore, and then tell others. Are there breaches in the wall of your life? Have you not lost something very precious in this world? Are you not ashamed in your heart of hearts? Would you not like to be whole, to be holy, to be clean, to be true, to be able to see through life, through death, and to know God and enjoy him? There is only one way – go back direct to him. And as masses of people shall do so, so the moral and the social and the economic and the industrial and all the other problems will begin to be solved. Look to your Maker!

18

From the Mirage to Christ[1]

And the parched ground shall become a pool.

Isaiah 35:7

So the statement we are to consider reads in the Authorised Version. In the Revised Version we find, 'The glowing sand shall become a pool.' But I think the best translation may be the one which is suggested in the margin of the Revised Version where you find, 'And the mirage shall become a pool.' Now here we find ourselves on the first Sunday night of a new year, and we are all of us quite instinctively and inevitably thinking about life and facing the future. I want to suggest to you that there is no better way in which we can do that than to consider these striking words which are to be found in this verse.

In the entire chapter the prophet Isaiah is giving a preview of some of the glorious and wonderful results of the coming of Christ and the great salvation which he shall bring. He describes it all with picturesque imagery. 'He will come and save you', says the prophet, or 'He himself will come and save you', and the result of his coming will be that 'the eyes of the blind shall be opened, and the ears of the deaf shall be unstopped. Then shall the lame man leap as an hart, and the tongue of the dumb sing: for in the wilderness shall waters break out, and streams in the desert. And the mirage shall become a pool.'

Now this is a very typical and characteristic Old Testament way of looking at life. It is a typical Eastern way of looking at life. The Easterner as we find, not only in the Bible, but in other literature, very naturally and instinctively viewed life as a great journey. Many

[1] Westminster Chapel, 5 January 1947.
This sermon is also currently published in booklet form by the Evangelical Movement of Wales, Bridgend, entitled *Water in the Desert*.

of them were nomadic people who were accustomed to taking journeys. Not infrequently it happened that they had to cross a desert and wilderness which was not only trackless but also, and more serious, without water. There was no experience to which the typical Easterner was more accustomed than just that travelling through the desert with the broiling sun beating upon his head, making for a destination that never seemed to arrive, beginning to feel tired and weary, longing for some water to try to slake his thirst, to revive his drooping spirits, to give him new energy and fresh power. As he thus went across these sandy wastes, with the sun beating down upon him, ever and anon he saw a marvellous pool of water. It quickened his heart and he said to himself, 'I have only to arrive there and I shall find all the water I need – I shall be able to rest in that oasis and satisfy my every want and then go on with the journey.' But when he arrived at that point he found nothing there but glowing sand – there was no water. That is what is meant by a mirage, it is one of those peculiar natural phenomena that are found in desert places – the sun shining upon the sand in such a way and in such a manner as to give the appearance of a sheet of water though no water is there. It is a mere appearance, a mirage, an illusion. Then the traveller would continue on his journey and again he would see another amazing sheet of water. Again he is filled with gratitude, but on arriving at that point once more he has the same experience. It is only a mirage – there is no water. On and on he would go and he might be deluded by mirage after mirage.

Now that is the picture we have in our text and the teaching of the Bible is that life is like that. There is nothing that is so typical of the biblical language as just this idea of life, arising, as I say, very naturally from Eastern conditions. *Man, according to the Bible, is like one taking a journey;* he enters into this world and he is making for a destination; he is a pilgrim, he is a sojourner. Those are the terms – he is a traveller. You find the same idea in our hymns. There is nothing so common in the hymn books as this self-same picture of life. But the Bible does not stop at that; it tells us that man as he goes through this journey called life is constantly facing what the Easterner so constantly experienced in his literal, physical journey through the actual wilderness or desert. We have not gone very far in this life and world, according to the Bible, before we begin to feel a little tired. We may have started out in life with rose-coloured spectacles on, and everything was going to be perfectly beautiful and wonderful. We may have thought there would be no real problems. But we have not gone very far before we have found that life has its problems and its difficulties, and we begin to know what it is to be tired and what it is to be weary. We have all known what it is to long for satisfaction. We are all looking for something, and as we go along, according to the Bible, we are constantly seeing these appearances of water and of supply. But its ultimate message is that apart from the gospel of our Lord and Saviour Jesus Christ they will all prove to be nothing but a mirage.

There are certain things for which everybody is looking. Everybody is looking for peace and for joy; everybody wants happiness. We all look for life in a real sense – life worthy of the name, life with certain satisfactions and with certain securities. We are here in the wilderness, in the desert, and, because of our experiences, because of our needs, because of our tiredness, we are looking for something to give us rest, relief, power and life. Now in that situation we are confronted by two possibilities. There is the offer made by the world and by life outside of God and outside of Christ; and on the other hand is the great offer of the gospel of Jesus Christ. Let us consider these two possibilities.

The world is constantly offering us these very satisfactions that we need. The world is catering for man as he is this evening. The world in many different ways is assuring us that if we only accept its message we shall obtain the very things we want. How does it do so? I have no time to give you an exhaustive list, but let me mention some of the ways in which men are trying to find these satisfactions, and the ways in which the world is offering them.

Take first the idea of pleasures – entertainments. There are large numbers who seem to believe quite seriously that everything that is needed in life can be obtained in that way. They live for one round of pleasure after another – reading novels, drinking, dancing, gambling, looking at films and football matches. Such are some of the offers the world makes to enable us to get rid of our troubles and problems and difficulties. The whole life of pleasure and entertainment, as it is so highly organised at the present time, is based on that supposition. You cannot read your morning newspaper without seeing that. People are seeking satisfaction and they believe that the world can really satisfy them along those lines.

To others it is satisfaction through the possession of wealth. They believe if they get money they will be able to buy happiness and pleasure. They seem to think that the royal protection against all troubles is an economic one. I am not only thinking of those who are wealthy in the customary sense but of all those who pin their faith to an economic solution. They believe that if only the money problem can be settled they will have everything that they need and everything that can be desired. That becomes their main end and object in life.

Others say that that is not the way to obtain satisfaction. The way to satisfaction and happiness is through learning, intellectual interests – art, music, philosophy, studying problems, debating and discussing – an intellectual life. 'There,' they say, 'if you only accept it and give yourself to it, you will ultimately find all the satisfaction you need.'

There are many who are seeking it in marriage and in family life. The whole life of many people in this country today is lived within the limits of the family. That is everything to them and there they find a temporary satisfaction. That has become the whole of life to them. They give themselves to the family and are confident that that is the way to live and enjoy life and to get ultimate satisfaction.

But then there are those who, having tried all these things and having found them wanting, are firmly convinced that what they need is a change. Given a change of environment and circumstances, a new start, a new beginning, all will be well. It is that idea which explains so much of what is happening in this modern world. Here is a person travelling through life in this world, feeling tired and miserable and unhappy. He wants to be happy, she wants to be happy. What is to be done? Suddenly they see a hope, an oasis, an appearance in the desert. What does it say? It says, 'make a new start, break this particular engagement you are in at the moment, get out of that marriage relationship, make a fresh one and there you will find happiness.' They are confident that if this first marriage is broken and another is started all is going to be well.

Others believe that if they just leave this country and go to another country that there they will find what they want. I need not elaborate. Am I not stating the facts concerning life tonight? 'What I need is a new beginning, a new job, all my troubles are due to the situation I am in. If only I could have a new beginning, a new marriage, a new country, a new job, something new – there it is away in the distance, if only I could get there I should have complete satisfaction.' That is the outlook.

Then think of it on a larger scale, in terms of the faith of mankind in new ideas. The history of the world in a sense is just the history of man clinging desperately to new hopes and ideas, believing that if only this new thing can be put into practice all his problems will be solved. You see it happening in the realm of the individual, in the realm of nations, and in the realm of the world at large. Some thirty years ago we said we really were fighting the last war, 'the war to end war'. We pinned our faith to the League of Nations and various other things – new ideas, new hopes springing from new thoughts and ideas.

Then think of the way in which mankind so often believes that an improvement in social conditions, or some political action, is really going to change everything. Is it not rather sad today to read some of the poets of the mid-Victorian period, but still sadder to read the statements of the statesmen and politicians during the last sixty years ! How certain they were that if only certain things were done in Westminster, paradise would be achieved – 'If only, if only . . .' – then all would be well.

Now I have hurriedly reminded you of some of the ways in which men and women, individually and collectively, are made to believe by the world that their needs can all be answered and satisfied. We are all, I say, in the journey; we are all aware of this feeling of fatigue and tiredness and of dissatisfaction; and we have all seen these things that are offered to us there in the future. But isn't the Bible stating the simple truth when it tells us that the promised satisfaction always proves to be nothing but a mirage? Isn't this the case in the life of the individual? Isn't it a fact in the life of the world generally? Look back on your history books, read the biographies, study the history of man, do you not find that all along it has just proved to be a mirage! Haven't you observed that people become a pool? The thing you see is going to be real; it is not an appearance, it is actually going to happen. The first claim of the gospel is that it really does do for us and supply to us the very things we need. 'The mirage shall become a pool'. How does it do it? Well, the gospel does it like this. It starts by making us understand the real nature of life. The gospel, in other words, is the exact opposite of everything I have been trying to say. The first thing the Bible does is to make a man take a serious view of life; it makes a man see himself. It reminds us quite simply of the fact we constantly forget, that we have all started in life and we have all to end it. Now the gospel just starts there. It makes us see the real nature of life as a journey, a travelling, a pilgrimage. It gets rid of all those superficialities – the brightness and the glitter of it all – and it says, 'Man, you are here tonight but you may not be here tomorrow.' It tells us we have within us an immortal soul and spirit which goes on beyond death and the grave into eternity.

Then *this message brings us immediately and directly to Christ.* That is the very essence of the gospel. May I put that negatively, on this first Sunday night of a new year. The gospel does not in the first instance ask us to make any new resolutions. It is the world that does that. The gospel of Jesus Christ is not an appeal to us to start living a better life because it is the first Sunday of a new year. The gospel of Jesus Christ only asks you to do one thing and that is to come to Christ and to submit to him. Let me tell you why the gospel does not ask you to make new year resolutions. I will do so in some words written by the great Dr Samuel Johnson. This is what he says: 'I have now spent fifty-five years in resolving, having, from the earliest time almost that I can remember, been forming schemes of a better life. I have done nothing. The need of doing, therefore, is passing, since the time of doing is short.' What an honest confession! And what was true of Dr Johnson has been true of all. We have all made our new year resolutions; how often have we decided to be better but we are not better! The gospel tells us that it cannot be done that way. The gospel of Jesus Christ is something entirely different, it pictures us in the desert with the sun blazing upon us. We are all tired and weary and exhausted; we have been running after mirages. We have tried pleasures and we have had our fill. They have taken something out of us and have left us empty. We have searched here and there; we are staggering in this desert called life. What is the use of asking such a person to make a new year resolution? What is the use of asking such a man suddenly to climb a mountain? What is the use of asking such a man to be perfect? We cannot do it – we are tired and weary. What we need is rest, peace, refreshment and a new life. And if I say nothing else, may this be abundantly plain and clear, the gospel does not ask you to do anything in the first instance but just to come to Christ. There you are in the wilderness, in the desert; and there, I tell you, is the very thing you need. It is there in a Person. 'But,' you say, 'I have been deluded by mirages so often, isn't this just another mirage?' My reply is, Come to Christ, and 'the mirage shall become a pool'. This is different. This message does not ask you to do something impossible; it assures you that he can give you everything you need and much more. It assures you that if you just come you will find it is the oasis it appears to be – that the blazing sand illusion has become a veritable pool.

How does Christ do this? He does it first of all by putting me right with God. I said just now that the trouble with all the other methods is that they forget God. The gospel starts there. The gospel reminds us that we are not only in this life and world, but that we are also facing God. The first problem is how can I be put right with God? The difficulty is that I have sinned against him; I have deliberately forgotten him; I have done things I know to be wrong; I have cursed God in so many ways; I have deliberately turned my back upon him – how can I get right with him? I cannot undo my past. What I have done, I have done. I cannot undo my past, I cannot erase what I have written, I have blotted my book of life. How can I get right with God? There is only one answer, Jesus of Nazareth is the Son of God, and when he went to that cross he went there for you and for your sins. He has borne your sins; he has borne your guilt and punishment; he has died that death that you and I should be put right with God. The first essential thing, without which nothing can be put right, he has done, he has died for our sins; he puts us right with God.

But he not only puts us right with God, he also puts us right. *He gives us a new nature,* he gives us a new life. The gospel of Jesus Christ, I say again, is not an appeal to us to adopt a new moral, ethical code. Thank God, the gospel offers a new life – we can be born again, we can receive a new nature. This leads to a new outlook and to our being filled with new desires – we no longer desire the things we used to, and we desire things that are good. Beyond that it gives us power and strength to overcome; it enables us to defeat old enemies that have got us down through the long years of the past. It enables us to smile at foes and to be more than conquerors in spite of them.

The gospel puts me right with God, it puts me right, and above all he, Christ, satisfies my every need. He never fails, he never changes – whatever I may need in this life Christ can give me and he won't leave me in the hour of death. Look at these other things, death robs us of them – every one. Pleasure will not help you, philosophy will not help you, at that hour. You see a dear one suddenly taken from you and what is the value of money and art and music and all other noble and excellent things? They do not help you when your heart is bleeding and when you seem to have lost everything in life and in this world. They have nothing to give you; but Christ is with us in life and he will be with us in death, he will be with us through the countless ages of eternity. There he is in the desert. He comes to meet you. He has entered into the world and he offers to give you tonight everything you need: rest, peace, satisfaction, happiness, joy, power and a hope that can never fade away. Everyone who has ever met him is ready to say this:

> *O Christ, in Thee my soul hath found,*
>   *And found in Thee alone,*
> *The peace, the joy I sought so long,*
>   *The bliss, till now unknown.*
>
> *I sighed for rest and happiness,*
>   *I yearned for them, not Thee,*
> *But, while I passed my Saviour by,*
>   *His love laid hold on me.*
>
> *I tried the broken cisterns, Lord,*
>   *But, ah, the waters failed!*
> *E'en as I stooped to drink they fled,*
>   *And mocked me as I wailed.*
>
> *The pleasures lost I sadly mourned,*
>   *But never wept for Thee,*
> *Till grace the sightless eyes received*
>   *Thy loveliness to see.*
>
> *Now, none but Christ can satisfy,*
>   *None other name for me!*
> *There's love, and life and lasting joy,*
>   *Lord Jesus, found in Thee.*

'But is it really true', asks someone – 'are you just standing there painting a wonderful picture? Isn't it just another mirage ? Can I be sure that if I come to him and believe your message and yield my life to Christ that he really will prove to be what I need? Will the mirage become a pool?' Let me answer you in the words of another hymn:

> *Finding, following, keeping, struggling,*
> *Is He sure to bless?*
> *Saints, apostles, prophets, martyrs,*
> *Answer: yes!*

All who have ever come to him and tried him have ever found in him full, complete, and final satisfaction.

My dear friends, the mirage shall become a pool at last – it really does happen when you seek it in Christ.

19

Facing Reality

The heart is deceitful above all things, and desperately wicked: who
can know it? I the LORD search the heart, I try the reins, even to
give every man according to his ways, and according to the fruit of
his doings ... Heal me, O LORD, and I shall be healed; save me, and
I shall be saved: for thou art my praise.

Jeremiah 17:9, 10, 14

Of all the charges that are brought against religion from time to
time there is none which, to me, is quite so inexplicable as that
which suggests that religion and Christianity are somehow divorced
from life, and that they thrive and persist only to the extent that
men and women allow themselves to be drawn into and drugged by
the false unreal atmosphere which they create. It is the charge
which is most difficult to understand, I say, but yet it is, perhaps,
the charge which is most frequently heard during these present
days. Regarding the Bible as an admixture of mythology and
history, with more of the former than the latter in the mixture, men
and women today feel that it is more or less a waste of time to
consider what it has to say. They have no time, they say, to study
or to interest themselves in persons and events, the occurrence
and existence of which is, to say the least, doubtful – life with its
attendant circumstances and problems demands all their immediate
attention. 'Conditions of life in the days of the Old Testament',
they tell us, 'were so different, their categories so strange to our
modern ears; likewise the setting and background of the New
Testament were obviously so different from what we know today
that immediately one begins to consider what the Bible has to say
and to look upon life in the light of and in the terms of the Bible,
one immediately is entering into an atmosphere which, from the
standpoint of life today, is unreal and somewhat artificial.'

In other words, there is a large number of persons today who regard religion and Christianity as a superstition or dope – something which, for the time being, helps people to forget their trials and troubles by transporting them into some imaginary Elysian atmosphere where all is well and all sorrows are ended. And, accordingly, the people who still attend their places of worship are those who, lacking real moral stamina and the guts and courage needed to face life honestly and squarely without flinching and without any artificial stimulant, avail themselves of anything which for the time being can bring them relief. They are never too scrupulous or careful about the honesty and integrity of what is provided as long as it does give the relief. That is the way in which our meeting here Sunday after Sunday would be explained and is being explained by many people in this town today – we come here merely to get away from life and to avoid its problems. Religion does for us what novel reading does for them, and what pleasure and sport do for a still larger number. They regard it as our safety valve. We have all known, at some time or other, the stimulating and tonic effect that reading a certain type of novel can have upon us. How one of Scott's romances can make us forget our troubles and see a greater hope for life for the time being! 'Well', say these people, 'your religion does precisely the same thing and operates upon you in exactly the same way. It carries you into a false, unreal atmosphere, where face to face with romantic joy and love, you for the time being forget all that makes you sad. But it is only "for the time being" for no sooner do you have to face life, as it is, once more than you realise how artificial it all was.'

Now they claim that they themselves are realistic, they face life as it is and at its worst. They do not attempt to lull themselves into a false sense of security or of happiness, and regard us not so much with hatred as with mingled contempt and pity. They even go further, at times, and are prepared to grant that, after all, it is a good thing perhaps that we find our relief in this harmless way rather than in some other way which might be more dangerous. They only become infuriated and annoyed when we claim that this and this alone is reality and that all else is blindness and sham.

Now in honesty and fairness we must grant that there is much in what such people say that is perfectly true of many of us who call ourselves religious people. The mistake they make is that they confuse true religion with the abuse of religion – what they say of the latter is entirely true, but how false it is of the former! The fact that many people do indeed make use of religion as a drug does not mean that religion itself is of that nature. It can never be stated too often or too clearly that the business of religion is not to give people a nice comfortable feeling and to make them feel happy for a few hours once a week. There is a tendency in many quarters in these days to emphasise this aspect of religion and to make religious services quiet and soothing for we know how people turn instinctively to the church when faced with death, either their own or a relative's. Now it is not for me or for anyone else to dictate in these matters, but of this I am certain, that people who only turn to God when things go wrong are people who have never known him and are never likely to until they have been changed. The object and business of religion and the preaching of the gospel is not to make you forget your troubles for the time being, but to remove them once and for all, to help you to overcome them. If you merely *forget* your problems while here every Sunday, singing the hymns and listening to the sermon, you have not yet known true religion, for its function is to *solve* your problems. If hitherto your history has been that week after week you have in this hall registered vows that henceforward you will be a different and a better person but still you have gone on in the same old way, I say you have not, so far, felt the power of the gospel, for it is the object and function of the gospel not so much to provoke resolutions as to produce reformation.

The real tragedy of religion in these days is not so much that the masses do not believe in it. It is that they who do profess to believe in it are not changed by it, but rather use it to suit their own convenience. Present-day religion far too often soothes the conscience instead of awakening it; and produces a sense of self-satisfaction and eternal safety rather than a sense of our unworthiness and sinfulness and the likelihood of eternal damnation. Emotionalism is ever the most real, because the most subtle, enemy of evangelicalism. These abuses of religion, these perversions of the pure gospel, lend much colour to the popular charge against religion that it helps in life precisely because it avoids life and that which we call salvation is nothing but self-flattery and a sense of contentment based upon a delusion.

[235]

How false that charge against religion itself really is, any intelligent person who, without prejudice and bias, reads the Bible can readily discover. What often amazes me is how anyone can possibly read the Bible without a shudder and without an awful fright, for while it displays God in all his perfection, it most certainly displays man as he is and at his worst. If there is any one claim which one can safely make concerning the Bible it is that it not only faces but seems to delight in exposing life as it is and at its very worst. For what is it after all but the record of the sinfulness, baseness, hypocrisy, folly, madness and hopelessness of human nature? Is that pleasant reading? There is no sin known to human nature but that you will find it recorded here; delicacy and all restraints seem to be abandoned as we are shown from room to room and department to department. It is a complete and full picture of life – never content with merely recording the virtues and extolling the merits of its heroes, it tells us of their faults and vices also. It presents to us kings and princes amidst the pomp and show of their thrones, and, a few minutes later the very same men grovelling in sin and crime. It shows the glory and the infinite possibilities open to human nature, and, at the same time, the shame and awful potentialities, and it goes further and tells us clearly that if we do not accept the former as the free gift of God we shall inevitably fall into the latter as our destiny. What a drug! What an odd sort of romance this, in which we are told the naked truth about ourselves, are held face to face with our own failures and deficiencies, are shown our own nature and are given an occasional terrifying glimpse into that awful abyss into which, apart from the grace of God in Christ Jesus, we shall inevitably fall. What literature is there in existence that is as terrible as this? Show me the worst morbidly and sordidly realistic book that you can find, it can easily be equalled and surpassed by one out of many stories told in the Bible. And, in addition, there is always this additional fact to be remembered. The men and women who claim that they face life and see it as it is, and who say the very worst about it in their talk and their books, generally have this great consolation that they regard death as the end. The tragedy for them ends in death, but not so in the Bible. In a sense, in the Bible, the tragedy begins at death. 'Life is terrible to those who think', say the moderns, 'full of tragedy and disappointment and evil but cheer up and let's make the best of it for soon we shall be dead and out of our misery.' 'Yes,' the Bible seems to say, 'life is terrible but the real tragedy lies in the fact that death is not the end but merely the point of transition to what will be an eternal destiny.' If there is any document that tells us the truth about life and about ourselves, it is the Bible. It tells us the very worst and then shows us the best. And the business of preaching is not to hide sin but to expose it; not to tell men and women that all is right, that 'God is love' and that they need not worry at all; but to tell them that as things are, as we all are, all is wrong, that God is our Judge and that unless we are so worried and frightened and appalled by the prospect there is no hope for us.

That is the message of religion, seen everywhere in this Book, seen here in these verses which I have chosen as my text tonight and which I pray that by God's grace we may all see before we leave here. Religion is not content with dissecting and analysing life – it does that but does not stop at that. Having exposed life, having revealed its terrible depths, having analysed it to its ultimate components, it does not leave it in shreds but by the divine revelation of God in Jesus Christ it shows the glorious possibility of a new synthesis, a new beginning, a new birth, yes, a new manhood and a new life. The need of that synthesis is made abundantly clear in these verses.

1. *How rarely are we truly conscious of our own natures and of the depths and deceitfulness of our own minds!* We are indeed most 'fearfully and wonderfully made' (*Psa.* 139:14). No wonder that the prophet having said, 'the heart is deceitful above all things, and desperately wicked', should have gone on to ask, 'who can know it?' What depths there are within us! No one really knows us but ourselves – there is an ultimate loneliness and solitariness about each one of us, however gregarious we may be by nature and however highly our social instincts may be developed. Our very nearest and dearest do not know everything about us – we do not tell them everything, however much we may like to think that we do. Just think of this for a moment and you will find how true it is of you, for it is true of each one of us. You tell your best friends and those that are dearest to you everything, all your innermost secrets – so you like to think, but do you actually in deed and fact? Is everything that is to be known about you known to someone? We well know

that that is not the case – there are certain things which we all reserve to ourselves. Certain things about us, certain things we have done we hide from our friends as well as our enemies; from our friends because knowledge of them would grieve and pain them, from our enemies because they would provide a lever whereby they might ruin us and destroy our characters for ever.

What remarkable beings we are! There are certain things of which we never speak to anyone except ourselves. Has this final and ultimate loneliness of your own nature and personality ever struck you? We are born into families and communities and yet how markedly individual we all are. We have secrets that our parents, brothers and sisters, husbands and wives, and children will never know and never discover. When someone tells you that he or she has told you all his or her secrets you can always be sure that that is never the case. However frank and open a person may be there is always something which is held back and reserved. That is why we are always found talking to ourselves particularly after a burst of frankness with someone else! Have you not felt this on many an occasion, that when you have been trying your utmost to be most frank and open you are somehow giving a very false impression of yourself? That is our nature. How deep we are! No one can ever truly understand us. No one knows all the things we have done, leave alone all the things we have thought and have contemplated. Others may know a lot about us, but no one will ever know the whole truth – 'the heart is deceitful above all things, and desperately wicked: who *can* know it?' And on this the majority of men live and trade. What concerns them is not so much right and wrong but rather the question of whether they will be found out or not. On this make-shift and make-belief they go through life, knowing what they call 'the devil's own luck'. If only these things were known and discovered! But they are not, they are covered over, we tell no one about them and keep them secret to ourselves.

It is because of this fact that this society keeps going, for if we only saw right into the depths of each other's mind and thoughts it would all collapse in a moment. What keeps it going is that we do not *know* what is in other people's minds, knowing our own we can guess, but we never know for certain. There is that man smiling in your face and paying you compliments. How honest and transparent he appears to be! Yet who knows what is passing in the recesses of his mind! However much he says he thinks of you, you can be quite sure that he thinks more of himself! Nothing we do is disinterested, we ourselves colour everything. We have motives and interests that the world knows not of, there are depths within us known only to ourselves, struggles with ourselves and our passions, suggestions and thoughts rising from some dark hidden corner in our souls! But enough of this! These are the things we do not mention. These are the things that are to be kept secret and quiet while we go on living as we are, and as we seek to enjoy life. Is that not a true picture? Are we not all as happy as we are merely because all the facts about us are not known? 'The heart is deceitful above all things and desperately wicked: who can know it?'

2.   Yes, there is no doubt but that we are all very clever and very deep, but, and this is the whole point of the message of the prophet here – God is deeper. All the time that we continue being satisfied with the thought that these secret actions, thoughts and ideas of ours are unknown to anyone but ourselves, *we forget the presence and existence of God*. On we go, congratulating ourselves on our cleverness, little realising that in the meantime God, who 'searches the heart and tries the reins', is observing us and watching us and carefully recording everything. You cannot move but that God sees you, you cannot act but that he is watching you, no thought enters into your mind but that he is aware of it. He not only sees you but sees through you, to the very depths of your being. We are as an open book before him. We can hoodwink and fool the whole world, can appear as one thing before it and be in reality something else, but how vain and foolish it is to do so. What is the point and object of doing that when all the time God knows the full facts about us? When we get into difficulties with each other, we quickly manage to extricate ourselves by putting forward some made-up explanation or excuse which satisfies, and we congratulate ourselves on the cleverness and cuteness which we displayed in doing so – we all have a great reserve of ability at our command in such emergencies.

But how ridiculous it is, for we must be finally face to face with God who knows all and who will 'give every man according to his ways and according to the fruit of his doings'. In other words, you will spend eternity exactly along the very same lines upon which you have proceeded in this world. If it has been a patchwork and a make-believe here, it will be the same there. If it has been a sham and a fraud here it will continue the same - we get precisely that which we deserve and have prepared for ourselves.

3.　Is it surprising that the prophet should have prayed, 'Heal me, O Lord, and I shall be healed; save me, and I shall be saved'? He had suddenly realised what a fraud his life was and how un-satisfactory it was, and prayed to be released from it once and for all. *No longer content with fooling and satisfying others, this man faced himself and God.* He looked at himself in a mirror and was horrified. There was nothing solid in his life, nothing lasting, nothing on which he could depend. There were things in his nature which he hated and which he could not understand. He surprised even himself, his own baseness alarmed him; he wondered why he still hankered after certain old sins that he thought he had finished with years ago. The world thought highly of him, he was universally respected. But that did not help him at all for he knew of things within himself which, if the world but knew of them, would put an end to its respect and admiration at once. More than that, he realised that God knew of them. He had done his best to cleanse himself of these things, had read good books, had attended lectures and demonstrations on morality, had talked to good people, had made friends of nice and godly people, had indeed surrounded himself with everything and everybody good that he knew of. Still he was no better. He sinned less perhaps but his mind was still the same. With a great effort of the will he had been able to control the frequency of his failures, fear of offending his good friends had helped greatly, but still he felt unsafe. 'It is only a kind of patchwork', he said, 'I am not healed, I am not whole, I am not safe, I cannot trust myself. I am tired of make-believe, I am tired of pretence, I am tired of a hand-to-mouth moral existence, tired of crying over my sins and then returning to them, tired of trying to cure myself and of being cured by other people, tired of trying to play "hide and seek" with thee, O God, when I know that it does not work and that you can see it all so plainly.' 'Heal me, O Lord, and I *shall be healed;* save me, and I *shall be saved.*'

Oh, that we also might see ourselves as this man saw himself. Oh, that we might see the madness of thinking that we are clever and smart when we are not found out. Oh that we might see the deception and trickery that is within our own souls, and above all, see that our case is so desperate, our plight so terrible that there is no human agency which can save us and rid us of our baser nature. For it is only those people who have realised all that who utter this prayer and who, having prayed it, are healed and saved to all eternity through and by the grace of God in Jesus Christ our Lord. May we be found amongst them. For his name's sake.

20

The Amazing Gospel

Thus saith the LORD; Behold, I will bring again the captivity of Jacob's tents, and have mercy on his dwellingplaces; and the city shall be builded upon her own heap, and the palace shall remain after the manner thereof.

And out of them shall proceed thanksgiving and the voice of them that make merry: and I will multiply them, and they shall not be few; I will also glorify them, and they shall not be small.

Jeremiah 30:18, 19

I take these two verses because I am anxious to call your attention to some of the great essentials of the gospel of our Lord and Saviour Jesus Christ. There is no need for any apology for doing that through the medium of an Old Testament text. To the spiritual eye the Old Testament contains as many and in a sense as glorious evangelical texts as does the New Testament itself. Those who fail to see the gospel in the Old Testament and regard it merely as a history of the Jewish people generally do so because they also fail to see the real gospel of the New Testament. The dispensations are different, but it is the same God who acts and his graciousness is as evident in embryo in the Old Testament as it is in its full bloom and development in the New Testament. And here in this text in Jeremiah, whose very name has become a synonym of pessimism and melancholy to the ignorant and thoughtless, we find a great example and illustration of the gospel. At once and on the very surface these words fix our attention upon what are the great underlying and vital truths concerning the gospel. As I note them I desire also to indicate how sadly these aspects of the matter are being ignored, forgotten and even denied at the present time by those who tend to talk glibly about re-stating the gospel in modern terms. The principles are not only clearly stated in this text, they are of the very essence of the New Testament message and have invariably been recognised and extolled throughout the centuries by all sections of the church which are at all entitled to use the name Christian.

The first principle is that the gospel is something which comes from God: 'Thus saith the Lord'. I shall deal with this principle more in detail later on. What I desire to indicate here and now is that if we fail to realise that the gospel and all it professes is primarily an activity on the part of God, and not on the part of man, we have entirely failed to understand it. Of course, man has something, and indeed much, to do in the scheme of salvation but all that is secondary. Man only begins to act after God has first acted and has rendered man capable of action. What is the Bible after all but an account of God's activity and action in the matter of human salvation. It is not a manual of instructions designed to tell us how to save ourselves, it is a revelation and a proclamation of what God has done in order to bring that salvation to pass. Salvation then is something which is already complete and entire in God's hands. It is something which he has to give and which he is willing and ready to give. He has done the work, he has taken the action and you and I, if we are Christians, recognise and acknowledge gladly and with thanksgiving that we are what we are and have what we have solely and entirely by 'the grace of God'.

This comes first. Before you begin with your good deeds, before you begin to prepare your programmes and plans and set out after your high ideals – stop! Have you listened to what God says? Do you understand this, 'Thus saith the Lord'? Are you planning in accordance with what he announces or are you drawing merely on your own ideas and imaginations? That which starts with man and his attempts to find God, instead of starting with God's way of finding and saving man, is not gospel. Had you realised that? The gospel starts with God and comes from him.

And because of that we are able to announce as our second controlling principle that the gospel is essentially supernatural as regards both its nature and also its mode of action. It is a miracle. 'The city shall be builded upon her own heap.' Salvation according to the Bible is something large, something vast. And there is no better test which can be applied to anything that professes and offers itself as the gospel as this test of greatness or of scope. It is so great according to New Testament writers that no terms are quite adequate to describe it except such terms as rebirth, renovation, regeneration. It is something which makes all things new. The gospel is not merely meant to make us a little better and to hold out ideals for us. It does not offer itself as a mere veneer on our lives. It is something which completely and entirely changes us. It is face to face with this truth that all the vapid idealisms and moralisings that so frequently pass as the gospel today are seen to be so hopelessly inadequate.

But because the gospel is essentially miraculous and super-natural it follows that it is not only large and vast in its scheme and its action, it must also be something that comes as a surprise to man and which in its essence is incomprehensible to man. It is marvel-lous, astonishing and invariably moves all who truly see it to a cry of wonder and amazement. Here again we have only to recall one of those great exclamations of a man like Paul as he contemplates the gospel. 'Great is the mystery of godliness', he cries (*1 Tim.* 3:16). Then again, 'O the depth of the riches both of the wisdom and knowledge of God!' (*Rom.* 11:33). And with him all the saints at all times and everywhere have owned themselves as being 'lost in wonder, love and praise' as they contemplate the gospel. But if the gospel is merely something that exhorts us to live a better life and to be good and kind, if it is but a social and ethical scheme, something which primarily asks us to do something rather than an announce-ment of what God has done, it cannot possibly evoke such a response. It then becomes just one among a number of philosophies and schemes of life which we may affirm, but it definitely ceases to be something which breaks in upon us and overwhelms us with its majesty and its graciousness. But this is always the effect of the gospel which announces God's action. He amazed Abraham and Jacob and David and the prophets and all the New Testament saints as we have already seen. Does what you have always regarded as the gospel do that to you? Has the Word of God come to you and has it filled you with 'wonder, love and praise'. The apprehension of God's action always leads to that.

But the word 'praise' reminds us of our third general principle, which is that the gospel always comes, as its very name implies, as 'good news'. Every action of God is not good news, for he announces his law and his wrath, his displeasures and his punishment. But in the gospel he states something that has not only amazed and surprised men but has also led them to sing in praise and thanksgiving, and to be filled with joy unspeakable. Here again is a vital test. Merely to prescribe an ethical code and to give instructions with respect to social conditions, etc., is never good news and cannot be in and of itself. Indeed, the very calling to such duties in itself leads to much heart-searching and fear because of the greatness of the task and our fear of our failure to accomplish it. And yet, face to face with the demand of the most exalted code of life that the world has ever known, Christian people have nevertheless been bright and happy, cheerful and buoyant. Confronted with circumstances which are enough to break the stoutest heart they still remain the same. Why is this? There is only one answer. The good news they have received from God more than compensates for whatever news, however bad that may be, which comes to them from men.

There then we see three of the essential qualities of the gospel. It announces God's action for men; an action which is marvellous, wondrous and sublime; and which comes to men as the most glorious good news they have ever heard. Had you realised that? Has it so come to you? That it may come in that way to all under the blessing of God, let us consider it as it appears in this great evangelical announcement of the prophet Jeremiah. The circumstances of the children of Israel at this point must be well known to all. Their country and the city of Jerusalem were being attacked by an enemy that was fierce and relentless. Day by day they were becoming weaker and weaker. Jeremiah had had clearly revealed to him by God the subsequent course of events which literally and actually came to pass. The city was to be captured and destroyed by the enemy, and the children of Israel carried away captive to Babylon. Yet, and this is the amazing thing, after seventy years the captivity was to end, the captives were to return and their city should be 'builded upon her own heap'. That is the good news, the amazing news of God's action. Let us consider it and apply it along the following lines.

1.   *Consider in the first place, the task with which the gospel is confronted.* The city of Jerusalem was in ruins, in a heap. Jerusalem was the city of God and the pride of the people, the city of which the

psalmist had so frequently sung and whose virtues and excellences had been so regularly acclaimed. She was indeed a wondrous city, rightly regarded as in every respect the earthly habitation of God himself. For in Jerusalem was the temple where all the people met to worship and whither they came with their offerings and sacrifices. There the great festivals were all celebrated and the highest hours in the lives of the people had been experienced. It was there they had felt the presence of the living God, it was there they had communed with him and thanked him for his blessings. In addition, the city was remarkable for its strength and power: its commanding position on the rocks, its towers and turrets, its walls and buildings. Furthermore, it was a city that had never been conquered. But alas, owing to the sin of its people, owing to the disobedience and the falling away from God, owing to their neglect of his commandments both in their individual lives and the life of the city, the defences had become weak and the people themselves indolent. At last, the enemy from the outside, taking advantage of all this, had attacked them and sacked their city and reduced it to ruins. The temple had been destroyed and its marvellous treasures of gold and silver carried away. The altar had been broken down. Everything had been demolished. The walls were razed to the ground, the turrets and towers had come crashing to earth – the city of God was in a heap. All that had been the proud boast of the Jews for centuries was now nothing but a mass of ruins. The glory had departed, the greatness had gone, the most marvellous city on earth was a formless, shapeless mass of refuse.

'What has all this to do with the task of the gospel?' asks someone. The answer is that what we have just described is a perfect picture of the soul of man as the result of sin. In biblical typology, Jerusalem frequently stands for the soul, as John Bunyan, amongst others, was not slow to see. God made man perfect. Any other view is of necessity dishonouring to God and utterly subversive of the central theme of the gospel which describes the fall of man, his deserved punishment and God providing a way of escape. Man was made lord of creation. He was to rule and to dominate the life of the world. Like Jerusalem set high upon a rock, so man was to stand out in greatness and in majesty above all else in the world. Furthermore, God had endowed him with powers and faculties that were to make him unique and remarkable. While possessing many of the same instincts and powers as the animal, man was to differ by having the high power of reason and therefore of discipline and control. To him alone was given the power of being able to think, to regard even himself objectively and to ponder and in a measure to understand the whole meaning of life, being and existence. And then above all was given to man that unique quality described as the soul or the spirit. By means of this man was to be capable not only of thought and reason and of means of communication with other men like himself, but also capable of holding communion with God, of walking with him. Such is the biblical view of man and of the soul. Man is not a creature, an animal who is gradually stretching and reaching out to something higher and better and who with the passage of the ages is gradually leaving that which is low and animal and becoming increasingly noble and more like God. Rather, the reverse is the case. Man was created with all these unique and distinct powers and possibilities – and what is infinitely important for us to realise is that he will be judged according to that standard. As God gave the city of Jerusalem to the children of Israel, so he gave to men their souls. As he held the children of Israel responsible for what they had done with, and made of, their city, so he holds us responsible for what we have done with his greatest gift to us – the soul. What *have* we done with it? What is true of us? What of the state of your soul?

Let us face that question in terms of this picture and let us ask a few simple questions. The first is general. Do you find that you conform to that exalted standard? Had you realised that that is the true nature of man and that that is what you were meant to be? How have you thought of yourself and of your life? Has it been in terms of God and of the infinite possibilities open to your soul, or has it been merely in terms of the world and the flesh and the things of the senses? Have you realised that your life is a great, noble and exalted thing, higher than anything else in this world? Are you aware of the privilege of being a living soul and of being a unique and special creation of God?

But let us come to the details and to the important particulars. What of the wall around the city of your soul, what of the turrets and battlements and defences? Are they all intact? You know of the enemy, do you not? As soon as we begin to think for ourselves at all we are aware that we are surrounded by enemies that are constantly attacking us. Temptation and sins and suggestions to evil begin to assail and to bombard our defences. You have known it. But what has happened? Have you kept your defences intact? Have you held the enemy at bay? Are there any breaks in the wall? Have you preserved your purity and chastity? Have you maintained your character? Looking back across your life what do you find? Has not the enemy come in? Have not the walls and the towers been smashed and broken? But still more closely, what of these gorgeous palaces and buildings which once were the pride of Jerusalem? Are they still standing? What has happened to the powers that God implanted within man and therefore in you? What have you made of them and what has become of them? What real use have you made of your mind? To what occupation and tasks have you put it? Has it been used as it was meant to be used for the contemplation of the great things of life, for thoughts and ideas that should be ennobling and uplifting? And what of the other faculties? What direction have your emotions and susceptibilities taken and all the strong powers which God has given us? What of these palaces, these great buildings? In whose possession are they? Indeed, are they still standing?

Why do I ask these questions? Simply because of what is to be seen round and about us at the present time. All these great powers and faculties that God gave us are being used to the gratification of the flesh only. Mind and ingenuity, cleverness, feeling and emotion – all the great gifts of man – have been prostituted to the service of the self and the body. The very powers that were meant to be the glory of man have become his shame. But face it personally and individually. To what do you give your time and your energy and your money? What is it that really appeals to you and pleases you? To what use do you put your mind and intellect and these other powers? Are they really standing at all? But come right to the centre! What of the temple? For that was the chief glory of Jerusalem after all – its temple. What of the temple of your soul? The place of God? The place of communion with the Eternal, the place of hearkening to his voice? What of it? You may have felt that you could argue that some of the wall is still standing and that some of the great buildings are still intact, but what of the greatest building of all – the temple? Do you know God? Is God real to you? Is there a 'holy of holies' within you where he lives and dwells?

Is there an altar in your life? These are not mere idle questions. Neither are they meant merely for certain people. They apply to all. God meant man to dwell with him and to commune with him. He made and created man with that possibility and therefore holds him responsible for that. What of the soul, my friend? What of the city? Is it not in ruins? As you compare yourself with what you see you ought to be must you not admit that? The enemy has broken down the defences, has entered in and captured the city and demolished its buildings and plundered and destroyed its temple. There is no need to argue, we have but to face the facts. Sin has ruined the soul, the city is in heaps, the enemy has carried us away captive. Such is the task that awaits and confronts the gospel. The soul of man is in that state and condition. It has fallen, it is ruined and destroyed, it is in heaps.

2.   *That being the task, we proceed in the second place to point out that it is a task with which the gospel alone can deal.* Our analogy of the city of Jerusalem makes this abundantly clear. The children of Israel after the destruction of their city were carried away captives to Babylon. Their position was one of utter and complete helplessness. Their city was in ruins and they themselves were not only far away from it, but they were also in the hands of a powerful enemy. They are powerless and can do nothing whatsoever. There is no need to elaborate. But can you see that precisely the same thing is true of the soul? Of course, there were some amongst the children of Israel who did not desire to go back to Jerusalem – they were content to be slaves. We are not discussing them. We are concerned with those who did desire to go back, and who longed and yearned to be back, but were utterly helpless and powerless. Alas, there are thousands today who are not aware of the state of their souls and who, when told, do not care. Nothing awaits them but destruction. But I speak now on the assumption that you are alive and awake to the situation, that you see that your soul is in a desperate plight and that you long to be what you know you ought to be. Have you realised your helplessness and that the gospel alone is equal to the task? If not, face it again and see what a perfect parallel is provided by the condition of the children of Israel of old! Can you not see that you cannot even commence upon the task? You may decide to turn over a new leaf and live a better life, but

that is no more dealing with the situation than certain schemes of moral reformation among the children of Israel in Babylon would have been. For the question of the past still remains. You cannot start from where you are for that still leaves the old legacy untouched. What has happened has happened, and the ruins are there, and to start building elsewhere and on a new foundation is of no value. But you cannot deal with the past. Nothing that you may do can affect it. There it remains and you are helpless. Before you commence to struggle with the power of sin, face the prior question of the guilt and the pollution of your past sin.

But to prove this still further, let us turn again to the details. Can you rebuild these old walls and defences? Can you shake off the power of the enemy? Can you by your own effort recapture the right use of all these powers and propensities which you have so long neglected and perverted? Can you recreate within yourself an interest in and an enthusiasm for the nobler and higher pursuits of the mind and of the soul?

How easy it was thirty and forty years ago for the idealist to talk about uplifting mankind. All that was necessary, they said, was education and training. All that was needed was to print and publish good literature and provide means for culture and improvement for the people and they would at once rise to it. But the passage of the years alone has completely revealed the fallacy of that light assumption. Men prefer the easy, the superficial, the enjoyable and cannot make the sustained effort essential to real advancement and progress. It may be argued that just a few by means of a great effort of the will can succeed up to a point. But can they succeed in the greatest thing of all? Can they find God? Can you find God? Can you rebuild the ruined altar of your soul? Can you bring back the holy of holies and recreate that which is most sacred and spiritual? It is just here that every human system and ritual utterly breaks down. Man is meant for God and as St Augustine put it so long ago, 'we cannot find rest until we find our rest in thee'. We cannot deal with the past, we are defeated in the present, we fear the unknown future. Deep within us is a sense of failure and of sin. When we cease to argue and to be clever and listen to the voice of our better self we know that we are failures, miserable and wretched. We have disobeyed the noblest promptings and yielded to our lowest desires in spite of the warnings of conscience; we have sold the pass, we have been conquered. We are failures.

And over and above that there is within us that voice of God, that feeling that he is, and that we are responsible to him, and that we shall have to face him. But oh, how can we find him? What right have we even to look for him at all? But we long to know him! Our sin has not only allowed the enemy to reduce that city of our soul to a heap, it has also made us miserable, wretched and unhappy. We see an occasional saint and hear and read of others. Oh, how wonderful it would be to be like that we think. Oh, that we might be like that! Oh, that we might know God and feel his presence nigh. Oh, that we might experience his strength and power and feel our souls being cleansed and renewed by him. Above all, Oh, that we might be like the saint who, far from fearing death, can look forward to it calmly and serenely because he knows that beyond it lies the Father's face and an eternity of bliss.

Have you not felt like that? Do you not feel like that even now? Are you not like these Israelites in Babylon? Too late you see your mistakes and your folly. But you can do nothing. There you are in Babylon a prisoner and Jerusalem is so far away. You think of it, you long for it, you yearn for it, but all seems to be in ruin. The city is in a heap, and you are helpless. The task is too great. All the efforts of men and of the world together cannot give man what he really needs and what in the depths he longs and yearns for – the world in its cleverness can do much but it cannot even start upon the work of building a new Jerusalem, of renewing our soul.

3. *That is a task to which the gospel alone is equal. Let us now observe how it does it.* Let us return again to the picture. There are the children of Israel in their utter helplessness in Babylon. The situation seems hopeless. But to them in that very situation comes the message. 'Thus saith the Lord; Behold I will bring again the captivity of Jacob's tents, and have mercy on his dwellingplaces; and the city shall be builded upon her own heap, and the palace shall remain after the manner thereof . . .' And it actually happened. It was actually fulfilled. When the men themselves had utterly and completely failed, God came in and gave them their heart's desire. He brought them back to Jerusalem and actually upon the old site, in the former position, the new city was built with its walls and battlements, its palaces and buildings, even its temple. On the very

heap and ruins of the old city the new city was built. The old site, but a new city.

All this is but a picture, a parable, as I have been pointing out right through, of what God does to the soul. He offers to do the impossible. And he does the impossible. He comes to us and speaks to us in our deepest trouble and woe. He comes to us when we are defeated and helpless and miserable, realising what we have done and our desperate plight. He comes to us and announces what he purposes to do. It is his moment, his action, his initiative. He announces that he is going to work a miracle upon us – 'the city shall be builded upon her own heap'. He promises us life and joy. Just when we are most unhappy and forlorn the wondrous Word comes.

How does it come? In and through Jesus Christ, the Son of God. How does he do it? Our picture illustrates it perfectly. What do we need? First and foremost we need to be brought back to Jerusalem and to have the rubbish and ruins of the past cleared away. That is ever our first problem. How can the guilt of our past, the wreckage of our life be dealt with? How can it be removed? Remorse and sorrow cannot remove it. Efforts in the present and the future cannot atone for it. There it remains. How can it all be cleared away? There is only one answer:

> *There is a fountain filled with blood,*
> *Drawn from Immanuel's veins;*
> *And sinners plunged beneath that flood,*
> *Lose all their guilty stains.*

Jesus Christ, the Son of God, by dying that death on Calvary's hill has cleared away the ruins and the wreckage. He has borne your guilt and borne it away. He has paid your penalty and died your death. 'He is the propitiation for our sins: and not for ours only, but also for the sins of the whole world' (*1 John* 2:2). You cannot deal with your past. He can and has done so. The old site has been cleared from the ruins and the wreckage of the past. The old foundation is again revealed. He has cleared away the rubbish.

But he does not stop at that. That is merely the beginning, the preliminary work. Alas, there are many who seem to think that that is the whole story of the gospel, that it just tells us that God will forgive us. As if God were to do no more than clear away the ruins and wreckage produced by the work of the enemy and then leave the old site vacant. But a site, however clean, is not a city and for God to end there would really mean that he had been defeated by the enemy. But he does not stop there. He only starts there! 'The city shall be builded upon her own heap'! Jesus Christ the Son of God not merely died for our sins, he rose again and ascended into heaven, and from heaven he sent the Holy Spirit who brings us a new birth and a new life, who creates us anew and makes of us new men and women in Christ Jesus. You are offered not merely pardon and forgiveness, but a new start and a new life. A new Jerusalem is built on the old site. And you can become new.

Let me emphasise the word 'you'. For it is the great word here and expresses the whole marvel and wonder of the gospel. A city bearing the name of Jerusalem is not built somewhere else, but actually on the old site, in the same place, on its 'own heap'. A new city on the old site. Still Jerusalem but a new Jerusalem. *You*, the same person with the same essential personality and individuality, *you* are offered a new nature and a new life with new desires and interests, new hopes, new possibilities and above all a new temple, a new altar. What could appear to be more impossible than that creatures such as we have been, soiled by sin and alienated from God, could ever hope to commune with him and to find joy in doing so! But that is precisely the miracle of grace. Having forgiven you, God assures you that you are his child. He smiles upon you, blesses you and even dwells within you. You still have the same name, you are still the same essential individual in your natural make-up, but you are a completely new man. The site is the same, but the city is new. You say, therefore, with Paul – 'I live; yet not I, but Christ liveth in me' (*Gal.* 2:20). But it does not stop even there. 'What of the old enemy?', you ask. 'He will still be there and will try to defeat me again and I am afraid of him.' You are quite right. The enemy remains and will remain, but God in Christ offers to make you more than a conqueror. Before, you fought him alone and you were too weak. He conquered you. But now the One who conquered him offers to dwell within you and to strengthen you. He will be your strength and your stay. He will nerve and empower your feeble arm. He will renew your strength again day by day. And he will never leave you nor forsake you. 'The city shall be builded upon her own heap.' Yes, in the very place and places where you were formerly defeated you shall now triumph and prevail.

Such are the blessings offered you by the gospel. In spite of your condition, 'with God all things are possible', and that is what he offers to do. All who realise their condition will gladly accept.

21

No Feasting: No Christianity

Thus saith the LORD of hosts; The fast of the fourth month, and the fast of the fifth, and the fast of the seventh, and the fast of the tenth, shall be to the house of Judah joy and gladness, and cheerful feasts; therefore love the truth and peace.

Zechariah 8:19

The real significance of the message contained in this text can only be grasped and appreciated when we bear in mind the context and the exact occasion on which it was uttered. There is nothing that so tends to rob us of the full benefit of some of the greatest passages which are to be found in Holy Writ as the present tendency to doubt and to query the exact historicity and historical background, and to say that the actual facts as events in history do not really matter one way or the other as long as we receive the spirit of the message and the teaching. That is a position which has been often taken up during the past one hundred years. 'The history of the Old Testament', these critics say, 'not only may be wrong but actually is wrong, very frequently, but that really makes no difference so long as we grasp the message and the teaching.'

Now that attitude leads to our missing the real greatness of the message. For the Bible is not a book of romance or a novel which just pictures and imagines certain situations and difficulties, and then solves them by some encouraging word. It is something infinitely greater. It is a record of actual facts and events and happenings. That is of vital importance to us. When we read a novel or a story we tend to say, 'Ah yes, all that is wonderful but it isn't true to life and it doesn't happen in life. It is all right as an idea, but it is imaginary, not real'. And with respect to the novel and the film that is a perfectly true criticism. But when you come to the Bible it is entirely false – for here are events in history, stories of what has actually happened. Shake my faith in the facts and you shake my

[255]

faith in the teaching. It is no use presenting to us the salvation with which God is prepared to deliver us in terms of his deliverance of the children of Israel from Egypt if that event was a mere fancy. Did he deliver them or not? Did he work these miracles through Moses or not? Did he divide the Red Sea and speak from Mount Sinai? Did he divide Jordan and cause the walls of Jericho to fall miraculously? These questions are vital and it is only to the extent that I accept the records as facts that they are of value to me as indications and illustrations of what God is prepared to do and can do for me also. The history is all-important and nowhere more so than in this particular text.

Here is the command to these people to turn their days of fasting into days of joy, gladness and cheerful festivity. When was it given? The exact time and context, as I shall show you, are of vital importance. This message was given through the prophet Zechariah who is one of the so-called post-exilic prophets. His words are addressed to the remnant of the Jews that had returned to Jerusalem from the captivity of Babylon. You will remember the facts. Owing to their sin and their disobedience to God, the Jews, after many warnings, had been attacked and conquered by the forces of Babylon. Their city had been sacked and ruined, and they themselves had been carried away as slaves and captives. Their temple had been destroyed and all their ancient glory and power had vanished. Realising this in Babylon they had introduced these different fasting days mentioned in the text. The first as a reminder of the capture of Jerusalem, the second as a reminder of the day on which the temple had been destroyed, the next to commemorate with shame a base act of treachery against one of their own best men, and the last a fast to recall the day in which the blockade of Jerusalem had commenced.

In Babylon they remained for seventy years in misery, remorse and repentance. And then in his own time and in his own miraculous manner God had intervened as he had promised to do and had delivered them. He opened a way by which all who desired to do so could return to Jerusalem, and a remnant of the people did so. And here we find them back in Jerusalem, in a sense surrounded by ruins and difficulties.

What were they to do about these fasts which they had kept during the captivity? The answer is provided in our text. This is

God's Word to them. Do you realise its significance? Do you catch its real meaning? Let us consider it together remembering as we do so what I have said already, namely, that these fasts are recorded along with all Scripture in order, as Paul says, that we may profit (*2 Tim.* 3:16). What God said here to these people through Zechariah, he has said and is saying in a still more glorious way and manner to us in his Son, Jesus of Nazareth. The great message of the gospel of God is essentially the same in the Old Testament and in the New. The real difference between the two is simply in the mode of expression – faint and indistinct in the Old Testament, and clear and loud in the New. How we should thank God that we live in the gospel dispensation. But do we? It depends upon whether we realise and believe what the gospel has to say. What is it? We can answer that question by making the following observations.

1. *The ultimate effect produced by the gospel in its dealings with men is joy and a spirit of rejoicing.* I say 'ultimate effect' because it is of vital importance, as I shall show you, that we should realise that this is not the only effect produced by the gospel or indeed its more immediate effect and concern. The joy and the spirit of happiness and rejoicing produced by the gospel are end-products. They follow as the direct result of something else. That is where the gospel differs initially from so many, and indeed, all of the cults that offer to make men happy. They are concerned about happiness alone. That is the sole object and purpose which they have in mind and they go directly to that point. The gospel is primarily interested in something else. Its concern is with righteousness and truth, and to get us into a right relationship with God. It is only as these primary conditions are fulfilled that the joy and the happiness can follow. But given these, and a conformity to its laws and to its ways, the gospel is out to make us happy, joyful and glad. It is vitally important that we should realise the exact nature of this proposal and see that it is something which is essentially positive. What is proposed in this text for the children of Israel is not a mere lessening of the number of the days of fasting, nor even an ending of the days of fasting altogether, but something which goes infinitely and gloriously beyond that. They are not merely to stop fasting, they are to commence feasting and rejoicing. What is proposed is not merely that they shall be a little less miserable and

unhappy, but that they should be positively joyous and happy. Indeed, the claim of the gospel everywhere is that it alone can really make us happy:

Solid joys and lasting pleasures
None but Zion's children know.

Now there can be no doubt at all that a statement like that comes with a real sense of strangeness and surprise to most people today, for their conception of the gospel and religion is something which is strangely different. I suppose the most common idea regarding religion is that it is something which makes people positively miserable and unhappy: it is regarded as something which stands between us and anything which makes life enjoyable and happy. Most people who dismiss religion with contempt do so because they see it as something which makes life small and dull and uninteresting; something which cramps life and prevents self-experience and the full enjoyment of life; something which prohibits everything that is life-giving in a real sense. It is conceived of as an idea which would have us perpetually confront the facts of death and the grave, and our future life and existence, but which has nothing to give us or to offer us now. That is why it is said that religion is all right for old people who have had their day and who, having lost their health and their vigour, have nothing more to do but to die. To take up religion, therefore, when you are young is to make yourself prematurely old and to rob yourself of all the real sweetness of life. But I need not elaborate. You are all familiar with the view. It is because they regard religion as something which makes life dull and miserable and boring that they not only reject religious talk but also treat it as a subject fit only for jokes and for contempt. There is no epithet that is so frequently hurled at Christians as the word 'miserable'. To forsake religion when they reach a certain age is regarded by most people as an act of liberation and emancipation. For such people to be told that the gospel proposal is to turn our fasting into feasting and rejoicing is to confront them with something which they regard as being utterly incredible.

There are others to whom it is equally incredible – only for a different reason. The real proposal and ultimate objective of the gospel comes as a surprise not only to the irreligious, but also to a large number who are religious and believe in religion. I refer to the large number of people who turn to religion in their need and in their trouble. They may have done so for many varied reasons. It may be that as a result of a process of thought they have seen the utter hollowness of the previous position which we have just described. Their intelligence alone, or their knowledge of history and of life, have shown them that there is a tragic element in life and that life itself, far from being a mere trifle through which we can lightly trip our way, is rather a grim fight and struggle which calls forth all our powers and resources. Or it may be that the actual experience of life has brought them to that conclusion in spite of themselves and their own ideas. Illness and disease, trouble and trial, sorrow, bereavement and death have come and in their helplessness and weakness they have turned to religion. There was nothing else that could help them so they turned to this. Why? To be comforted, to be soothed, and to be helped. But alas! they go no further, or rather, they see no further. The function and business of religion, to them, is to lessen our sorrow, to comfort us in our grief, to keep us from utter despair and perhaps suicide, and to provide us from week to week with new courage and fortitude with which to face the weary business of living. In a word, the function of religion is to produce in us a state of contented resignation and calm. I would not be unfair to such people and to such a view. My whole point is that this corruption of religion is quite as wrong and as fallacious as that of the first group with which I have dealt. For this second group, religion is still something purely negative. They do not, like the other foolish, flippant, ignorant people, regard it as something which actually makes people miserable. No, life has done that for them! They are grateful for anything from religion which helps to drown their misery and to assuage the grief somewhat.

But still the conception is purely negative. Religion only lessens the grief, it merely mitigates the suffering. It does not transform life, it simply helps to make it endurable and possible. Or in terms of my text, it does not proceed beyond lessening the fasting or abolishing the fasting – it does not go on to proclaim feasting and rejoicing. And yet that is precisely what the gospel proposes and offers to do. Its claim is not that it can improve life but that it can change it, revolutionise it and utterly transform it. Fasting is to be turned into feasting and misery into joy.

Why is it that this false view of religion is so widely held? Why is it that the very glory of it all is missed? There can be no doubt that there are two main answers to that question. One is that people will persist in judging religion by what they see in some of its worst and most ignorant exponents: there is that constant fatal tendency to confuse nominal religion and mere respectability with true Christianity.

But perhaps the real cause is to be traced to an utter ignorance of what the Bible really says. People today talk about the Bible without ever having read it. They dismiss it on the basis of what they read anywhere and everywhere except in the Book itself. Open the Bible and hear its case. Read it from beginning to end and you will find that everywhere it offers as its ultimate effect happiness, joy, peace. Indeed, it is the greatest insult that we can ever offer to the holy name of God to suggest that he desires our misery and that to obey him and live the life he would have us live is the direct road to unhappiness. No, he is the Father. He loves his children and nothing will satisfy him except to see his children rejoicing and happy. And he has made a way to bring that to pass, as all know who accept that way. Listen to the psalmist celebrating that experience and still more all the saints of the New Testament in the book of Acts and in the various epistles. See it in the lives and stories of the saints. Indeed we would go further and say that God not only desires our happiness but actually commands us to be happy. This text was a command to these Jews in exactly the same way as Paul commands the Philippians to rejoice evermore and in all conditions, even in tribulations and trouble. In other words, this is so central in the whole teaching of the Bible that we must regard it as the acid test of our profession. A Christian is not merely one who is a little less miserable than he was. He is one who rejoices. Our Lord in his last discourses told his disciples, and through them all who follow him ever since, that their sorrow shall be turned into joy, and he would so deal with them after his death and resurrection that 'your heart shall rejoice, and your joy no man taketh from you' (*John* 16:22). Again he says, 'Ask and ye shall receive, that your joy may be full' (*John* 16:24), and 'In the world ye shall have tribulation: but be of good cheer; I have overcome the world' (*John* 16:33). That is what he offers – positive joy in spite of everything. Not a little less sorrow and a little comfort, help and strength, not a mere modification of the fasting, but the turning of the fasting into feasting! He does not encourage us merely to be calm, strong and sturdy, resigning ourselves to the grim business of life with stoic resignation and fortitude. He offers us conquest and victory, triumph and joy. To represent Christ and his religion, therefore, as offering us anything less than that, and to call ourselves Christians while possessing and experiencing anything less than that is to be false to him and to his cause. The Christian is not only meant to be happy, he is commanded to be happy! The claim of the gospel is that it alone can make us happy in spite of life, in spite of everything. Is that true in your life? Have you experienced it? Do you know it? If not, why not?

2.   *We can help to answer that question by considering the type of person in whom the gospel produces this ultimate effect of happiness.* In a word, it is only in those who have been miserable. It is only to those who have fasted that the command comes to feast! Nowhere is the exact history more important than in connection with these fasts and we must emphasise it because it is just here that so many go astray and, in the words of Peter, 'wrest ... the scriptures, unto their own destruction' (*2 Pet.* 3:16). For this command to feast and to rejoice is not made indiscriminately to all and sundry; and it is not made to all sorts at all times. There are always conditions attached to the promises of God and it is because men ignore these conditions that they fail to obtain the blessing. Those who make happiness the primary condition of their life never truly find it, and those who come to religion primarily to be comforted never really experience the full joy of the gospel. It is only to those who had been through the state of fasting that there was the command to start feasting and rejoicing.

Let me put it to you quite definitely and historically in the case of the children of Israel. Read the prophecies of Isaiah before the captivity and the prophecies of Jeremiah, Ezekiel, Hosea, Joel and all who prophesied before the captivity. Do they command the people to feast and to rejoice? Is happiness offered to them? Anyone who knows the writings of these prophets even superficially knows that such is not the case. The message to the people before Babylon is one of wrath and condemnation. It is the foretelling of impending doom and disaster. Ah yes, occasionally there are appeals and exhortations, some of them couched in the most tender and loving terms to be found anywhere in the Bible, but in each case, together with the offer of pardon and forgiveness, is the call to repentance and to the forsaking of their sin. But the people would not listen. They continued in their sinful, disobedient course and the Word of God, the burden of the Lord, became more menacing, more threatening, until at last disaster came and they were carried away captive and the city and temple were destroyed. Too late, the people realise their sin and folly. They see the madness of ignoring God and worshipping idols; they recognise now how they have broken the law and sinned against God. They awaken to their true condition. What all the preaching and appeals of the prophets had failed to achieve their finding themselves by the rivers of Babylon soon brought to pass. Yes! There, they wept when they remembered Zion and hung their harps upon the willows (*Psa.* 137:1, 2). Like the prodigal son, they came to themselves in the strange land and saw their sin and their folly. And it was in the light of that that they instituted these days of fasting. Even this, the prophet tells them, was not as thorough as it might have been and as it should have been. Even then they were more concerned about their suffering than about their sin, but they had seen it and recognised it up to a point. Then came the deliverance and the return to Jerusalem and it is only then that God addresses them in words like these and, even here, you observe on top of the fasting there is coupled with the promise a stern word of warning and of ethical exhortation.

The fulfilment of all the most gracious and glorious prayers in all the prophets, all those magnificent evangelical promises, refer to Judah *after* her captivity. This is a point which is vital to the true understanding of the gospel. Repentance precedes pardon and it is only to those who have become miserable because of their sin that the gracious Word of God in Christ offering pardon and joy and peace ever comes. The direct way to feasting is preliminary fasting; it is ever 'sorrow' that is turned into 'joy' by the intervention of Christ. Let us clearly grasp this fact. It is only those who have been miserable on account of their sin who can experience the joy of salvation, and, as we have already seen, it is doubtful whether there is such a thing as salvation without the joy of salvation.

Now we may try to avoid the fast and the trouble by saying that this is not a universal principle but merely something which is true of certain types and kinds of persons. There are those who argue that it is only those who have committed violent crimes and then experience a dramatic kind of conversion who experience this joy. It is not meant for everyone, they think, and certainly not for people who have always been brought up in religion and who have never sinned very violently. They suppose repentance is either a matter of temperament and psychology, or else it is dependent solely upon the amount of sin or the mode of sinning. The introspective, morbid, serious type of person who tends to react violently, and the sinner who has sinned violently, are the only ones who are to find the joy of salvation. The average, ordinary person is not meant to do so. And that is why this average, ordinary person is so prone not only to admire the Christian convert who was once a violent sinner and to make a hero of him, but also at times almost to covet his past sinful experience.

All that cuts right across the teaching of the gospel and is an utter travesty of what it says. Nothing but a complete failure to understand the gospel can ever account for such a view. It can be clearly refuted and dismissed by the following consideration: it is simply not true to say that only people of a certain type, or of a certain temperament, experience the joy of salvation, for the fact is that all types and kinds of men have experienced it in the past and still do so. The circle of the apostles alone shows all the possible differences of background and temperament but they all had the same joy and so it has continued ever since. These psychological details sound very important and very plausible in theory – the history of the church deals with facts. The introverts and the extro- verts alike have had the same joy, and the change from fasting to feasting has been as common – if not commoner – among people brought up in church (as Luther, Wesley and others were) as in those who have lived a godless, sinful life of violence and crime. But apart from that, the New Testament does not limit the offer to certain people only. It offers it to all. It draws no distinctions between one type and another, and assures us all that 'the same God over all is good unto all'. God does not reward extra sin by giving an extra measure of joy afterwards. To suggest that he does is not only to impute an immoral action to God but also to insult his holy name. But the real trouble with people who hold such ideas is that they form their opinion from the standpoint of inward feeling instead of from the standpoint of objective eternal realities.

Let me illustrate my meaning. Imagine two men in trouble and difficulty at sea, and both are at the very point of drowning. Both are rescued by a man who risks his life in order to save them. Is it seriously suggested that their respective joy, happiness and gratitude are to be determined solely by their temperament? Surely temperament and psychology scarcely enter into the matter at all. What counts is the man's realisation of his position; his realisation first of the danger and then of the fact of his safety. The most phlegmatic, stolid and unemotional type of person becomes alarmed when he thinks he is drowning and sees his position to be hopeless, and his joy and his gratitude know no bounds when he realises that he has been saved. It is not the man's state nor feeling that matters but his apprehension and appreciation of the position and the situation. It is precisely the same in connection with religion. Have you realised your position? Forget all about your temperament and make-up. Forget all about your up-bringing and all the sin you have never committed. Forget the violent sinner, forget other people and just consider your own case. Have you realised how you stand at this moment? Are you miserable because of your sin? Have you ever been? If not it is not because you are not a sinner but simply because you have not realised that you are a sinner. Infants are not afraid of fire, people ignorant of electricity are not aware of the danger of touching a live wire – fools step in where angels fear to tread. But the ignorance does not affect or change the facts to the slightest extent. And the facts are these: the Bible says that we are all born in sin; that we have all actively sinned against God; that, even though we have not been violent sinners in the world's estimate, we have all come short of the glory of God and broken his law. Have you honoured him as you should have done? Have you worshipped him and adored him as Jesus Christ did? Has he been supreme in your life? Have you felt your entire and utter dependence upon him and have you thanked him constantly for all his goodness to you?

Above all, face this question – have you felt your utter un-worthiness before God? For all the saints have felt that. It is only people like the Pharisees, whose sin was condemned by our Lord in such strong terms, who felt pleased and satisfied with themselves.

The greatest proof of all of utter sinfulness is self-satisfaction and a failure to see our desperate need of the grace of God. It is only those who see that need who rejoice and are glad when they see the grace and understand its offer. Has the gospel of Christ made you happy? Is there a song in your heart? If not it is solely due to the fact that you have never seen your need of it. But consider that need again. How are you to face God? How are you to dwell in heaven and enjoy its purity? How are you to satisfy the demands of the law? A Saul of Tarsus felt hopeless; young Luther who had renounced the world, lived in a cell, fasted and prayed felt there was no hope; a virtuous John Wesley felt more and more conscious of his sin. The same thing has been true for all the most saintly people that the world has ever seen. And are you satisfied and contented? Do you not see your terrible and alarming position? Humble yourself. Weep for your sin. Fast and repent. Do you see it now? Are you concerned? Are you terrified? Do you see the hopelessness and helplessness of your position? Well, if you do, the gospel has a most glorious word to say. For, wonder of wonders, it is to people like you that it sends out this glorious command to abolish the fasting and to start feasting. 'Not the righteous, sinners Jesus came to save'. Those who can swim and save themselves will never be helped, it is only the drowning and the desperate who can have the joy of being taken hold of by the everlasting arms of God in Jesus Christ. It was for these alone that the Son of God not merely risked his life but actually gave it as a ransom. Yes, in spite of the sin and the disobedience which had led to the destruction of the temple and of Jerusalem itself, and to the captivity in Babylon – in spite of all the disobedience and the sin – once these people saw it, regretted it, repented of it and, filled with shame, spent their days in fasting, God forgave all and gave the command to start feasting and rejoicing. If you, tonight, know yourself to be a sinner, if your sins grieve you and torment you, if at long last you have seen your folly and your iniquity, if you feel you are beyond forgiveness and beyond hope – this Word is to you: Rejoice! The essential preliminary to feasting is fasting and you have fulfilled it!

3.   'But how can this be?' you say. Let me show you. Just here we come to the very heart of the glorious gospel message. *The command to feasting, rejoicing and happiness is not based upon feelings*

and emotions. These people in Jerusalem were not feeling happy at the moment but that made no difference, God commands them to be happy. Neither was this happiness based upon anything that they had done, for all they had done was to sin and to disobey God and thereby incur his wrath, finding themselves in Babylon and its hopeless misery and despair. The happiness and joy were clearly not based upon any action or activity on their part. As far as they were concerned they would still be in Babylon. Their own effort could never have taken them from there or ever have procured liberty for them. It was God's action that had made all the difference and the command to feasting and rejoicing is always based in the fact of what God has done. It is failure to appreciate that which accounts for the misery and unhappiness in the lives of many very good people who strive to live the godly and the religious life. That is exactly what John Wesley discovered. He was doing everything that a man could do, yet he could not find happiness. But suddenly he possessed it. What was it due to? Simply to the realisation of what God had done in Christ. When Wesley realised this, his heart was renewed and he became happy. The same is true of Luther, Bunyan and all others. If you regard the gospel merely as a plan and scheme of life, whether social or personal; if you regard it merely as something that calls you to the high and the heroic and to a certain order of morality; you will never know the joy and the happiness which it offers. Regard the Christian life as being something primarily that you have to do and far from making you happy it will make you miserable, for you will be constantly aware of your own failure. But the glory of the gospel is that it is based upon something that God has done once and for all in Christ. What has he done? It is perfectly illustrated in the case of these Jews at this point. Why does God command these people to rejoice and to be happy and to cease fasting and feast?

(a) He does so because the cause of the fasting has been removed. Why did they fast? Because of their guilt, because of their shame and because of the fact that they were in Babylon instead of being in Jerusalem. But God had intervened and in his own way had brought them back to Jerusalem. He had restored them to their old position and place. Clearly, therefore, he had forgiven their guilt and was offering them a new start and a new beginning out of their shame. 'Rejoice and feast', says God. 'The cause of your fasting and misery I have removed.' That is primarily what he says to us in Jesus Christ his Son. God has acted. He has sent his only begotten Son into the world to live and die and rise again for us and for our salvation. 'How can I feast and rejoice?' Look unto Jesus Christ on the cross and see your guilt borne by him and wiped out by him. 'How can I be happy', you say, 'when I am so filled with a sense of shame because of what I have been?' To which the gospel answers:

> *The past shall be forgotten,*
> *A present joy be given.*

In Christ there is a new beginning and you are no longer the slave of sin. And, in like manner, it tells you that your whole status and your situation are also changed. In Christ you become a child of God and are regarded as such by him. You have been an enemy and an alien but now you are a son. Do not look to your own feelings, or your own record. Look to God and the record of what he has done in Jesus Christ. Rejoice, sing, cry aloud, be glad, Christ has cleansed away your sin and restored you to the favour of God which you had lost. Yes, the rejoicing is based purely upon what God has done.

(b) But it is also based upon what God will do. These Jews now here in Jerusalem did not have much immediately round and about them to cheer them. The temple was still not rebuilt and they were surrounded by difficulties and trials and troubles in every respect. The prospect and situation was not very cheerful and promising. But God commands them to rejoice and feast and to be happy. Why? Partly, as we have seen, because they were back in Jerusalem. To be back in Jerusalem even in ruins is better than to be in the palaces of Babylon. But there is a much stronger reason than that for feasting and rejoicing. The bright and glorious prospect for the future! The God who had delivered them from Babylon, from that impossible situation, could surely be relied upon to keep them and to sustain them right on to the end. Had they trusted to themselves and to their own powers only, with all the enemies round and about them, the picture would be ominous and fearful. But God was with them and the God who had saved could also keep. 'Though things are as they are', says God to these people, 'rejoice, I am with you. Trust me. Celebrate your victories even before you get them.' That is the message which Paul in writing to the Romans puts like this: 'If, when we were sinners, we were reconciled to God by the death of his Son, much more, being reconciled, we shall be saved by his life' (*Rom.* 5:10).

'How can I be happy', you say, 'while I am so weak and frail and the enemy is so strong and so powerful? And what of tomorrow and the future?' Leave it all to him! Rely upon him! 'Sufficient unto the day is the evil thereof' (*Matt.* 6:34). The Christ who died in order to deliver you and give you a new life and a new start will not desert you. He will be with you to the end! He will hold you and guide you! It is because of that that Paul could say, 'For I am persuaded, that neither death, nor life ... shall be able to separate us from the love of God, which is in Christ Jesus our Lord' (*Rom.* 8:38, 39). Before writing that he had said, 'O wretched man that I am!' (*Rom.* 7:24). But Christ turns the wretched into the joyful and makes the weak strong. Are you finished with yourself and your sin and do you feel weak and helpless? Look to Jesus Christ and what he has done and commence to sing and to rejoice!